Lecture Notes
in Business Information Processing   128

Series Editors

Wil van der Aalst
  Eindhoven Technical University, The Netherlands
John Mylopoulos
  University of Trento, Italy
Michael Rosemann
  Queensland University of Technology, Brisbane, Qld, Australia
Michael J. Shaw
  University of Illinois, Urbana-Champaign, IL, USA
Clemens Szyperski
  Microsoft Research, Redmond, WA, USA

Lecture Notes
in Business Information Processing 29

Natalia Aseeva
Eduard Babkin
Oleg Kozyrev (Eds.)

Perspectives in Business Informatics Research

11th International Conference, BIR 2012
Nizhny Novgorod, Russia, September 24-26, 2012
Proceedings

 Springer

Volume Editors

Natalia Aseeva
Eduard Babkin
Oleg Kozyrev
National Research University
Higher School of Economics
Nizhny Novgorod, Russia
E-mails:
naseeva@hse.ru
eababkin@hse.ru
okozyrev@hse.ru

ISSN 1865-1348   e-ISSN 1865-1356
ISBN 978-3-642-33280-7   e-ISBN 978-3-642-33281-4
DOI 10.1007/978-3-642-33281-4
Springer Heidelberg Dordrecht London New York

Library of Congress Control Number: 2012946039

ACM Computing Classification (1998): J.1, H.3.5, H.4

Typesetting: Camera-ready by author, data conversion by Scientific Publishing Services, Chennai, India

Printed on acid-free paper

Springer is part of Springer Science+Business Media (www.springer.com)

Preface

This book consists of selected papers presented in the framework of the 11th International Conference on Perspectives in Business Informatics Research (BIR 2012), held in Nizhny Novgorod, Russia, September 24–26, 2012. The BIR conference series was established 11 years ago as the initiative of some German and Swedish universities with the aim of supporting the global forum for researchers in business informatics for their collaboration and exchange of results.

This initiative seems to be very successful. Today, the BIR conference is a well-known forum and the level of its proceedings is very high quality. In 2012 we received a great number of proposals to be included in the conference agenda and we selected 15 to be published in LNBIP.

The topics covered the most significant zones for business informatics research:

1. Business, people, and system interoperability:
   - Philosophical and social perspectives of interoperability
   - Ontological foundations of business informatics
   - Systems theory and principles
   - Conceptual modeling
   - Human-oriented systems
   - Emerging technologies and paradigms
   - Methods, architectures, and communication technologies supporting interoperability
   - Enterprise modeling and virtual organizations
   - ERP, CRM, and SCM systems
   - e-commerce, e-business, e-government
2. Business and information system development:
   - Business process modeling
   - Model-driven architecture (MDA)
   - Service-oriented architecture (SOA)
   - Requirements engineering
   - The synergy of agile and model-driven (MDA) development
   - IS modeling, testing, and verification
   - Object-oriented techniques and methodologies
   - Unified modeling language (UML)
   - Workflow management
   - Quality of business software
   - Business rules
3. Business intelligence:
   - Business excellence and business intelligence solutions
   - Data warehousing
   - Reporting

- Decision support systems
- Healthcare/medical informatics
- Competing on analytics

4. Knowledge management and Semantic Web:
   - Knowledge management in an interconnected world
   - Semantic Web methods
   - Ontology modeling languages and tools
   - Ontology applications in business
   - E-learning and learning organizations

5. Contextualized evaluation of business informatics:
   - Feasibility of existing standards, techniques, and languages
   - Contextualized value and quality
   - User acceptance of new technology
   - Teaching business informatics
   - Curriculum design and implementation issues
   - Case studies and experience reports
   - Project management issues

It is very promising that BIR now attracts researchers from the fields of both economics and management. It is evidence that we are doing well.

We hope that the discussions at BIR 2012 stimulated new ideas for the success of business informatics and for new cooperations.

July 2012

Natalia Aseeva
Eduard Babkin
Oleg Kozyrev

Organization

Program Committee Chair

Oleg Kozyrev   NRU HSE in Nizhny Novgorod, Russia

Program Committee

Jan Aidemark	Växjö University, Sweden
Esma Aïmeur	University of Montreal, Canada
Natalia Aseeva	NRU HSE in Nizhny Novgorod, Russia
Eduard Babkin	NRU HSE in Nizhny Novgorod, Russia
Per Backlund	University of Skövde, Sweden
Jānis Bārzdiņš	University of Latvia, Latvia
Peter Forbrig	University of Rostock, Germany
Boris Goldengorin	NRU HSE in Nizhny Novgorod, Russia
Horst Günther	University of Rostock, Germany
Markus Helfert	Dublin City University, Ireland
Kalinka Kaloyanova	University of Sofia, Bulgaria
Valery Kalyagin	NRU HSE in Nizhny Novgorod, Russia
Dimitris Karagiannis	University of Vienna, Austria
Mārīte Kirikova	Riga Technical University, Latvia
Andrzej Kobylinski	Warsaw School of Economics, Poland
Oleg Kozyrev	NRU HSE in Nizhny Novgorod, Russia
Vladimir Krylov	NRU HSE in Nizhny Novgorod, Russia
Yannis Manolopoulos	Aristotle University, Greece
Lina Nemuraite	Kaunas University of Technology, Lithuania
Jacob Nørbjerg	Copenhagen Business School, Denmark
Enn Õunapuu	Tallinn University of Technology, Estonia
Nava Pliskin	Ben-Gurion University of the Negev, Israel
Alessandro Ruggieri	University of Viterbo, Italy
Kurt Sandkuhl	University of Rostock, Germany
Christian Stary	University of Linz, Austria
Victor Taratoukhine	SAP CIS, Russia
Benkt Wangler	University of Skövde, Sweden
Stanislaw Wrycza	University of Gdansk, Poland
Jelena Zdravkovic	Stockholm University, Sweden

Organizational Committee Co-chairs

Natalia Aseeva	NRU HSE in Nizhny Novgorod, Russia
Eduard Babkin	NRU HSE in Nizhny Novgorod, Russia

Steering Committee

Kurt Sandkuhl	University of Rostock, Germany (Chair)
Eduard Babkin	NRU HSE in Nizhny Novgorod, Russia
Per Backlund	University of Skövde, Sweden
Rimantas Butleris	Kaunas University of Technology, Lithuania
Sven Carlsson	Lund University, Sweden
Peter Forbrig	University of Rostock, Germany
Horst Günther	University of Rostock, Germany
Mārīte Kirikova	Riga Technical University, Latvia
Harald Kjellin	Kristianstad University College, Sweden
Lina Nemuraite	Kaunas University of Technology, Lithuania
Jyrki Nummenmaa	University of Tampere, Finland
Eva Söderström	University of Skövde, Sweden
Bernd Viehweger	Humboldt University, Germany
Benkt Wangler	University of Skövde, Sweden
Stanislaw Wrycza	University of Gdansk, Poland

Sponsoring Institutions

Mera NN, Nizhny Novgorod, Russia
SAP CIS, Moscow, Russia
TECOM, Nizhny Novgorod, Russia

Table of Contents

Knowledge Management and Semantic Web

Business and Information Systems Development

Business, People and Systems Interoperability

Business Intelligence

Online Recommender System
for Radio Station Hosting

Dmitry I. Ignatov[1], Andrey V. Konstantinov[1], Sergey I. Nikolenko[2,3],
Jonas Poelmans[1], and Vasily V. Zaharchuk[1]

[1] National Research University Higher School of Economics
dignatov@hse.ru
http://www.hse.ru
[2] Steklov Mathematical Institute, St. Petersburg, Russia
[3] St. Petersburg Academic University, St. Petersburg, Russia

Abstract. We describe a new recommender system for the Russian interactive radio network FMhost. The underlying model combines collaborative and user-based approaches. The system extracts information
from tags of listened tracks for matching user and radio station profiles
and follows an adaptive online learning strategy based on user history.
We also provide some basic examples and describe the quality of service
evaluation methodology.

Keywords: music recommender systems, interactive radio network, e-
commerce, quality of service.

1 Introduction and Related Work

Music recommendation is an important topic in the field of recommender systems. Recent works in this area can be found in the proceedings of the International Society for Music Information Retrieval Conference (ISMIR) [1], the
Workshop on Music Recommendation and Discovery (WOMRAD) [2,3], and the
Recommender Systems conference (RecSys) [4]. Several broadcasting services including LastFm, Yahoo!LaunchCast and Pandora are well known and work on
a commercial basis. The latter two of them do not broadcast for Russia. Despite
the many high-quality papers on different aspects of music recommendation,
there are only few studies devoted to online radio station recommender systems.

This work is devoted to the Russian online radio hosting service FMhost and,
in particular, its new hybrid recommender subsystem. Recently, the focus of
computer science research for the music industry has shifted from music information retrieval and exploration [5,6,7] to music recommender services [8,9]. The
topic is not new (see, e.g., [10]); however, it is now inspired by new capabilities
of large online services to provide not only millions of tracks for listening to, but
even radio station hosting. Social tagging is also one of the important factors
which allows to apply new tag-similarity based recommender algorithms to the
domain [11,12].

N. Aseeva, E. Babkin, and O. Kozyrev (Eds.): BIR 2012, LNBIP 128, pp. 1–12, 2012.
© Springer-Verlag Berlin Heidelberg 2012

Recently, a widely acclaimed public contest on music recommender algorithms, KDD Cup, was held by Yahoo! (http://kddcup.yahoo.com/). In KDD Cup, track 1 was devoted to learning to predict users' ratings of musical items (tracks, albums, artists and genres) in which items formed a taxonomy. Each track belonged to an album, albums belonged to artists, and together they were tagged by genres. Track 2 aimed at developing learning algorithms for separating music tracks scored highly by specific users from tracks not scored by them. It attracted a lot attention from the community to problems which are both typical for recommender systems and specific for music recommendation: scalability issues, capturing the dynamics and taxonomical properties of items [13]. The current trends of music recommender systems reflect advantages of hybrid approaches and show the need for user-centric quality measures [14]. For instance, in [15] an interesting approach based on a "forgetting curve" to evaluate "freshness" of predictions was proposed. In [16], the authors posed an important question, namely how much metadata do we need in music recommendation, and after a subjective evaluation of 19 users the authors concluded that pure content-based methods can be drastically improved by using genres.

In [17], the authors proposed the music recommender system Starnet for social networking. It generates recommendations based either on positive ratings of friends (social recommendations), positive ratings of others in the network (non-social recommendations), and it also makes random recommendations. Another interesting online music recommendation system we can mention is Hotttabs [18], dedicated to guitar learning. Some authors aim at improving music recommender systems by using semantic extraction techniques [19,20]. In [21] the author describes a system of genre recommendation for music and TV programs, which can be considered as an alternative channel selector. The authors of [22] proposed a recommender system GroupFan which is able to aggregate preferences of group users to their mutual satisfaction.

Many online services (e.g., Last.fm or LaunchCast) call their audio streams "radio stations", but in reality they produce a playlist from a database of tracks based on a recommender system rather than actually recommend a radio channel. FMhost, on the other hand, provides users with online radio stations in the classical meaning of this term: there are human DJs who perform live, a radio station actually represents a strategy or mood of a certain person (DJ), they play their own tracks, perform contests etc. Thus, the problem we are solving differs from most of the work done in music recommendation, and some of the challenges are unique.

The paper is organized as follows. In Section 2, we describe our online radio service FMhost. In section 3, we propose our new recommender model, two basic recommender algorithms, and describe the recommender system architecture. Quality of Service (QoS) measurement for the system and some insights on FMhost user behaviour are discussed in Section 4. Section 5 concludes the paper.

2   Online Service FMhost.me

2.1   A Concise Online Broadcasting Dictionary

Before we proceed, we need to shortly explain some basic domain terminology.

A *chart* is a radio station track rating; for example, the rock chart shows a certain number (say, 10) of most popular rock tracks, ranked from the most popular (rank 1) to the least popular (rank 10) according to the survey. A *live performance* (or just *live* for short) is a performance to which one or several *DJs* (*disk jockeys*) are assigned. They do it from their own PCs, and the audio stream is being redirected from them to the Icecast server and then everywhere. Also they may have their own blog for each live, where people may interact with DJs who perform live. *LiquidSoap* is a sound generator that broadcasts audio files (*.mp3, *.aac etc.) into an audio stream. *Icecast* is a retranslation server that redirects an audio stream from one source, for example LiquidSoap, to many receivers.

2.2   The FMhost Project

FMhost is an interactive radio network. This portal allows users to listen and broadcast their own radio stations. There are four user categories in the portal: (1) unauthorized user; (2) listener; (3) Disk Jockey (DJ); (4) radio station owner.

User capabilities vary upon their status. Unauthorized listeners can listen to any station, but they cannot vote or become DJs. They also cannot use the recommender system and the rating system.

Listeners, unlike unauthorized users, can vote for tracks, lives, and radio stations. They can use a recommender system or rating system. They can subscribe to lives, radio stations, or DJs. They also can be appointed to a live and become a DJ.

There are three types of broadcasting: (1) stream redirection from another server; (2) AutoDJ translation; (3) live performance.

Stream redirection applies when a radio station owner has its own server and wants to use FMhost as a broadcasting platform, but also wants to broadcast using his own sound generator, e.g., SamBroadcaster (`http://spacial.com/sam-broadcaster`), LiquidSoap (`http://savonet.sourceforge.net/`) etc. AutoDj is a special option that allows the users to play music directly from the FMhost server. Every radio owner gets some space where he can download as much tracks as he can, and then LiquidSoap will generate the audio stream and the Icecast (`http://www.icecast.org/`) server will redirect it to the listeners. Usually the owner sets a radio schedule which is being played.

Live performances are done by DJs. Everyone who has performed live at least once can be called a DJ. He can also be added to a radio station crew. Moreover, a DJ can perform lives at any station, not only on his own station where he is in a crew.

FMhost was the first project of its kind in Russia, starting in 2009. Nowadays, following FMhost's success, there exist several radio broadcasting portals, such as

http://frodio.com/, http://myradio24.com/, http://www.radio-hoster.
ru/, http://www.taghosting.ru/, http://www.economhost.com/, and even
http://fmhosting.ru/. In late 2011, FMhost was taken down for a serious
rewrite of the codebase and rethinking of the recommender system's architecture. In this paper, we describe the results of this upgrade.

The previous version of the recommender system experienced several problems, such as tag discrepancy or personal tracks without tags at all. A survey
by FMhost with about a hundred respondents showed that more than half of
them appreciated the previous version of our recommender system and more
than 80% of the answers were positive or neutral (see Table 1); nevertheless,
we hope that the new recommender model and algorithms provide even more
accurate recommendations and make even less prediction mistakes.

Table 1. FMhost's recommender system satisfaction survey

User opinion	Number of respondents (%)
I like it very much, all recommendations were relevant	54 (49%)
Good, I like most of the radio stations	22 (20%)
Sometimes there are interesting stations	16 (14%)
I like only few recommended radio stations	9(8%)
None of the recommended stations was satisfactory	10 (9%)

2.3   FMhost Conceptual Improvements

The new version features a more complex system of user interaction. Every radio
station has an owner who is not just a name but also has the ability to assign
DJs for lives, prepare radio schedule, and assign lives and programs. There will
be a new broadcasting panel for DJs that will allow them to play tracks with
additional features that were not available before, such as an equalizer or fading
between tracks. A new algorithm for the recommender system, a new rating
system, and a new chart system will be launched.

The rating system has been developed to rank radio stations and DJs according to their popularity and quality of work. A new core is being implemented
and a new concept of LiquidSoap and Icecast is being designed. The system is
designed such that all problems that have surfaced in the previous version were
eliminated.

3   Models, Algorithms and Recommender Architecture

3.1   Input Data and General Structure

Our model is based on three data matrices. The first matrix $A = (a_{ut})$ tracks
the number of times user u visits radio stations with a certain tag t. Each
radio station r broadcasts audio tracks with a certain set of tags T_r. The sets
of all users, radio stations, and tags are denoted by U, R, and T respectively.

The second matrix $B = (b_{rt})$ contains how many tracks with a tag t a radio station r has played. Finally, the third matrix $C = (c_{ur})$ contains the number of times a user u visits a radio station r. For each of these three matrices, we denote by v^A, v^B, and v^C the respective vectors containing sums of elements: $v^A = \sum_{t \in T} a_{ut}$, $v^B = \sum_{t \in T} b_{rt}$, and $v^C = \sum_{r \in R} a_{ur}$. We also denote for each matrix A, B, C the corresponding frequency of visits matrix by A_f, B_f, and C_f; the frequency matrix is obtained by normalizing the matrix with the respective visits vector, e.g., $A_f = (a_{ut} \cdot (v_u^A)^{-1})$. Our model is not purely static; the matrices A, B, and C change after a user u visits a radio station r with a tag t, i.e., each value a_{ut}, b_{rt}, and c_{ur} is incremented by 1 after this visit.

The model consists of three main blocks: the Individual-Based Recommender System (IBRS) model, the Collaborative-Based Recommender System (CBRS) model, and the End Recommender Systems (ERS) that aggregates the results of the former two.

Each model has its own algorithmic implementation. Since both our previous works [23,24] and this work implicitly use biclustering ideas, we continue to name our general algorithms with the RecBi acronym; this time it is the RecBi3 family. We call the resulting algorithms for the three proposed models RecBi3.1, RecBi3.2, and RecBi3.3, respectively. Here we do not use the notation from formal concept analysis, but refer to [25] for the basic notation used in our previous algorithms RecBi2.1 and RecBi2.2.

3.2   IBRS

The **IBRS** model uses matrices A_f and B_f and aims to provide a particular user $u_0 \in U$ with top N recommendations represented mathematically by a special structure $Top_N(u)$. Formally, $Top_N(u_0)$ is a triple $(R_{u_0}, \preceq_{u_0}, \text{rank})$, where R_{u_0} is the set of at most N radio stations recommended to a particular user u_0, $\preceq_{u_0}$ is a well-defined quasiordering (reflexive, transitive, and complete) on the set R_{u_0}, and rank is a function which maps each radio station r from R_{u_0} to $[0, 1]$.

The **RecBi3.1** algorithm computes the 1-norm distance between a user u_0 and a radio station r, i.e. $d(u_0, r) = \sum t \in T |a_{u_0 t} - b_{rt}|$. Then all distances between the user u_0 and the radio stations $r \in R$ are calculated. Further the algorithm constructs the relation $\prec_{u_0}$ according to the following rule: $r_i \preceq r_j$ iff $d(u_0, r_i) \leq d(u_0, r_i)$. The function rank operates on R_{u_0} according to the following rule:

$$\text{rank}(r_i) = 1 - d(u_0, r_i) / \max_{r_j \in R} d(u_0, r_j).$$

Finally, after selecting N radio stations for N greatest rank values in the set R_{u_0}, we have the structure $Top_N(u_0)$ which represents a ranked list of radio stations recommended to the user u_0.

As shown in Fig. 1, our model takes into account not only "listened tracks" but also "liked tracks", "liked radio stations", and "favorite radio stations". To refine the IBRS submodel we tune it with the SMARTS algorithm known from decision making theory [26]. According to the method and expert decisions, we

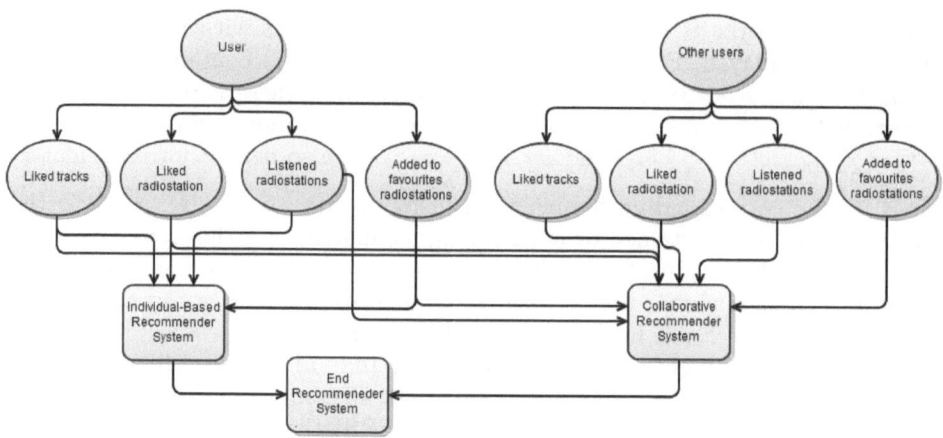

Fig. 1. The recommender system architecture

should count each track tag of a "listened radio station", "liked radio station", "liked track", and "favorite radio station" with a different weight. The SMARTS procedure provided us with the four weights for "listened radio station", "liked radio station", "favorite radio station", and "liked track" according to our experts' assessment of mutual criterion importance, namely 0.07, 0.16, 0.3, and 0.47. In the SMARTS method, we consider each tag type as a criterion with two terminal values 0 and 100% on a real number scale. Some tag t may have some or even four of these types simultaneously; in this case, the algorithm adds to a_{ut} the total weight of the tag (i.e., the sum of weights) after a user u visits some radio station with this tag. In case there are several elements with the same rank so that $Top_N(u)$ is not uniquely defined, we simply choose the first elements according to some arbitrary ordering (e.g., the lexicographic ordering of station names).

3.3 CBRS

The **CBRS** model is based on the C_f matrix. The matrix also yields a vector n^C which stores the total number of listened stations for each user $u \in U$. This vector also changes over time, and this value is used as a threshold to transform matrix C_f to distance matrix D as follows:

$$d_{ij} = \begin{cases} |c_{fir} - c_{fjr}|, & if\ c_{fir} \geq n_i^{-1} and\ c_{fjr} \geq n_j^{-1} \\ |c_{fir} + c_{fjr}|, & if\ c_{fir} > n_i^{-1} and\ c_{fjr} < n_j^{-1} or\ vice\ versa \end{cases} \quad (1)$$

This distance takes into account the frequency n_u^C of all radio station visits for user u and considers its inverse value as a threshold to decide whether a particular station r should be considered as popular for this user. Thus, users with different signs of $c_{fir} - n_i^{-1}$ and $c_{fjr} - n_j^{-1}$ become more distant than for the conventional absolute distance. This distance d_{ij} actually serves as a sort of polarizing filter, and in Section 4 we compare it with common approaches.

After computing D, the algorithm **RecBi3.2** constructs the list $Top_k(u_0) = (U_{u_0}, \preceq_{u_0}, \text{sim})$ of k users similar to our target user u_0 who awaits recommendations, where $\text{sim}(u) = 1 - d_{uu_0} / \max\limits_{u' \in U} d_{u'u_0}$. We define the set of all radio stations user u_0 listened to as $L(u_0) = \{r | c_{fur} = 0\}$. In a similar way, we define

$$Top_N(u_0) = (R_{u_0}, \preceq_{u_0}, \text{rank}), \text{ where}$$
$$\text{rank}(r) = \text{sim}(u^*) \cdot c_{fu^*r} \text{ and}$$
$$u^* = \arg \max\limits_{u \in U_{u_0}, r \in U/L(u_0)} \text{sim}(u) \cdot c_{fur}.$$

It is worth mentioning that rank $: r \mapsto [0, 1]$. The problem of choosing exactly N topmost stations is solved in the same way as in the IBRS submodel.

3.4   ERS

After IBRS and CBRS have finished, we are left with two ranked lists of recommended stations $Top_N^I(u_0)$ and $Top_N^C(u_0)$ for our target user u_0 from IBRS and CBRS respectively. The **ERS** submodel proposes a simple solution for aggregating these lists into the final recommendation structure $Top_N^E(u_0) = (R_{u_0}^E, \preceq_{u_0}^E, \text{rank}^E)$. For every $r \in R_{u_0}^C \cup R_{u_0}^I$, the function $\text{rank}^E(r)$ maps r to the weighted sum

$$\beta \cdot \text{rank}^C(r) + (1 - \beta) \cdot \text{rank}^I(r),$$

where we let $\beta \in [0,1]$, $\text{rank}^C(r) = 0$ for all $r \notin R^C$ and $\text{rank}^I(r) = 0$ for all $r \notin R^I$. The algorithm **RecBi3.3** adds the best N radio stations according to this criterion to the set $R_{u_0}^C$.

4   Quality of Service Assessment

To evaluate the quality of the developed system, we propose a variant of the cross-validation technique [27]. Before we proceed to the detailed description of the procedure, we discuss some important analyses that we conducted on the FMhost data for the period from 2009 till 2011.

4.1   Basic Statistics

It is a well-known fact that social networking data often follows the so called power law distribution [28]. To decide which amount of active users or radio stations we have to take into account for making recommendations, we performed a simple statistical analysis of user and radio station activity. Around 20% of the users (only registered ones) were analysed.

Table 2 shows p-values of statistical tests, which were performed by means of Matlab tools from [28], show that the power law does fit the radio station

Table 2. Basic parameters of the user and radio visits datasets, along with their power-law fits and the corresponding *p-value*

Dataset	n	$\langle x \rangle$	σ	x_{max}	$\hat{x}_{min}$	$\hat{\alpha}$	n_{tail}	*p-value*
User dataset	4187	5.86	12.9	191	12 ± 2	2.46(0.096)	117	**0.099**
Radio dataset	2209	11.22	60.05	1817	46 ± 11	2.37(0.22)	849	**0.629**

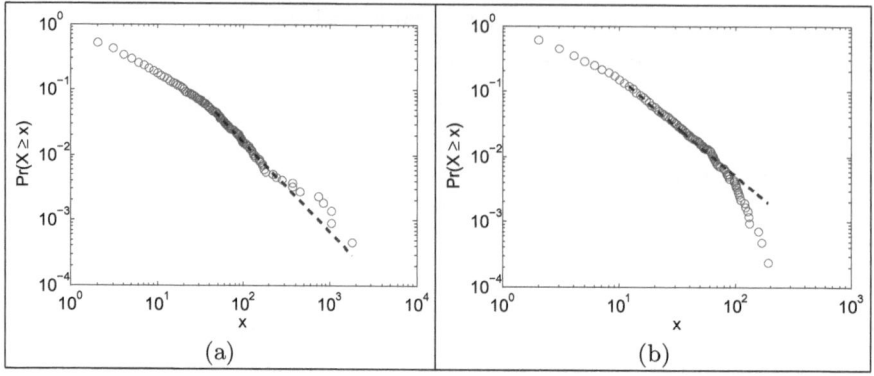

Fig. 2. Cumulative distribution functions $P(x)$ and their maximum likelihood power-law fits for the FMhost two empirical data sets. (a) The frequency distribution of radio station visits. (b) The frequency of visits of unique users.

dataset, and the probability to make an error by ruling out the null hypothesis (no power law) is about 0.1 for the user dataset. Thus, the radio station visits dataset is more likely to follow the power law than the user visits dataset, but we should take it into account for both datasets; Fig. 2 shows how the power law actually fits our data.

This analysis implies useful consequences according to the well-known "80:20" rule:

$$W = P^{(\alpha-2)/(\alpha-1)},$$

which means that the fraction W of the wealth is in the hands of the richest P of the population. In our case, 50% of users make 80% of all radio station visits, and 50% of radio stations have 83% of all visits. Thus, if the service tends to take into account only active stations and users, it can cover 80% of all visits by considering only 50% of their active audience. However, new radio stations still deserve to be recommended, so this rule can only be applied to the user database.

4.2   Quality Assessment

To evaluate QoS for the IBRS subsystem (RecBi3.1 algorithm), we count average precision and recall on the set $R_N \subset R$, where N is a number of randomly "hidden" radiostations. We suppose that for all r in R_N and every user $u \in U$

the algorithm does not know whether the radio stations were liked, added to favorites, or even visited, and we change A_f and R accordingly. Then RecBi3.1 attempts to recommend Top-N radio stations for this modified matrix A_f.

Top-N average precision and recall are computed as follows:

$$\text{Precision} = \frac{\displaystyle\sum_{u \in U} \frac{|R_u^I \cap L_u \cap R_N|}{|L_u \cap R_u^I|}}{|U|},$$

$$\text{Recall} = \frac{\displaystyle\sum_{u \in U} \frac{|R_u^I \cap L_u \cap R_N|}{|L_u \cap R_N|}}{|U|}.$$

To deal with CBRS, we use a modification of the leave-one-out technique. At each step of the procedure for a particular user u, we "hide" all radio stations $r \in R_N$ by setting $c_{fur} = 0$. Then we perform RecBi3.2 assuming that $c_{fu'r}$ is unchanged for $u' \in U/u$. After that we compute

$$\text{Precision} = \frac{\displaystyle\sum_{u \in U} \frac{|R_u^C \cap L_u \cap R_N|}{|L_u \cap R_u^C|}}{|U|},$$

$$\text{Recall} = \frac{\displaystyle\sum_{u \in U} \frac{|R_u^C \cap L_u \cap R_N|}{|L_u \cap R_N|}}{|U|}.$$

To tune the ERS system, we can use a combination of these two procedures trying to find the optimal β as

$$\beta^* = \arg\max_{\beta} \frac{2 \cdot \text{Precision} \cdot \text{Recall}}{(\text{Precision} + \text{Recall})}.$$

We suppose that in one month of active operation we will have enough statistics to tune β and choose appropriate similarity and distance measures as well as thresholds. We suppose that the resulting system will provide reasonably accurate recommendations using only a single (last) month of user history and only 50% of the most active users. For quality assessment during the actual operation, we will compute Top-3, Top-5, and Top-10 Precision and Recall measures as well as whether the system provides a user only with Top-10 items with a highest rank. In addition, online surveys can be launched to assess user satisfaction with the new RS system.

5   Conclusion and Further Work

In this work, we have described the underlying models, algorithms, and the system architecture of the new improved FMhost service. We hope that the developed algorithms will help a user to find relevant radio stations to listen to. In future optimization and tuning, special attention should be paid to scalability issues and user-centric quality assessment. We consider matrix factorization techniques as a reasonable tool to increase scalability, but it has to be carefully adapted and assessed taking into account the folksonomic nature of tracks tags. Another attractive feature of the developed system is that it can serve as a kind of World of Music map built on track-to-track similarity matrices with tags [7]. Another important issue is dealing with the triadic relational nature of data (users, radio stations (tracks), and tags), which constitutes the so called *folksonomy* [29], a primary data structure in tagging resource-sharing systems. As shown in [30], this data can be successfully mined by means of triclustering, so we also plan to build a tag-based recommender system by means of triclustering.

Acknowledgments. We would like to thank Rustam Tagiew and Mykola Pechenizkiy for their comments, remarks and explicit and implicit help during paper preparations. The work of Sergey Nikolenko has been supported by the Russian Foundation for Basic Research grant 12-01-00450-a, the Russian Presidential Grant Programme for Young Ph.D.'s, grant no. MK-6628.2012.1, for Leading Scientific Schools, grant no. NSh-3229.2012.1, and RFBR grants 11-01-12135-ofi-m-2011 and 11-01-00760-a. The study was implemented in the framework of the Basic Research Program at the National Research University Higher School of Economics in 2012 and in the Laboratory of Intelligent Systems and Structural Analysis.

References

1. Klapuri, A., Leider, C. (eds.): Proceedings of the 12th International Society for Music Information Retrieval Conference, ISMIR 2011, Miami, Florida, USA, October 24-28. University of Miami (2011)
2. Anglade, A., Baccigalupo, C., Casagrande, N., Celma, Ò., Lamere, P.: Workshop report: Womrad 2010. In: Amatriain, X., Torrens, M., Resnick, P., Zanker, M. (eds.) RecSys, pp. 381–382. ACM (2010)
3. Anglade, A., Celma, O., Fields, B., Lamere, P., McFee, B.: Womrad: 2nd workshop on music recommendation and discovery. In: Proceedings of the Fifth ACM Conference on Recommender Systems, RecSys 2011, pp. 381–382. ACM, New York (2011)
4. RecSys 2011: Proceedings of the Fifth ACM Conference on Recommender Systems, 609116. ACM, New York (2011)
5. Hilliges, O., Holzer, P., Klüber, R., Butz, A.: AudioRadar: A Metaphorical Visualization for the Navigation of Large Music Collections. In: Butz, A., Fisher, B., Krüger, A., Olivier, P. (eds.) SG 2006. LNCS, vol. 4073, pp. 82–92. Springer, Heidelberg (2006)
6. Gleich, D.F., Rasmussen, M., Lang, K., Zhukov, L.: The world of music: User ratings; spectral and spherical embeddings; map projections. Online report (2006)
7. Gleich, D.F., Zhukov, L., Rasmussen, M., Lang, K.: The World of Music: SDP Embedding of High Dimensional data. In: Information Visualization 2005 (2005), Interactive Poster
8. Brandenburg, K., Dittmar, C., Gruhne, M., Abeßer, J., Lukashevich, H., Dunker, P., Gärtner, D., Wolter, K., Grossmann, H.: Music search and recommendation. In: Furht, B. (ed.) Handbook of Multimedia for Digital Entertainment and Arts, pp. 349–384. Springer US (2009)

9. Celma, Ò.: Music Recommendation and Discovery - The Long Tail, Long Fail, and Long Play in the Digital Music Space. Springer (2010)
10. Avesani, P., Massa, P., Nori, M., Susi, A.: Collaborative Radio Community. In: De Bra, P., Brusilovsky, P., Conejo, R. (eds.) AH 2002. LNCS, vol. 2347, pp. 462–465. Springer, Heidelberg (2002)
11. Symeonidis, P., Ruxanda, M.M., Nanopoulos, A., Manolopoulos, Y.: Ternary semantic analysis of social tags for personalized music recommendation. In: Bello, J.P., Chew, E., Turnbull, D. (eds.) ISMIR, pp. 219–224 (2008)
12. Nanopoulos, A., Rafailidis, D., Symeonidis, P., Manolopoulos, Y.: Musicbox: Personalized music recommendation based on cubic analysis of social tags. IEEE Transactions on Audio, Speech & Language Processing 18(2), 407–412 (2010)
13. Koenigstein, N., Dror, G., Koren, Y.: Yahoo! music recommendations: modeling music ratings with temporal dynamics and item taxonomy. In: Proceedings of the Fifth ACM Conference on Recommender Systems, RecSys 2011, pp. 165–172. ACM, New York (2011)
14. Celma, O., Lamere, P.: Music recommendation and discovery revisited. In: Proceedings of the Fifth ACM Conference on Recommender Systems, RecSys 2011, pp. 7–8. ACM, New York (2011)
15. Hu, Y., Ogihara, M.: Nextone player: A music recommendation system based on user behavior. In: [1], pp. 103–108
16. Bogdanov, D., Herrera, P.: How much metadata do we need in music recommendation? a subjective evaluation using preference sets. In: [1], pp. 97–102
17. Mesnage, C.S., Rafiq, A., Dixon, S., Brixtel, R.P.: Music discovery with social networks. In: Workshop on Music Recommendation and Discovery 2011, pp. 1–6 (October 2011)
18. Barthet, M., Anglade, A., Fazekas, G., Kolozali, S., Macrae, R.: Music recommendation for music learning: Hotttabs, a multimedia guitar tutor. In: Workshop on Music Recommendation and Discovery 2011, pp. 7–13 (October 2011)
19. Tatlı, I., Birturk, A.: Using semantic relations in context-based music recommendations. In: Workshop on Music Recommendation and Discovery 2011, pp. 14–17 (October 2011)
20. Knees, P., Schedl, M.: Towards semantic music information extraction from the web using rule patterns and supervised learning. In: Workshop on Music Recommendation and Discovery 2011, pp. 18–25 (October 2011)
21. Knopke, I.: The importance of service and genre in recommendations for online radio and television programmes. In: Workshop on Music Recommendation and Discovery 2011, pp. 26–29 (October 2011)
22. Popescu, G., Pu, P.: Probabilistic game theoretic algorithms for group recommender systems. In: Workshop on Music Recommendation and Discovery 2011, pp. 7–12 (October 2011)
23. Ignatov, D.I., Poelmans, J., Zaharchuk, V.: Recommender System Based on Algorithm of Bicluster Analysis RecBi. In: Ignatov, D., Poelmans, J., Kuznetsov, S. (eds.) CDUD 2011 - Concept Discovery in Unstructured Data. CEUR Workshop proceedings, vol. 757, pp. 122–126 (2011)
24. Ignatov, D.I., Kuznetsov, S.O.: Concept-based Recommendations for Internet Advertisement. In: Belohlavek, R., Kuznetsov, S.O. (eds.) Proc. CLA 2008. CEUR WS, vol. 433, pp. 157–166. Palacký University, Olomouc (2008)
25. Ganter, B., Wille, R.: Formal Concept Analysis: Mathematical Foundations, 1st edn. Springer-Verlag New York, Inc., Secaucus (1999)

26. Edwards, W., Barron, F.: SMARTS and SMARTER: Improved Simple Methods for Multiattribute Utility Measurement. Organizational Behavior and Human Decision Processes 60(3), 306–325 (1994)
27. Ignatov, D.I., Poelmans, J., Dedene, G., Viaene, S.: A New Cross-Validation Technique to Evaluate Quality of Recommender Systems. In: Kundu, M.K., Mitra, S., Mazumdar, D., Pal, S.K. (eds.) PerMIn 2012. LNCS, vol. 7143, pp. 195–202. Springer, Heidelberg (2012)
28. Clauset, A., Shalizi, C.R., Newman, M.E.J.: Power-law distributions in empirical data. SIAM Rev. 51(4), 661–703 (2009)
29. Vander Wal, T.: Folksonomy Coinage and Definition (2007), http://vanderwal.net/folksonomy.html (accessed on March 12, 2012)
30. Ignatov, D.I., Kuznetsov, S.O., Magizov, R.A., Zhukov, L.E.: From Triconcepts to Triclusters. In: Kuznetsov, S.O., Ślęzak, D., Hepting, D.H., Mirkin, B.G. (eds.) RSFDGrC 2011. LNCS, vol. 6743, pp. 257–264. Springer, Heidelberg (2011)

OWL Orthogonal Extension

Renārs Liepiņš, Janis Barzdins, and Lelde Lace

Institute of Mathematics and Computer Science, University of Latvia,
Raina blvd. 29, LV-1459, Riga, Latvia
{Renars.Liepins,Janis.Barzdins,Lelde.Lace}@lumii.lv

Abstract. It is critical for knowledge bases to capture the reality in direct and intuitive way. OWL ontology language was designed for this goal. In this paper we study the limitations of the OWL open world semantics for the task of knowledge capture and retrieval. We propose a new mechanism based on the closed world semantics that alleviates part of the limitations. Further we describe a system where both OWL and the new mechanisms interoperate together. Finally, we outline some immediate applications and further research directions.

Keywords: OWL, Reasoner, Extension.

1   Introduction

OWL [1] is a powerful modeling language for representing knowledge about the world. It was initially designed for Semantic Web applications where the knowledge is distributed, and it is a norm that only a small part of the whole knowledge is available. Therefore OWL adapted the so-called open world assumption. It means that, if something is not known, then it does not follow that it is false. For example, let us assume we only know that Bob is a person. From this we can neither say that Bob is a student nor that he is not one. Our knowledge is incomplete, and it can be correctly represented in OWL.

OWL has attracted the interest of the community of business knowledge base. They hope that it will allow them to capture their domain knowledge more precisely, infer new information and ease the integration with outside knowledge bases. None of this is possible, when the information is stored in a relational database.

In the knowledge base settings one of the main tasks is the knowledge retrieval. The best way to make it easier is to store the data in terms that are intuitive for the end-users. In OWL these terms are represented with classes. There are two types of classes, namely, primitive classes and class expressions. Only a human can decide what objects belong to a primitive class – it is done by intuitive interpretation of the class name. In contrast, class expression allows us to define new classes from primitive classes, and the objects belonging to them can be found algorithmically. However, there are many types of intuitive classes that cannot be expressed using OWL constructs.

Specifically, they are classes that deal with some form of the closed world reasoning, e.g. objects for whom it is not known if they have a data property value or not. Due to

N. Aseeva, E. Babkin, and O. Kozyrev (Eds.): BIR 2012, LNBIP 128, pp. 13–25, 2012.

the open world assumption OWL can only define either a class of objects for whom it can be proven that they must have a property value, or a class of objects for whom it can be proven that they cannot have a property value. It is also impossible to define classes that involve conditions on aggregations, e.g. objects for whom the sum of attribute values is equal to some value.

The prevailing attitude in the "reasoner community" is that such cases should be handled outside the ontology by either adding the additional information in the preprocessing step, or calculating it later in the application. Such attitude is good for the logical purity of the language, but bad for practical adaptation, since the end-users want to treat the knowledge base as a black box [2] specifying everything in an ontology and letting the knowledge base decide, what to calculate using a reasoner and what to derive using something else. The results should be retrievable by asking for instances of a class.

In this paper we propose an OWL extension for specifying classes that cannot be described using only OWL constructs. It is inspired by Object Constraint Language (OCL) [3] for UML models, but with semantics adapted to OWL. We also show how this extension can be integrated with a reasoner in practical applications.

The rest of the paper is structured as follows. In Section 2 we introduce the example ontology on which the current OWL modeling shortcomings are shown and on which the proposed language and integration with a reasoner will be later presented. Section 3 describes the proposed extension language, the extension of ontology graphical notation with a place for this language, and how it can be serialized in OWL form. In Section 4 we discuss how the proposed extension can interoperate with a reasoner and the design tradeoffs that were made to make it practical. Section 5 discusses related work. Finally, we describe future work in Section 6.

2   Motivating Example – University Ontology

To better understand the proposed language we will start with a motivating example. Let us suppose that we are modeling a knowledge base of a university information system. It will be used for data storage, data validation and query answering. The ontology (shown in Figure 1 in the OWLGrEd [4, 5] notation) will have primitive classes: Teacher, Professor, Student, AcademicProgram, Course and Grade. These classes are all that is needed for the purpose of data storage. However, the end-users will want to make queries not only about all students, but also about students that have some specific features, e.g. students that take some course or students that have graduated. Usually a feature set describes some intuitive concept with a name, e.g. students that take some course correspond to a concept ActiveStudent. Many intuitive concepts can be defined in OWL as derived classes using class expressions, e.g. the class ActiveStudent (from Figure 1) can be defined with an OWL expression "takes some Course". A derived class can later be used not only for answering queries, but also for defining other intuitive concepts.

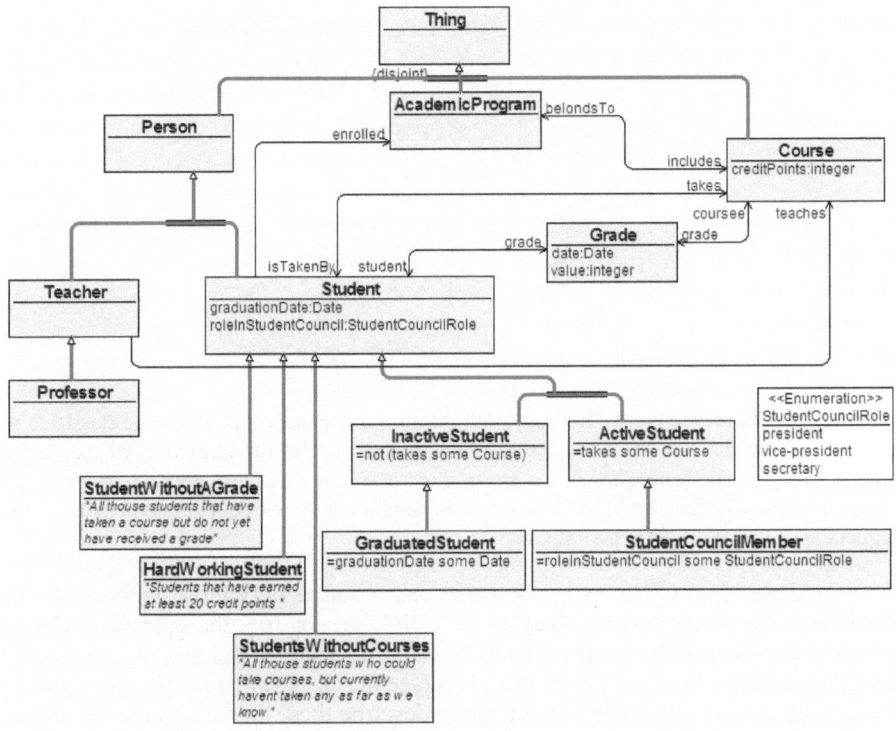

Fig. 1. Simplified University Ontology

However, some class descriptions are impossible to specify in OWL. Nevertheless they are intuitive and useful for knowledge base users. For example, suppose that we want to define a class whose instances will be students that have not yet registered for courses (assume that we want to send them a reminder that they will be expelled if they do not register). It would seem that it is sufficient to define two classes, namely, *ActiveStudents* – those who take some course, and *InactiveStudents* – those who currently do not take any courses. Let us look at a fragment of the university ontology shown in Figure 2 where those two classes are defined. We must be careful with what exactly is meant by these definitions from the perspective of the open world assumption. Let us look at the individuals from the class *Student* in Figure 2. The individual *s2* has a link *takes* to the course instance *c1*, therefore it can be inferred that it is also an instance of the defined class *ActiveStudent*. What about the individual *s1*? There are no outgoing links from it. From the perspective of the open world assumption it means that we do not know about any outgoing links, it may be that there actually are some. Hence, we cannot infer either that the individual *s1* is an *ActiveStudent* or that he is an *InactiveStudent*. Consequently it is better to read expressions like "takes some Course" and "not takes some Course" as "all individuals for whom it can be proved that they take some Course" and "all individuals for whom it can be proved that they <u>cannot</u> take a course". When read in such a way and assuming we have partial information in our knowledge base, it becomes quite intuitive why the individual *s1* can be classified as neither *ActiveStudent* nor as *InactiveStudent*.

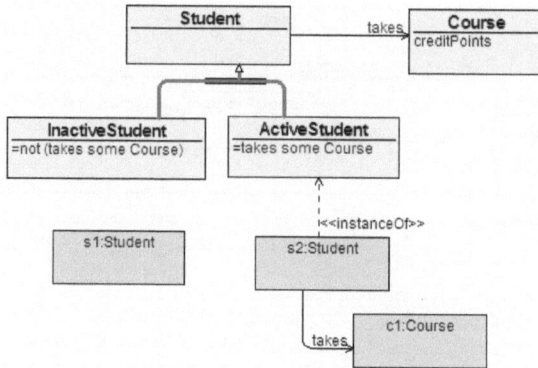

Fig. 2. Fragment of the University Ontology with instances. The individual *s2* can be classified as an *ActiveStudent* because it has a link *takes* to the course *c1*. But the individual *s1* cannot be classified as either an *ActiveStudent* or as an *InactiveStudent* because there is no enough information about whether the individual *s1* takes some course or not. This demonstrates the consequences of the open world assumption.

Actually there is no OWL expression that can describe only those individuals for whom it is not known whether they have a link or not [6], therefore knowledge engineers can only introduce a primitive class and provide an annotation in a natural language to explain what is meant by this class (see the class *StudentWithoutCourses* in Figure 1). Our goal is to present a language to describe these classes. In the rest of the paper we will call such type of classes ***IntrospectiveClasses***.

3   Proposed Extension Language – lQuery

As we saw in the previous chapter, OWL can only refer to individuals about whom we can prove that they have some feature or to individuals about whom it can be proved that they <u>cannot</u> have some feature. But there is no way to refer to individuals about whom there is no information whether they have some feature or not. In this chapter we present a language (lQuery) that can be used to define classes that belong to the category of *IntrospectiveClasses* and also classes that involve conditions on aggregations. Later we will use these defined classes in classification tasks.

The core of the lQuery is selector expressions. They are build using lQuery selectors, a list of most commonly used selectors is given in Table 1 and a selector expression grammar is shown in Figure 3. They are always evaluated in a context of some object collection (e.g. individuals of the class *Thing*), and each object that matches the selector is returned in the result collection of the selector expression. Thus a selector expression defines a new class of objects. Two main types of selector expressions are filters and navigators. Filters are used to return a subset of the initial collection based on some condition. Navigators are used to get a new collection of objects from the initial collection. Examples of filter selectors are the following: filter by class membership (i.e. there is an explicit *instanceOf* assertion in the ontology) and filter by data-property value. Examples of navigation selectors are the following: the collection of objects that are reachable from the current collection by a given object-property and the collection of values of some data-property.

Table 1. lQuery selectors

Operator	Description
.ClassName	all objects from the context collection that have an instanceOf link to a class with the name *ClassName*; (filter by type) (the dot can be omitted when there is no ambiguity)
/roleName	collection of objects reachable from the context collection by a object-property with the name *roleName*; (navigation)
@attrName	collection of data values for all objects in the context collection; (data property selector)
[*selector* **op** selector_or_const]	all those objects from the context collection for which the expression evaluates to true; (op: ==, !=, <, >, >=, =<); (filter by condition)
:**not**(sel)	all those objects from the context collection for which the sub-selector *sel* returns an empty collection; (filter by a negative selector result)
sel1 sel2 ... selN	a selector that applies each of the supplied selectors in order, first selector gets applied to the initial collection, and each subsequent selector is applied to the result of the previous selector; (selector chain)
:**count**()	number of elements in the context collection
:**sum**()	sum of the data values in the context collection

```
              <lQuery_expr> ::= <object_selector_expr>
      <object_selector_expr> ::= <class_name>
                               | <object_selector_expr> "/" <role_name>
                               | <object_selector_expr> "." <class_name>
                               | <object_selector_expr> "["
                                     <object_selector_expr>
                                     <obj_op>
                                     <object_selector_expr>
                                     "]"
                               | <object_selector_expr> "["
                                     <data_sub_selector_expr>
                                     <data_op>
                                     <constant>
                                     "]"
                               | <object_selector_expr> "not("
                                     <object_sub_selector_expr>
                                     ")"
  <object_sub_selector_expr> ::= "/" <role_name>
                               | "." <class_name>
                               | <object_sub_selector_expr>
                                 <object_selector_expr>
    <data_sub_selector_expr> ::= <object_sub_selector_expr> ":count()"
                               | <object_sub_selector_expr> ":sum()"
                    <obj_op> ::= "==" | "!="
                   <data_op> ::= "==" | "!=" | "<" | ">" | "=<" | ">="
```

Fig. 3. The lQuery selector expression grammar in a BNF notation

Besides the primitive selectors there are also selector combinators, such as a selector chain and a condition on selector result. The selector chain is a concatenation of primitive selectors. It will apply the first selector to the initial collection, then pass the result of that evaluation to the next selector and so on through all the selectors. For example, a selector expression "Professor /teaches" matches all courses that are taught by professors.

There are also aggregation operators for summing data-property values, getting the count of objects in collection, etc.

3.1   Integration with Ontology

Now that we have defined a language, in which it is possible to define classes that OWL cannot describe, we need some way for the ontology designers to use it. One of the best ways to intuitively capture the reality is through a visual representation. For OWL such a notation that is inspired by UML class diagrams is OWLGrEd graphical ontology notation [4]. In the OWLGrEd ontology notation classes are represented by boxes, and there is a field (starts with "=") under the class name where a class description can be added in the OWL Manchester syntax [7]. We extend this notation with a possibility to write there lQuery expressions. To distinguish them from the expressions written in the Manchester syntax, the lQuery expressions are enclosed in the symbols «» (see Figure 4).

HardWorkingStudent
"students that have taken at least 20 credit points"
=«Student [/takes@creditPoints :sum() >= 20]»

Fig. 4. Demonstration of the OWLGrEd syntax extension for the lQuery expressions

The lQuery expressions are serialized in ontology files using OWL annotation properties [8]. Annotation properties allow to attach arbitrary information to any OWL entity or assertion. The lQuery expressions are always added to a named class. We introduce an annotation property *lQueryEquals* whose domain is an OWL Class, and range is *lQueryExpression*. When the ontology is exported from the OWLGrEd ontology notation to an OWL file, the lQuery expressions will be exported as such annotations. Figure 5 shows the example from Figure 4 serialized in the Manchester syntax.

```
Datatype: lQueryExpression
AnnotationProperty: lQueryEquals

----------
Class: PassedStudent
    Annotations:
        lQueryEquals "Student:has(/grade/course@creditPoints:sum() >= 20)"^^lQueryExpression
        rdfs:comment "Students that have earned at least 20 credit points"
```

Fig. 5. lQuery expressions as annotation properties in Manchester syntax

3.2   Some Examples from the University Ontology

Now that we have seen a survey of the lQuery expressions and how they are shown graphically, we will look at some examples from the University Ontology that we were not able to define using OWL class expressions. First let us return to the example of students without known courses from the previous section. Figure 6 shows the same ontology fragment but with an additional class *StudentWith-NoKnownCourses* that defines the instances we could not get with OWL (this class belongs to the category of *IntrospectiveClasses*). Before we analyze the lQuery expression that describes that class, let us recall that the OWL definition of class *InactiveStudents* – "not (takes some Course)" – does not describe the instances we want because it will contain only instances for which it can be proved that they cannot have a link *takes*, but in this situation there is no information from which to prove that the individual *s1* could have a link or not. Therefore it is not classified as either *InactiveStudent* or *ActiveStudent*. In contrast, the lQuery selectors work only with the information that is directly known and assumes that everything that is not known is false.

Let us see how this example works step by step. The class *StudentWith-NoKnownCourses* is defined by the lQuery expression "Student :not(/takes)". This selector is a selector chain that consists of two primitive selectors – selector by class name and a negative filter selector.   The first part of the selector is a selector by class name "Student". It returns a collection of instances that have been classified as a Student. In Figure 6 that collection would contain the individuals *s1* and *s2*. The next selector in the chain is then evaluated in the context of the returned collection. In this case it is a negative filter selector ":not(/takes)". It leaves only those instances from the context collection for which the sub-selector ("/takes") returns an empty collection. In our example that would be only the instance *s1*. Finally, the query result is materialized as an *instanceOf* assertion from each instance in the result collection to the class *StudentWithNoKnownCourses* (shown as a red dotted line in Figure 5).

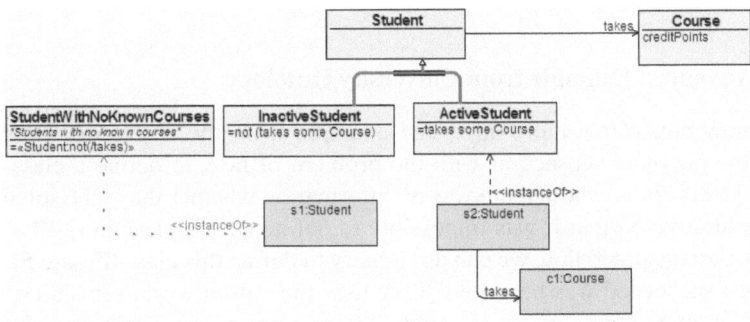

Fig. 6. Demonstration of the lQuery semantics in contrast to OWL semantics

Another feature that is missing from OWL is aggregation operations. Consequently many intuitive classes cannot be defined in OWL. For example, in the university ontology such a class would be *HardWorkingStudents* – "students that have taken at least 20 credit points". In lQuery this statement would be written as "Student

[/takes@creditPoints :sum() >= 20]". Let us look at how this expression is evaluated on an example in Figure 7. The selector consists of two parts – selector by class name and a filter by condition whose sub-selector is a selector chain. The result of the "Student" selector is a collection with instances *s1* and *s2*. Now let us look at the filter selector "[/takes@creditPoints :sum() >= 20]". It will return those objects from the context collection for whom the condition evaluates to true. In this case the condition is on the sum of data property values, i.e. the sum must be greater or equal to 20. The path "/takes@creditPoints" means that for each student we find all the courses that he *takes* and get values of the corresponding data-property *creditPoints*. The result is a collection of integers that is passed to the operation ":sum()". The result is compared to the value 20 and, if it is greater or equal, then the student is added to the result collection. In the current example the collection will contain only the individual *s2*.

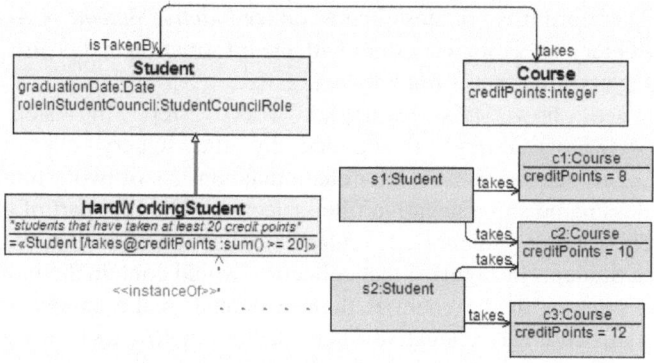

Fig. 7. Demonstration of the lQuery aggregation expressions

We could also define a more complex class, like "students that have taken at least 20 credit points and have no grade less then 4". It can be written in lQuery as follows – "Student [/takes@creditPoints :sum() >= 20] :not([/grade@value < 4])".

3.3   Advanced Example from University Ontology

Let us now consider a more advanced example from the University Ontology. We started the previous subsection with the problem of how to define a class with only those students about whom there was no information whether they take some course or not. We discovered that it was impossible to define such a class in OWL (Figure 2). Then we demonstrated how we can use lQuery to define this class (Figure 5). The main reason we succeeded was because lQuery uses the closed world semantics. From that example it may seem that we would always want to use only the closed world semantics. However, it turns out that the situation is much more subtle.

Let us suppose that we want to define a class of students to whom we want to send reminders to register to some course or they will be expelled. In this example the ontology (shown in Figure 8) will have two additional classes, namely, *GraduatedStudent* (those that have graduation date) and *StudentCouncilMember* (those that have some role in student council). For both of these classes there is a corresponding OWL definition of what it means for an individual to belong to that class. In addition, it is known that a *GraduateStudent* cannot take any courses because it is a subclass of *Inactive-Student* and *StudentCouncilMember* must take at least one course because it is a subclass of *ActiveStudent*.

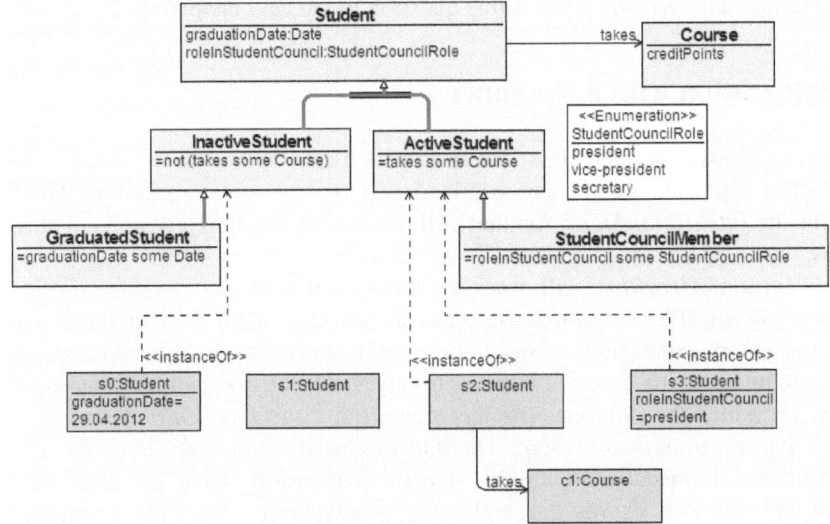

Fig. 8. Extended example from Figure 2

Let us look at what it means in terms of instances (remember that we are working under open world assumption). Now we have two additional students – *s0* and *s3* – for each of them we know an additional feature. For the student *s0* we know his graduation date and for the student *s3* we know his role in student council. Thanks to this additional information and the class definitions it can be inferred that *s0* is an *InactiveStudent* and that *s3* is an *ActiveStudent* (even though we do not know precisely which course he takes, we know that he is taking some course because otherwise he could not be a *StudentCouncilMember*). Therefore, if we return to our original example "students whom we need to send reminder to register to some course", we can see that the closed world assumption is not by itself sufficient to get what we need because then we would get all those individuals without a *takes* link, i.e. *s0*, *s1* and *s3*. But we actually want only the individual *s1* because there is no need to send reminders to students who have graduated (*s0*) or to students about whom we indirectly know that they are taking some course (*s3*).

As can be seen from the previous paragraph, the closed world assumption is not enough, and we need to be able to refer to the results of reasoning process to define the class that we want. Therefore we need to write the lQuery expression as follows – take all students then exclude all those students about whom it is known that they are   an *InactiveStudent* or an *ActiveStudent*, e.g.   "Student:not(InactiveStudent): not (ActiveStudent)". If the ontology contains all the *instanceOf* assertions that are shown in Figure 8, then that expression will return a collection with only one student – *s1* – which is exactly what we wanted.

However, it could be the case that the *instanceOf* assertions that allowed lQuery to get the correct result where not directly present in the ontology. Typically they are calculated by a reasoner. It is not required for those assertions to be explicitly present in the ontology all the time. Therefore it raises a question, how does a reasoner and the lQuery interoperate? We will answer this question in the next chapter.

4   Integration with a Reasoner

There are two kinds of derived classes in an extended ontology, namely, classes defined by OWL class expressions and classes defined by lQuery selector expressions. Now we will define the *IntegrationAlgorithm* that will use both types of expressions to classify instances.

The *IntegrationAlgorithm* will work as follows. It will start by classifying the ontology using an OWL reasoner. Because, as we saw in the end of the previous chapter, for lQuery expressions to work correctly they need all the inferred *instanceOf* assertions to be explicitly asserted in the ontology. After the reasoner has classified the ontology, i.e. added the inferred *instanceOf* assertions, the *IntegrationAlgorithm* will perform a lQuery classification step. The lQuery classification step first finds all the classes that are defined by an lQuery selector expression. Then for each class it evaluates the selector expression and gets a collection with the corresponding individuals. If the found collection is a strict superset of the currently asserted class individuals, then it adds *instanceOf* assertions for all the newly found individuals. But, if the class has an explicitly asserted individual that is not in the found collection, then it report a contradiction.

After the lQuery step has finished there will be new *instanceOf* assertions in the ontology that could be used by the reasoner to derive some additional information. Therefore we would want to run the reasoner one more time. Afterwards, of course, lQuery could again find some additional information, and so on. Now we will show that this algorithm always terminates with either a contradiction or an ontology where no new information can be deduced.

First, note that after running a reasoner there can be tree types of results, namely, the reasoner finds a contradiction, the reasoner finds new *instanceOf* assertions or it finds nothing new, i.e. every hidden assertion has been found, and there is no contradiction. The lQuery step can have the same three types of results. So both the lQuery step and the reasoner can only add new *instanceOf* assertions to the ontology. Therefore running them one after another in a loop will end in either a contradiction, or with an ontology where running one or the other will result in the same ontology.

5   Implementation

Data in the Semantic Web is stored in RDF [9] format in the so-called RDF data-stores. A universal way of working with such data is the SPARQL [10] query language. For a practical implementation of our extension we need an RDF data-store that supports update operations, such as Stardog [11], and a standard OWL reasoner, such as Pellet [12]. The proposed lQuery language is implemented as a library in the Lua programming language [13, 14]. A detailed explanation of the implementation of the lQuery language is given by the authors in [15] where a restricted subset of the language was used for the tool building task. Even though the described implementation was based on a domain specific repository, the base API can be easily translated to SPARQL queries. That allowed to transfer most of the library implementation ideas to an RDF data-store.

6   Related Work

The related work can be divided in two categories – query and rule languages for semantic web technologies, and OWL extensions with some closed world capabilities. First we will look at query languages that could be used in place of lQuery.

The most widely used query language for RDF data-stores is SPARQL [10]. Its main purpose is for retrieval and manipulation of RDF triples [9]. Because RDF is one of the standard serialization formats for OWL and almost all semantic web data is stored in RDF databases, SPARQL can also be used for writing queries for OWL data. The main problem with this approach is that we need to encode the RDF serialization of OWL expression in the query, thus making them "verbose, difficult to write, and difficult to understand" [16]. Thus SPARQL is unsuitable for being used in place of lQuery because our goal was an intuitive language in which the queries could be expressed using the ontology terms, not their underlying serialization in some other language.

Another language that can be used alongside OWL to define new classes is SWRL [17]. SWRL extends OWL with a new type of assertion – a rule that consists of an antecedent part and consequent part. Both parts consist of conjunction of atoms. Informally a SWRL rule can be read as if all atoms in antecedent part are true, then the consequent part must also be true. SWRL has the full expressive power of OWL-DL, combined with (binary) function-free Horn logic, consequently, it is undecidable [18], and there are no full implementations available. Additionally, because SWRL uses the same open world assumption on which OWL is based, it has the same problems for our purpose, i.e. it cannot describe classes of objects for which something is not known.

A similar language from a different domain, which largely inspired design of the lQuery, is the OCL [3] – a constraint language for UML. The main difference is that its semantics is tailored for constraint checking and not classification. Thus it always works on a single instance and not on all individuals.

There have also been attempts to extend OWL with operators to describe objects with unknown features (epistemic operators) [6]. It has largely been based on work on non-monotonic reasoning. Currently, only a partial success has been reached in this direction. The main advantage of introducing epistemic operators directly into OWL and writing a reasoner that understands it is that it could be possible to prove that the ontology is consistent. In our proposed system reasoner and the extension are only partially integrated – but it happens only on the instance level, i.e. a contradiction will be found only when a contradictory instance is added to repository. A reasoner that understands OWL and epistemic operators could find a contradiction only from class definitions.

7   Conclusions

In this paper we discussed the benefits and limitations of OWL for the task of knowledge capture and retrieval. The main emphasis was put on researching how suitable OWL is for defining derived classes that are intuitive for the end-users. The main advantage of OWL is the reasoners that can classify individuals given only partial information about them using the class definitions. However a reasoner can classify individuals only when it can be proven that either an object has some feature or that it cannot have a feature. Consequently it is impossible to define a class of exactly those individuals about whom some information is missing, e.g. students about whom we do not know what courses they have taken. Such *IntrospectiveClasses* are very natural and useful for practical applications.

We proposed an OWL extension that retains all the benefits of pure OWL, solves the problem of introspective class definitions and retrieval of their instances. The extension consists of two parts, namely, a selector language lQuery and an algorithm for integrating it with the existing reasoners. The proposed extension allows us to classify instances using either OWL semantics or lQuery semantics. One drawback of this solution is that it is no longer possible to prove that the extended ontology is consistent by looking only at the class level.

The primary advantage of the proposed extension is the ability to precisely define more derived classes at the ontology level and use them for the classification of individuals. These additional classes make it easy for end-users to write ad-hoc queries because they can select from a larger set of predefined intuitive classes instead of specifying them in a low level query. It is possible because our proposed algorithm can materialize both OWL inferences and lQuery inferences in an RDF data store. Thus higher-level RDF query languages, such as ViziQuer [19, 20], Facet Graphs [21], etc., can take advantage of the additional expressivity made possible by our extension without changing anything in their implementation.

Currently, the extended classification algorithm works in batch-mode just like most reasoners. In the future we plan to investigate how to make it incremental. Another research direction is whether it is possible to check the consistency of the extended ontology using only OWL and lQuery class definitions. Finally, since lQuery works orthogonally to a reasoner, and it is possible to easily extend it with new primitive operators, we will look for more patterns that are similar to the described *IntrospectiveClasses* and conditions on aggregations, that can be added to lQuery and thus help to more directly represent the intuitive classes in an ontology and use them for classification.

Acknowledgements. This work has been supported by the European Social Fund within the project «Support for Doctoral Studies at University of Latvia», and by the European Regional Development Fund within the project Nr. 2010/0325/2DP/2.1.1.1.0/10/APIA/VIAA/109, and by the Latvian National Research Program Nr. 2 „Development of Innovative Multifunctional Materials, Signal Processing and Information Technologies for Competitive Science Intensive Products" within the project Nr. 5 „New Information Technologies Based on Ontologies and Model Transformations".

References

1. OWL 2 Web Ontology Language. W3C Recommendation (October 27, 2009),
   http://www.w3.org/TR/owl2-overview/
2. Ng, G.: Open vs. Closed world, Rules vs. Queries: Use cases from Industry. In: OWL: Experiences and Directions (2005)
3. OMG Object Constraint Language, Version 2.3.1,
   http://www.omg.org/spec/OCL/2.3.1
4. Bārzdiņš, J., Bārzdiņš, G., Čerāns, K., Liepiņš, R., Sproģis, A.: UML Style Graphical Notation and Editor for OWL 2. In: Forbrig, P., Günther, H. (eds.) BIR 2010. LNBIP, vol. 64, pp. 102–114. Springer, Heidelberg (2010)
5. OWLGrEd – an Ontology Editor for Compact UML-style OWL Graphic Notation,
   http://owlgred.lumii.lv/
6. Grimm, S., Motik, B.: Closed World Reasoning in the Semantic Web through Epistemic Operators. In: OWL: Experiences and Directions (2005)
7. OWL 2 Web Ontology Manchester Syntax, W3C Working Group Note (October 27, 2009),
   http://www.w3.org/TR/owl2-manchester-syntax/
8. OWL 2 Web Ontology Language Structural Specification and Functional-Style Syntax. W3C Recommendation (October 27, 2009),
   http://www.w3.org/TR/owl2-syntax/#Annotation_Properties
9. RDF Primer, W3C Recommendation (February 10, 2004),
   http://www.w3.org/TR/rdf-primer/
10. SPARQL Query Language for RDF, W3C Recommendation (January 15, 2008),
    http://www.w3.org/TR/rdf-sparql-query/
11. Stardog: The RDF database, http://stardog.com/
12. Sirin, E., Parsia, B., Grau, B.C., Kalyanpur, A., Katz, Y.: Pellet: A practical OWL-DL reasoner. J. Web Sem. 5(2), 51–53 (2007)
13. The Programming Language Lua, http://www.lua.org/
14. Ierusalimschy, R., Henrique de Figueiredo, L.: Passing a Language through the Eye of a Needle. Communications of the ACM 54(7), 38–43
15. Liepins, R.: lQuery: A Model Query and Transformation Library. Scientific Papers, vol. 770, pp. 27–45. University of Latvia (2011)
16. Sirin, E., Bulka, B., Smith, M.: Terp: Syntax for OWL-friendly SPARQL Queries. In: Proceedings of OWLED (2010)
17. SWRL: A Semantic Web Rule Language Combining OWL and RuleML, W3C Member Submission (May 21, 2004), http://www.w3.org/Submission/SWRL/
18. Hitzler, P., Parsia, B.: Ontologies and rules. In: Handbook on Ontologies, 2nd edn., pp. 111–132. Springer (2009)
19. Barzdins, G., Rikacovs, S., Zviedris, M.: Graphical Query Language as SPARQL Frontend. In: Local Proceedings of 13th East-European Conference (ADBIS 2009), pp. 93–107. Riga Technical University, Riga (2009)
20. Barzdins, G., Liepins, E., Veilande, M., Zviedris, M.: Ontology Enabled Graphical Database Query Tool for End-Users. Selected Papers from DB&IS 2008. Frontiers in Artificial Intelligence and Applications, vol. 187, pp. 105–116. IOS Press (2009)
21. Heim, P., Ertl, T., Ziegler, J.: Facet Graphs: Complex Semantic Querying Made Easy. In: Aroyo, L., Antoniou, G., Hyvönen, E., ten Teije, A., Stuckenschmidt, H., Cabral, L., Tudorache, T. (eds.) ESWC 2010, Part I. LNCS, vol. 6088, pp. 288–302. Springer, Heidelberg (2010)

Transfer of Method Knowledge and Modelling in Distributed Teams – Lessons Learned

Magnus Lundqvist[1], Kurt Sandkuhl[1,2], and Ulf Seigerroth[1]

[1] School of Engineering at Jönköping University,
P.O. Box 1026, 55111 Jönköping, Sweden
{Magnus.Lundqvist,Ulf.Seigerroth}@jth.hj.se
[2] University of Rostock, Institute of Computer Science
Albert-Einstein-Str. 22, 18059 Rostock, Germany
Kurt.Sandkuhl@uni-rostock.de

Abstract. One of the traditional application areas for enterprise modelling is the context of improving business practice and management. In improvement situations an important dimension is better information flow in enterprises, i.e. to be able to provide the right information required to complete enterprise tasks. In order to systematically capture and analyse information demand, a method for information demand analysis has been developed. The subject of this paper is the use of this method in distributed teams of modellers, which requires transfer of method knowledge to the modellers, coordination of its application, systematic evaluation of lessons learned, and collection of change proposals for the method. The aim is to report on the process of method knowledge transfer and usage including the lessons learned and implications on the used method. The contributions are (1) lessons learned from the process of transferring method knowledge and performing the actual modelling in distributed teams, (2) implications for the method as such regarding alignment between different models-on-plastic (or paper) and electronic models, and (3) implications for the specific method notation.

Keywords: Enterprise modelling, information demand modelling, method knowledge transfer, method development, practice of modelling.

1 Introduction

Enterprise modelling, enterprise architecture, and business process management are three areas that for a long time have been part of a tradition where the mission is to improve business practice and management [1]. There are close relations between these areas and the information systems field in the aim to improve organisations [2]. This improvement process often involves activities such as understanding and evaluating the current situation of a business and then developing and implementing new ways of working [3]. In this context, business process management and enterprise modelling often are used and applied as techniques to perform a business diagnosis, often referred to as modelling and analysing the AS-IS situation, and to develop and implement

N. Aseeva, E. Babkin, and O. Kozyrev (Eds.): BIR 2012, LNBIP 128, pp. 26–40, 2012.
© Springer-Verlag Berlin Heidelberg 2012

improvements, often referred to as the TO-BE situation [3]. An important aspect of business diagnosis is the information flow within organisations, i.e. to analyse whether all organisational roles receive the information required for performing their work tasks and fulfilling their responsibilities.

One of the prerequisites for efficient business diagnosis and enterprise modelling projects is the use of a well-defined method, which guides the modelling procedure, defines the notation to be used for capturing modelling results, helps to identify important concepts and viewpoints, and supports identifying relevant stakeholders (cf. section 2.1). This paper addresses method use in distributed teams and in particular it focuses on experiences from the transfer of method knowledge. The experiences presented originate from the use of a method for information demand analysis (IDA), i.e. a method for analysing the information demand of organisational roles as a part of the information flow analysis. This method was developed in an iterative and incremental manner from 2006-2011 in two R&D projects, which included 7 industrial and academic partners.

In the context of another industrially driven project aiming at the improvement of information flow in enterprises, the IDA method had to be used in distributed teams of modellers, which required transfer of method knowledge to the modellers, coordination of its application, systematic evaluation of lessons learned, and collection of change proposals for the method. The aim of this paper is to report on the process of method knowledge transfer and usage including the lessons learned and method implications. The contributions of this paper are (1) lessons learned from the process of transferring method knowledge and performing modelling in distributed teams, (2) implications for the method as such regarding alignment between different models-on-plastic and electronic models, and (3) implications for the specific method notation.

The remaining part of the paper is structured as follows: Section 2 introduces the informing foundation for our work from method engineering and information demand modelling. Section 3 introduces the process and industrial cases of information demand modelling in distributed teams. Section 4 describes and discusses the lessons learned and method implications derived from the industrial cases. Section 5 summarizes our work and describes future activities.

2   Background

The informing foundation for our work presented in this paper consists of an understanding of "methods" as support for action (section 2.1), and of information demand modelling as specific perspective in enterprise modelling (section 2.2).

2.1 Methods as Support for Action

All actions are performed based on different motive´s and rational. There are different things that can influence, guide and inspire us, when we perform actions. The sources of guidance and influence can be more or less explicit. The support can be of a tacit nature in terms of different experiences that we have and that we are recalling in the actual work situation, in this paper enterprise modelling and especially information demand analysis. The support can also be explicitly formulated as different method descriptions that we follow. In our view methods are supposed to give us explicitly formulated guidance for cause of actions in terms of different method descriptions that we follow to achieve certain results. Somewhere between experiences and methods we also recognise theories that can influence our actions without giving such explicit prescriptive directives as methods. Theories can help us to focus and to direct our attention towards certain concepts and structure of concepts (focal areas). In this case the conceptualisation of information demand is built into the method for information demand analysis as a focal area. In addition to this we can also use computerised tools as guidance for actions since methods in many cases are implemented in different computerised tools. The use of methods, theories and tools can therefore be regarded as action knowledge that we can agree with and seek support from during enterprise modelling and information demand analysis. During modelling there is usually a need to document different aspects and therefore many methods include rules for representation, which often is called modelling techniques or notations, which has a central part in this paper. Methods also provide procedural guidelines, which many times are tightly coupled to notation. The procedure involves some concepts as process, activity, information, and object, which are parts of the prescribed work procedure. They are also parts of the semantics of the notation. The concepts are the glue that connects the parts work procedure and notation. Methods can thus be crystallised into: *Perform action A, in order to reach goal G.*

Methods are often a compound of several method components (focal areas), which could be referred to as methodology [5]. These different method components together form a structure called a framework, define the internal structure of a method. Method components often are considered as consisting of work procedure, notation, and concepts to be analysed [6]. The concept of method component is similar to the concept Method Chunk [7] and the notion of method fragment [8] (for further elaboration and explanation of the notion of methods, please c.f. [10] and [11]).

2.2 Information Demand Modelling

Enterprise Modelling as a discipline has a status as flexible and powerful approach to capture and describe many different aspects of enterprises. The purpose of describing an enterprise usually varies from case to case but common purposes are to improve quality, efficiency or to reduce cost and resource utilisations etc. Various methods and notations are in turn more or less suitable for modelling specific aspects of an enterprise, i.e. what we model, how we model, and how we express and represent the results highly dependant on the underlying purpose and scope. In some cases where the purpose is to improve quality it might be relevant to look at processes and in others to look at product variants and therefore we chose the approach and focus accordingly. Consequently there are a large number of different methods, notations and tools, focusing at such diverse aspects of enterprises as processes, information systems, concept domains, organisational structures etc.

In todays competitive business climate it has become increasingly important with lean organisations, shorter lead-times, geographically distributed and collaborative work teams, and a higher degree of market flexibility in general. There are also more and more technical solutions, such as Information Logistics, ERP-systems etc. that aim at better integration of information and the various tasks being performed in enterprises. Consequently, it has also become more important to focus on, and understand, how information flows within and between organisations and which consequences this has for the people working in such organisations.

We claim that, for such situations, where the information flow needs to be in focus, one relevant aspect to focus on is information demand. While there are modelling methods and notations, such as various IDEF-derivations, BPMN, EKD etc., which indeed do focus on information flow, they have a clear process-perspective. That is, many, if not most, process-oriented enterprise modelling (EM) -approaches mainly focus on workflow rather than information flow. When these EM-approaches deal with information they do so based on different process steps as unit of analysis to which information is related and grouped. This works perfectly well when we want to show the relationship between activities and information but not as well when we want to express and understand the relationship between information and the roles actually using and needing information when performing work tasks. Information Demand Analysis (IDA) is an EM-method defined with this purpose in mind and it defines, as one of its parts, how information demand and flow can be modelled from a role-perspective regardless of how the processes are defined. The method is documented in handbooks (cf. 3.1); the main characteristics are published in an article about modelling information demand in an enterprise context [4].

Many of the ideas presented in this paper are based on the authors' previous work on defining information demand from a theoretical and empirical perspective. In [9] these efforts are compiled into a number of conclusions regarding the nature and aspects of information demand. One of the major contributions of this work is the definition of an information demand context:

An Information Demand Context is the formalised representation of information about the setting in which information demands exist and comprises the organisational role of the party having the demand, work tasks related, and any resources and informal information exchange channels available, to that role.

That is to say, information demand has a strong relation to the context in which it exists. When we analyse information demand in an enterprise we do it from the perspective of the roles in the enterprise we do it. We furthermore look at the activities performed by roles and what resources they utilise in order to do so, i.e. to understand the information demand a role has in an organisation we need to understand the responsibilities that role has in the organisation and the tasks related to this responsibility.

Information demand relates to aspects of an enterprise that can be considered as traditional in the sense that they are the same concepts as most EM-approaches are concerned with. The difference mainly lies in the perspectives taken when modelling information demand as opposed to in approaches for process modelling. Following from this difference are of course also a number of additional differences in how the models are produces. The procedures used for deriving the information on which the models are based obviously have to reflect the difference in focus. It can therefore be argued that information demand modelling (IDM) is an EM-approach as any other but just as any other EM-approach it has to be supported by a method that describes how (procedures) and when (scope) the approach can and should be used, how the results should be expressed (notation) and what focus is put on (conceptual focus) as well as how all this is tied together (framework).

3   Information Demand Modelling in Distributed Teams

This section describes the context of information demand modelling in distributed teams forming the basis for lessons learned and experiences presented in this paper. This context includes industrial cases (section 3.2) and the process coordinating the modelling work (section 3.1).

3.1 Process of Modelling in Distributed Teams

The context for using the IDA method was the infoFLOW-2 project, which aims at improving information flow in small and medium-sized enterprises (SME) and has a runtime from 2010 - 2012. One of the main intentions of the project is to investigate, whether information demand-centric thinking can have advantages compared to process-centric thinking. When solving organizational problems, infoFLOW-2 starts from understanding and modelling the information demands in an organization, instead of modelling the work processes. The project includes two partners from automotive supplier industries, a system integrator specialized on IT-solutions for SME, a public-private partnership in information logistics research, a research institute and a university, responsible for the project management. Additional enterprises are involved on a case basis.

In the preceding project, infoFLOW-1 (2006-2009), the method for information demand analysis was developed. The method is documented in an English and a Swedish handbook. Both handbooks aim at supporting method use by describing each phase of the method with preconditions, steps to be performed, way of working, expected results and aids, if relevant. Since many participants in the infoFLOW-2 project are native Swedish speakers, the Swedish version was considered an important element to ease method application.

Work in the infoFLOW-2 project, including modelling in distributed teams, was coordinated by infoFLOW-2 project meetings with all project members attending. During the meetings, upcoming cases for information demand modelling were briefly introduced and the decision was made, who should perform and how the case should be performed. During the first part of infoFLOW-2, the basic strategy was to transfer method knowledge by always involving at least one modeller in the case who was part of the method development team, i. e. the handbook was basically considered as accompanying material for the cases in the first infoFLOW-2 phase. The other modellers involved in the cases were supposed to learn the method by observing the experienced modeller and by stepwise getting more responsibility for the case.

Later in the project, we added cases where only the method handbook served as means to provide the method knowledge or where the modelling teams did no longer include one of the initial method developers. In total, we so far performed 4 cases with involvement of method developers, 4 cases without method developers but with modellers who were involved in at least one of the first 4 cases, and 3 cases completely based on handbook use only. These 3 cases were outside the infoFLOW-2 project and using the English handbook version.

For all cases and during all phases of infoFLOW-2, the project meetings served as central coordination unit, i. e. the modelling results, experiences when performing the modelling, and improvement or change requests for the method and the method handbook were discussed during the infoFLOW-2 meeting in the project team and documented in the minutes. The infoFLOW-2 project includes 4 industrial and 2 academic partners. On average the meetings had 10 participants (5 from industry, 5 from academia). Among these 10 were 5 who were involved in the method development and the main method engineer.

3.2 Industrial Cases

The research work presented in this paper is motivated by a number of real-world cases, two of them were selected for brief presentation in this section. In both of the cases below we have used a final notation language for the information demand analysis according to the legend in the figure 1 below.

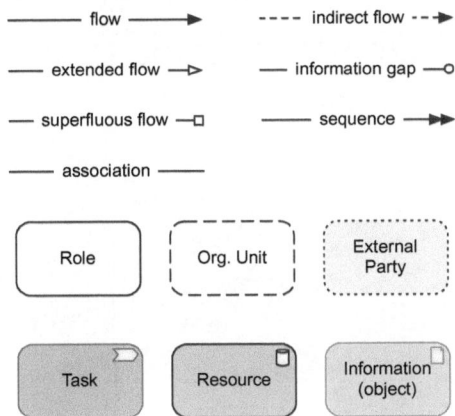

Fig. 1. Symbol legend for information demand analysis

3.2.1 The SAPSA Case

The SAP Swedish User Association (SAPSA) is a non-profit association for organizations that use the enterprise system SAP. The main purpose with SAPSA is to provide an arena for exchange of knowledge and experiences and networking for SAP stakeholders. SAPSA also aims at taking care of the member's demands for development of SAP software and services and third part products certified by SAPSA. The members have unlimited access to SAPSA's focus groups (groups with expertise within certain areas) and the annual SAPSA conference. The background for doing enterprise modelling and information demand modelling at SAPSA was an articulated need from SAPSA to elucidate their interaction with the focus groups, members, and other stakeholders. At the time of this case SAPSA experienced some difficulties in how to increase the activity and exchange between SAPSA central, the focus groups, the members, and other stakeholders. The core area for the modelling session therefore addressed the central roles; SAPSA, Focus groups, User companies, SAP consultancies, SAP Sweden, and SAP International. The people that were present at the information demand modelling seminar were, from SAPSA: the CEO, the Event coordinator, the economy administrator, and the secretary from the SAPSA board. From the research project we participated with one researcher. One representative also participated from the industry. The industrial project representative is also the secretary in the SAPSA board. The actual modelling seminar lasted for five hours including a scoping discussions (framing and setting the scene), the actual modelling, and validating discussions in the end of the seminar. The actual modelling session was divided into two phases. First we modelled the actual situation and how the different roles were interacting today (AS-IS), see figure 2 below.

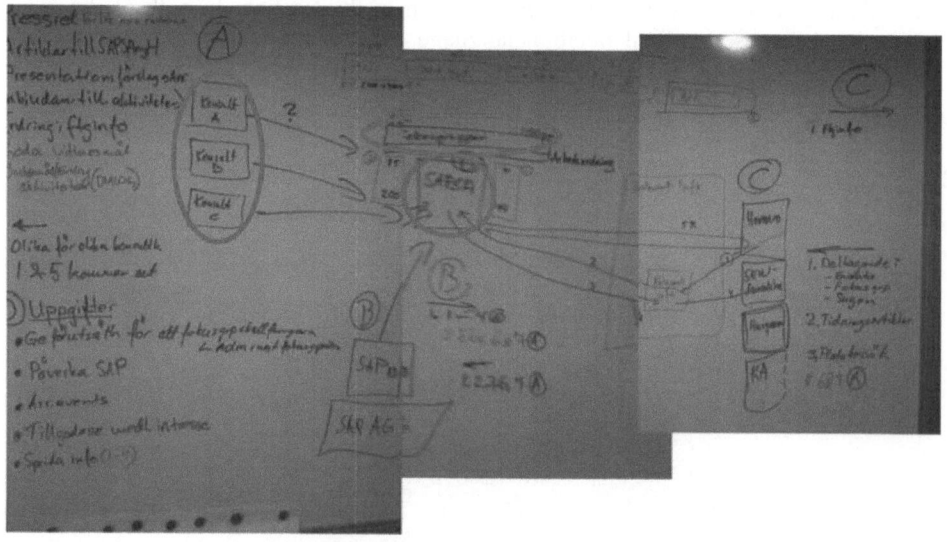

Fig. 2. Example of model from the first modelling phase

During this stage we also had an evaluating discussion about the current practice concerning the interaction between the involved roles. This evaluation resulted in a couple of core problems in relation to the exchange and interaction between the specified roles. Based on these problems we started to design a future interaction schema that could solve these problems. One important solution was to employ a new role at SAPSA, a Focus Group Coordinator. After the modelling seminar at SAPSA the models were then transformed into electronic versions, see figure 3 below.

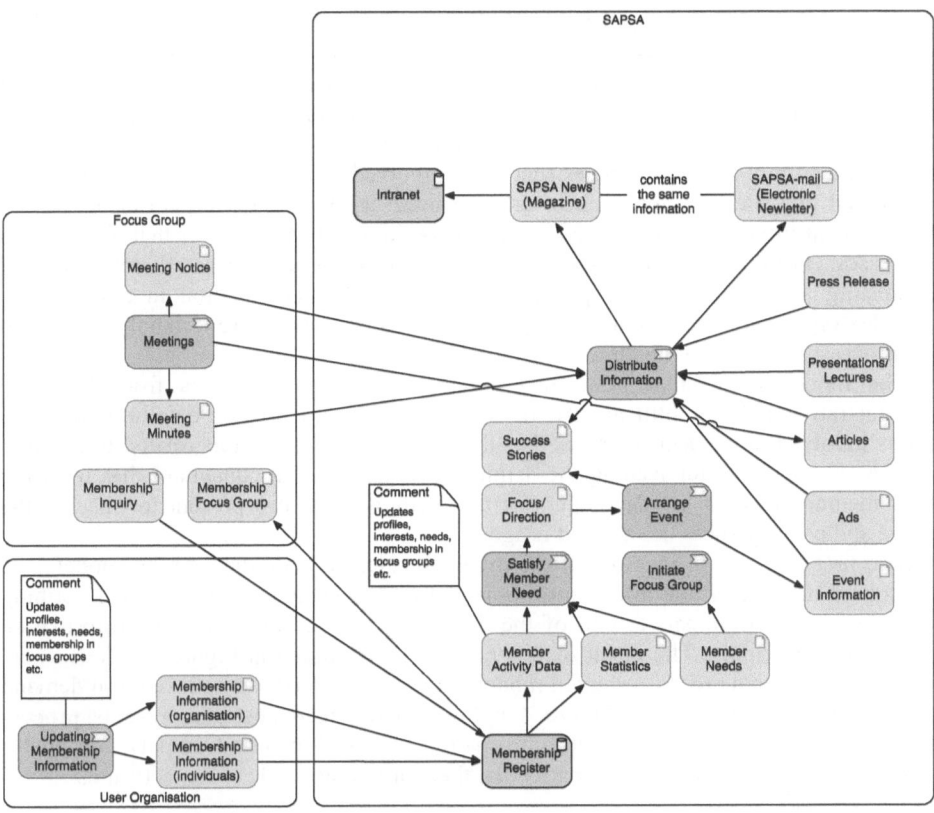

Fig. 3. Information demand model of the SAPSA case

As in a couple of other cases, we observed that there are somewhat troubling differences between the models that were developed on site, usually on plastic sheets or on whiteboard, and the models when they are transformed into electronic versions. It seems that the notation rules that are specified in the method for information demand analysis are a bit tricky to translate into the models during the actual modelling sessions. It seems, as there is a need for structural planning of the roles in the models, which is hard to do initially when the model starts to evolve. In some sense you need to have the whole picture before this type of structuring is possible.

3.2.2 The Mullsjö Municipality Case

In the Swedish society local aspects of government and administration concerning things like education, healthcare outside of hospitals, sanitation etc. are handled by a number of local authorities governed by locally elected officials. Such an administrative entity is called a municipality. One of the cases was to model the information flow in one process relating to administration of schools in one of Sweden's smallest municipalities, Mullsjö.

The purpose of the case was to clarify how information flowed during a case where municipality made a decision to close down a school in order to (1) understand how the decision was made and (2) identify what could have been done differently in terms of information to the citizens and transparency in the process. The complexity of the case does not lie in the actual process, which is quite straightforward, but rather in the many actors and administrative instances that were involved in the decision. It was therefore concluded that the best approach to analyse these aspects of the organisation was to focus on information flow and not to use a traditional EM-approach that focused on processes. From an InfoFlow-perspective this case was considered relevant and interesting as it provided an opportunity to apply the IDA-method in a case with complex organisational structures as opposed to earlier cases where it mainly have been the processes that have constituted the complexity.

The modelling seminar performed together with representatives from both the administrative and the political parts of the organisation focused on detailing all of the actors involved in the decision as well as the information these actors related to for their actions. Responsible for leading the seminar was an external consultant that used the IDA method. Two of the developers of the method were also present to observe the usage and consequences the method usage.

The first step was to identify all the involved roles and add them to the model. The consultant then added the information objects by having the representatives describing what happened from start to end of the decision process, connecting the information objects incrementally. The result of this process is illustrated in Figure 3 below where we ended up with a process-oriented model rather than a role based information demand model. This can be seen in Figure 4 below where green post-it represents process activities, orange post-it represents information objects (input and output), red post-it represents roles, and blue post-it marks that there are iterations between activities.

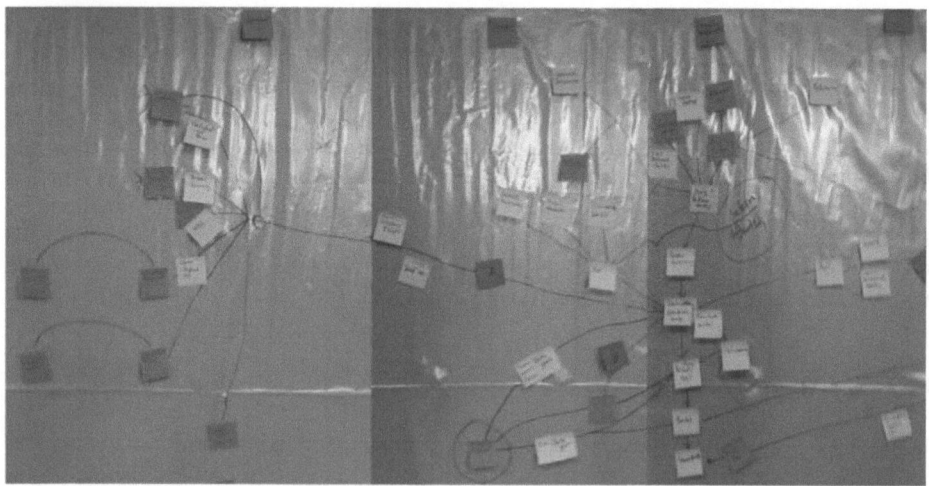

Fig. 4. Working draft of the model

This initial model turned out to be problematic from a number of perspectives, firstly, the notation used on the plastic sheets as depicted in Figure 4 had very little in common with notation language prescribed by the method, see Figure 5 below. When comparing the plastic sheets with the electronic model it is hard to see how the finished model relates to the initial model. The gap between the models is in this case bridged by situated knowledge captured during the modelling situation. There was a large amount of implicit knowledge of what was said during the seminar that neither was captured in the initial models nor is easily understood by anyone not present at the seminar. From an EM-perspective this is of course not preferable.

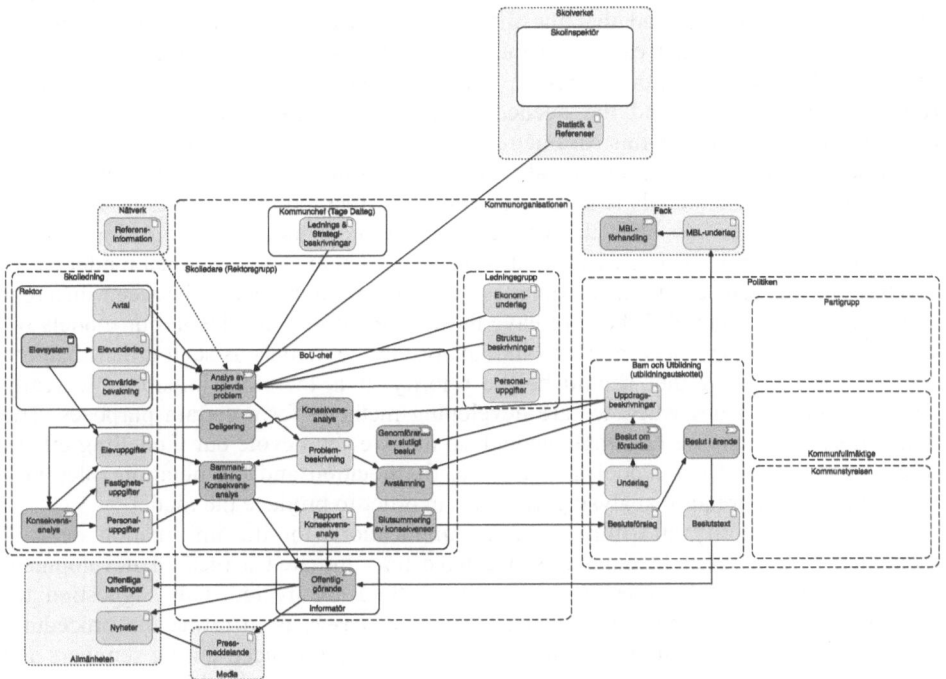

Fig. 5. Electronic version of the model

4   Lessons Learned and Method Implications

The lessons learned from distributed application of the information demand analysis method are presented in this section. This includes the necessity to avoid gaps between the electronic and pre electronic models (4.1), the importance of the model layout (4.2), and experiences from modelling in distributed teams (4.3).

4.1 How to Avoid Gaps between Pre Electronic and Electronic Models?

Based on practical experiences from the cases presented in section 3, we have recognised what we on a conceptual level would describe as model gaps. These knowledge gaps are closely related to the work procedure that is prescribed in the IDA-method. The normal work procedure in IDA, and many other modelling methods, is that the modelling is performed in two steps. In the first step we do the modelling on big plastic sheets or papers with post-it notes and white-board pens. The reason for this is to be able to do the modelling in an interactive manner together with different stakeholders. The goal is to get the stakeholders to be active in the actual modelling activities in different ways. In the second step the models on the plastic sheet is transformed into digital models in a modelling tool. As a result of this transformation process we have recognised that the differences between the plastic model and the transformed digital model can be of quite some difference. For information demand modelling this transformation process involves a restructuring of the models in terms of role-clustering of tasks and the needed information based on different rules. This clustering process could in this case be regarded as an analysis activity, which probably is not so easy to do during the actual modelling session. This structuring planning of clustered roles in the models is hard to do initially when the model starts to evolve. In some sense you need to have the whole picture (whole models) before this type of structuring is possible. This creates what we have chosen to call conceptual model gaps.

These model gaps are typical examples of alignment deficiencies between different work steps in the method. When we have these types of deficiencies in our models we will have to put down specific efforts into analysing the models as such rather than the specific case, which rather should be the priority. It is therefore important to really address notation issues when we are developing methods for a certain purposes. The notation should therefore be simple enough so that we can devote our modelling efforts to case analysis and not model analysis, i.e. the notation and the notation rules in a method should not require analysing activities in order to produce the model.

In order to identify and implement the implications for the information demand modelling method used in our cases, we have now initiated a method development activity where these alignment issues in the method are treated. Our suggestion for solution, which we already piloted in a number of cases, is to refine the procedural description of how both the initial draft of the model, as produced during seminars and the documentation of those into electronic models are constructed, which is supposed to ensure traceability between the different versions of the model.

More concrete, we started improvement work of the method with the following objectives:

- A more precise correspondence between the "paper-based" symbols used for models-on-plastic and the notation used in the electronic version. For all elements in the notation, a corresponding paper symbol has to be selected and labelled accordingly, e.g. colour, shape and print on the paper symbol have to be defined. This will at least ease the work of translating models-on-plastic to electronic ones.
- A checklist for supporting consistency and completeness of the models-on-plastic. In the modelling team, one member will have the task to assure at the end of the modelling session that the number of quality issues is as low as possible. Aspects to check include relations between model elements or additional textual descriptions of important concepts
- Guidelines for layout of models-on-plastic. Might be useful. However, this aspect has to be investigated carefully because standardizing the layout might hinder the user participation, which would be an unwanted effect.

4.2 Model Layout Matters – How to Best Visualize Information Flows

In order to remedy the shortcomings regarding model gaps discussed in previous sections effort has been focused on adapting and refining the notation and structure of the models as they are drawn in their initial state on plastic sheets. The idea behind this have been to find a way to work with and construct the initial models that results in something that better resembles the digital versions, thus making the relationship between the different versions clearer and more traceable for the clients and informants.

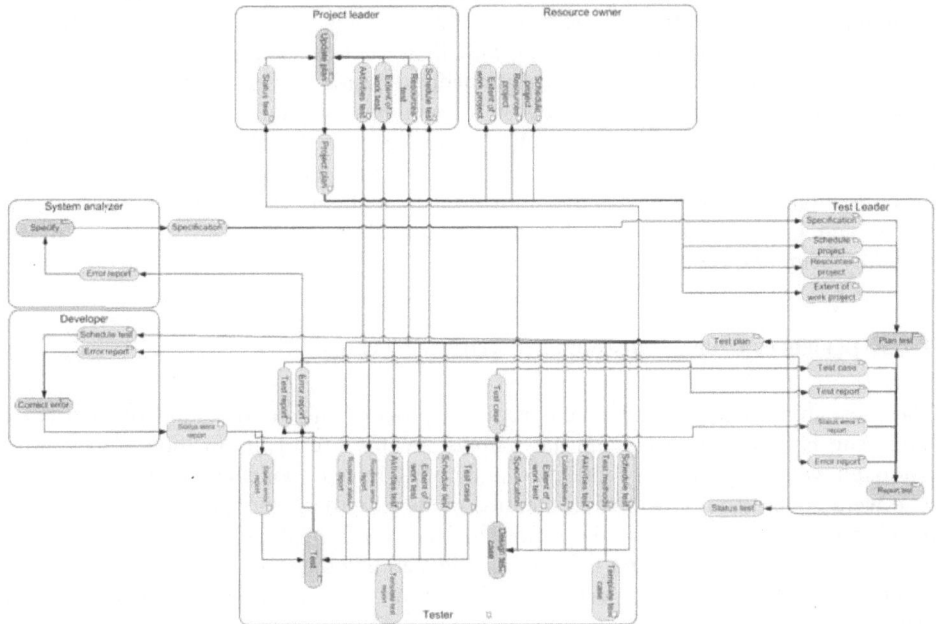

Fig. 6. Overview of new structure of initial models

One of the major problems with the initial models is, as mentioned in Section 3. that a relatively complete view of the model is needed before the modelled roles can be properly structured. As this post hoc property is one of the major reasons for the gaps between the different versions of the models, it is important to find an approach to easily changing the role structure already during the modelling seminars. Other problems we have seen during the cases are related to shared information objects and resources, i.e. such information or resources that are used by or related to several different roles. In the current approach these have been dealt with by letting them overlap the relevant roles, which works well with two roles but quickly becomes difficult with three or more roles.

As an experiment, a different approach was tested in a new case performed together with one of our project partners. The major change in this approach compared to the original one is how roles are structured. As illustrated in figure 6 above, the roles are structured around a blank centre area. The purpose behind this is two-fold, (1) the empty centre-area gives us an area to place such information and resources that are shared by several of the roles while such objects shared by only two roles still can be placed overlapping the relevant roles and (2) during modelling sessions we can move the different roles around in accordance to the developing model. The second point is further supported by the fact that we use a separate plastic sheet for each role placed on top on a larger one.

While this new approach makes it somewhat more cumbersome during the modelling sessions as the moving of roles also requires some redrawing of relationships between roles it also makes it a lot easier to keep consistency and traceability between the different iterations of the model. To reduce the need for redrawing of relationships when changing the structure of roles we propose that the bulk of the role-internal activities, information and relationships are dealt with first when possible, thus allowing for the restructuring of roles before the interrelationships are drawn. One problem with the new approach is that the relationships between roles on opposite sides of the centre area lead to decreased readability when shared objects are placed in this area. We suggest that this problem can be reduced if the tool used for constructing the digital version of the model supports hiding relationships as this allows for focus being put on specific parts of the model and hiding such details that do not contribute to the aspects of the model currently being viewed.

4.3 Experiences from Modelling in Distributed Teams

The most important lesson learned from the process and coordination of distributed modelling is that more tools and aids supporting the use of the method are required. Although we were in the very fortunate situation to have 6 modellers in the project team who were quite deeply involved in the method development, the transfer of this method to other modellers by joining the team and learning from the experienced ones had a number of problems. The experienced modellers all had the same IDA method steps and a joint perspective on how to perform the modelling in common, but they performed the actual modelling slightly differently, i. e. they did not share the practices of IDA originating from their own backgrounds. Examples of these differences are

- how to layout the models (see section 4.2),
- how to perform the scoping (start from an organizational unit or start from a work process?),
- how detailed to document terms and concepts (e. g. the responsibilities of roles), or
- how to schedule the modelling process (e. g. plan, interviews, modelling session and feedback workshop at the beginning of the process or one after the other)

These differences in practice basically are a consequence of the nature of methods, which are supposed to be support and a guideline for action, not a rigid and precise algorithm, since adaptation to situational requirements is considered an element of method success. However, when teaching a new method to modellers, these differences in practice often are perceived as deviations from the recommended method use or as inconsistencies in the method then as supportive practices. For relatively newly developed methods, like in our case the IDA method, variations in the practices should be made explicit by either offering alternative paths in the method descriptions or additional aids, like checklists or textual practice description, complementing the method handbook.

Our recommendation is to develop a training course for the method to be transferred (in our case the IDA method) and to include a detailed example for all steps of the method in the handbook. The training course will help to make the material and aids more detailed, the example will ease understandability of the handbook and help to identity gaps.

5 Conclusions and Future Work

Illustrated by two industrial cases, this paper presented experiences and lessons learned from transferring method knowledge and performing information demand modelling in distributed teams. These lessons learned mostly concern the practice of demand modelling and of transferring method knowledge. An important lesson learned is that method knowledge transfer "by heads" (i.e. by including persons experienced in the use of the method in a modelling team) does not substitute a good method handbook, since even these "heads" need some sort of normative ground to base their practice on.

Furthermore, a number of implications for the method as such can be derived from the experiences:

- Traceability between models-on-plastic and electronic models has to be improved, e.g. by correspondence between paper-based symbols and method notation, in order to avoid alignment deficiencies between different work steps
- The idea of a "blank centre area" as part of the secondary notation has to be further explored and developed, in order to ease the visualization and an understanding of role – information dependencies.
- more tools and aids supporting the use of the method are required, which make variations in the practice of different modellers explicit by either offering alternative paths in the method descriptions or additional aids, like checklists or textual practice description, complementing the method handbook

Implementation of the above changes and evaluating their effects in the practice of modelling constitutes the future work in this area.

Acknowledgement. The research presented in this paper was supported by the Swedish Knowledge Foundation (KKStiftelsen), grant 2009/0257, project "Demand Patterns for Efficient Information Logistics (infoFLOW-2)" and by the Swedish Foundation for Internationalisation in Higher Education and Research (STINT), grant IG2008-2011, project "Development and Evolution of Ontologies".

References

1. Harmon, P.: The Scope and Evolution of Business Process Management. In: vom Brocke, J., Rosemann, M. (eds.) Handbook on Business Process Management 1: Introduction, Methods, and Information Systems, pp. 83–106. Springer, Heidelberg (2010)
2. Seigerroth, U.: Enterprise Modelling and Enterprise Architecture – the constituents of transformation and alignment of Business and IT. Accepted for Publication in International Journal of IT/Business Alignment and Governance, IJITBAG (2011)
3. Hayes, J.: The Theory and Practice of Change Management. Palgrave Macmillan, Basingstoke (2007)
4. Lundqvist, M., Sandkuhl, K., Seigerroth, U.: Modelling Information Demand in an Enterprise Context: Method, Notation, and Lessons Learned. International Journal of Information System Modeling and Design (IJSMD) 2(3), 75–94 (2011)
5. Avison, D.E., Fitzgerald, G.: Information Systems Development: Methodologies, Techniques and Tools. McGraw Hill, Berkshire (1995)
6. Röstlinger, A., Goldkuhl, G.: På väg mot en komponentbaserad metodsyn (in Swedish). Presented at "VITS Höstseminarium 1994". Linköping University, Linköping (1994)
7. Ralyté, J., Backlund, P., Kühn, H., Jeusfeld, M.A.: Method Chunks for Interoperability. In: Embley, D.W., Olivé, A., Ram, S. (eds.) ER 2006. LNCS, vol. 4215, pp. 339–353. Springer, Heidelberg (2006)
8. Brinkkemper, S.: Method engineering: engineering of information systems development methods and tools. Information and Software Technology 37 (1995)
9. Lundqvist, M.: Information Demand and Use: Improving Information Flow within Small-scale Business Contexts. Licentiate Thesis, Dept of Computer and Information Science, Linköping University, Linköping, Sweden (2007) ISSN 0280-7971
10. Goldkuhl, G., Lind, M., Seigerroth, U.: Method integration: the need for a learning perspective. IEEE Proceedings - Software 145(4), 113–118 (1998)
11. Seigerroth, U.: Enterprise Modelling and Enterprise Architecture – the constituents of transformation and alignment of Business and IT. International Journal of IT/Business Alignment and Governance (IJITBAG) 2(1), 16–34 (2011)

Improving Quote Preparation in Project Management with Information Demand Patterns

Kurt Sandkuhl[1,2]

[1] The University of Rostock, Institute of Computer Science
Chair Business Information Systems, Albert-Einstein-Str. 22, 18059 Rostock, Germany
Kurt.Sandkuhl@uni-rostock.de
[2] Jönköping University, School of Engineering
Box 1026, 55 111 Jönköping, Sweden

Abstract. Among the many activities to be performed in the context of managing research and development projects preparing a quote for a call for tender can be considered as in particular information-intense. Some industrial methods and standards support the implementation of well-defined and efficient project management (PM). However, these guidelines primarily focus on work procedures and are not very detailed for quote preparation. This paper contributes to the area by proposing information demand patterns as a means to capture organizational knowledge about the desired information flow in project management with specific focus on quote preparation. The intention is to avoid wrong decisions, delayed actions and missing information in quotes caused by insufficient information supply. The contributions of the paper are (1) the concept of information demand pattern in the context of PM, (2) the information demand pattern for the role of a "quote responsible", and (3) lessons learned from validation.

Keywords: project management, process improvement, enterprise modeling, information logistics, information demand, pattern.

1   Introduction

Among the many activities to be performed in the context of managing research and development projects preparing a quote for a call for tender can be considered as in particular information-intense. In order to be successful, such a quote has to meet all requirements and expectations of the call's publisher (i.e. the potential customer if the quote is selected), include all wanted information, follow the given instructions, and have advantages compared to the competitors. Not meeting these requirements or delays in providing quote and supplements can lead to the rejection of the quote. In order to ease the implementation of well-defined and efficient project management, methods and standards, such as Prince2 [1] or PMBOK [2], provide guidelines and instruction contributing to avoid the problems mentioned. However, these guidelines are primarily focusing on work procedures and they are not very detailed for quote preparation as compared to other project management tasks.

N. Aseeva, E. Babkin, and O. Kozyrev (Eds.): BIR 2012, LNBIP 128, pp. 41–53, 2012.

This paper aims at contributing to the area by proposing information demand patterns as a means to capture organizational knowledge about the desired information flow in quote preparation and project management. The intention is to avoid wrong decisions, delayed actions and insufficient quality of quotes caused by insufficient information supply. The contributions of the paper are (1) the concept of information demand pattern in the context of PM, (2) an actual information demand pattern for the role of a "quote responsible" in order to illustrate the concept, and (3) lessons learned from validating this pattern.

The remaining part of the paper is structured as follows: the background for the work from information logistics and enterprise modeling is briefly introduced in section 2. Section 3 presents an industrial case motivating the research. The concept of information demand patterns and the method used for information demand analysis are introduced in section 4. Section 5 presents the information demand pattern for the role of a "quote responsible" including the validation activities performed. Conclusions and future work are discussed in section 6.

2   Background

Work from the areas information logistics and enterprise modeling form the background for the work presented in this paper and will be summarized in this section.

2.1   Information Logistics

Accurate and readily available information is essential in decision-making situations, problem solving and knowledge-intensive work. Recent studies show that information overload is perceived as a problem in industrial enterprises [8], i.e. many employees perceive that they receive too much and often not relevant information during their daily work, which makes it difficult to find the right information for a task at hand. Often information overload and information shortage can be observed at the same time when employees feel they receive too much information but cannot find the required information or did not receive it. It is expected that an improved information supply would contribute significantly to saving time and most likely to improving productivity.

The research field information logistics addresses the above mentioned challenge by using principles from material logistics, like just-in-time delivery, in the area of information supply. The main objective of information logistics is improved information provision and information flow. The research field explores, develops, and implements concepts, methods, technologies, and solutions for the above mentioned purpose. Contemporary research work in information logistics includes

- a method for information demand analysis in an enterprise context [7],
- patterns of information demand for efficiently constructing solutions [6, 24],
- technologies for matching information demand and content [5],
- applications for networks of automotive suppliers [4] or media industries [3].

2.2   Enterprise Knowledge Modeling

In general terms, enterprise modeling is addressing the systematic analysis and modeling of processes, organization structures, products structures, IT-systems or any other perspective relevant for the modeling purpose [9]. Lillehagen and Krogstie [10] provide a detailed account of enterprise modeling and integration approaches. Enterprise models can be applied for various purposes, such as visualization of current processes and structures in an enterprise, process improvement and optimization, introduction of new IT solutions or analysis purposes.

Enterprise knowledge modeling combines and extends approaches and techniques from enterprise modeling. The knowledge needed for performing a certain task in an enterprise or for acting in a certain role has to include the context of the individual, which requires including all relevant perspectives in the same model. Enterprise knowledge modeling aims at capturing reusable knowledge of processes and products in knowledge architectures supporting work execution [12]. These architectures form the basis for model-based solutions, which often are represented as active knowledge models. [13] identify characteristics of active models vs. passive models and emphasize that "the model must be dynamic, users must be supported in changing the model to fit their local reality, enabling tailoring of the system's behavior".

In most methods supporting enterprise modeling or enterprise knowledge modeling, information flow is analyzed as part of the business process. Examples of such methods are EKD [15] and MEMO [16]. With exception of the approach discussed in section 4, methods specifically focusing on information demand analysis do not exist, as confirmed by the survey published in [17].

3   Industrial Case

The proposed information demand pattern, which is presented in section 5 of this paper, is based on work in the R&D project InfoFlow-2, which includes 6 industrial and academic partners. Within InfoFlow-2, modelling of information demand was performed in a number of industrial cases in order to collect experiences from various situations and domains. This section will briefly discuss one of these cases in order to show the process of modelling, the organisational setting, and results. The industrial case selected is a sub-supplier to different first-tier suppliers in automotive and telecommunication industries who performs various surface treatment services of metal components. Surface treatment in this context includes different technical or decorative coatings to achieve certain functionality or appearance.

The case had the focus on the customer interaction in the surface treatment process, which includes engineering change management, quality assurance, and project management including preparation of new orders. The challenge is to manage the continuously incoming information from the customer side (e.g. change requests, specification information, order requests), from the own production (e.g. production status and problems, changes in schedule and in production systems configuration), and from the enterprise management (e.g. priorities for specific orders or policy updates). After modelling of the customer interaction process and its relation to the production processes, an information demand analysis of a specific part of the process (from quotation to production planning) was performed using the method described in section 4.

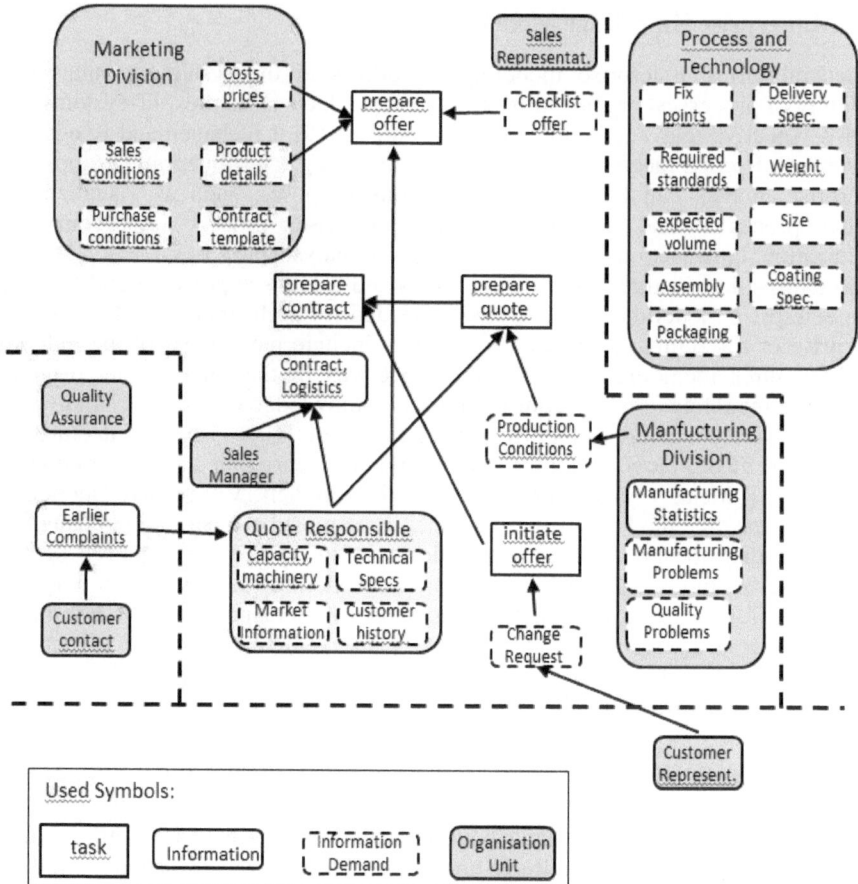

Fig. 1. Excerpt of an information demand model from the industrial case

The actual modeling, was divided into two main activities, 1) interviews, and 2) a facilitated modelling seminar. In these two activities, the head of quality, sales representative, technical support/technical in-house sales, production planner and two researchers were involved. The main purpose of the interviews was to set the stage and decide the focus for the following seminar. The major purpose of the modelling seminar was to understand the information demand for different roles based on their assignments in the process. The modelling seminar was performed in a participative way where the representatives from the industrial partner were actively involved in the modelling. The modelling was performed on plastic sheets with sticky notes and whiteboard markers. The result from the seminar has been used by the head of quality to elucidate and share knowledge among the employees about certain dimensions in the established process including quote preparation. The models have served as an instrument to develop shared knowledge amongst roles at the industrial partner about different aspects of the practice in terms of information demand and information flow.

Figure 1 is part of an information demand model developed in the case focusing on the customer interaction process in order preparation and sales (from quotation to production planning). It shows the different departments involved (production, marketing, process and technology, and sales) and illustrates their information demand and what information is produced. The whole process is initiated by a change request from a customer representative (depicted at the lower left corner on the right hand side) or by a call for tender published by an existing or potential future customer of the enterprise.

4   Information Demand Analysis and Patterns

This section introduces the concept of information demand patterns (section 4.2) and a method for analyzing the information demand of organizational roles in enterprises (section 4.2).

4.1   Information Demand Analysis

The understanding and definition of the term information demand used in this paper is based on empirical work performed during 2005-2007. Information demand will be used throughout this paper with the following meaning: *"Information Demand is the constantly changing need for relevant, current, accurate, reliable, and integrated information to support (business) activities, whenever and where ever it is needed."* [14, p.59] Furthermore, the empirical investigation confirmed the conjecture that information demand of a person is based on the roles and tasks this person has.

Understanding the information demand of an organization is a complex undertaking and has as such to be broken down in several interconnected phases that can be applied in a sequential and iterative manner depending on the given problem and desired outcomes. A method for information demand analysis was developed in order to supports this analysis based on a well-defined method notion and overall framework [18]. According to this method, the process of analyzing information demand starts with scoping the area of analysis, includes information demand context modeling, analysis and evaluation, and concludes in the application of the results in suitable software engineering and business process reengineering activities implementing an improved information flow.

The different phases have the following main characteristics [11]:

Scoping: Scoping is the activity of defining the area of analysis and is done with the purpose of selecting the part of an organisation or process to analyse with respect to information demand as well as identifying the individuals providing the necessary background information during the continued process of analysing.

Information Demand Context Modeling: The main purpose of this phase is to identify the basic information demands based on the core concept of information demand context, i.e. which role needs to do what tasks and what does this require in terms of resources.

ID-Context Analysis and Evaluation: Once the context related information is gathered this has to be analysed (and if necessary clarified and refined) and represented in a format useful for continued work. In addition to developing models, this step also allows for comparing the results to existing enterprise information if available. During this phase a choice has to be made whether or not the analysis should be continued and if so how in terms of what refinements to focus on.

Representation and Documentation: As the different analysis phases produce models and documents expressed in different notations the purpose of this phase is to collect and combine the results into a unified coherent representation that can be used to communicate the information demands as well as utilise them in activities aimed at improving information flow.

4.2   Information Demand Patterns

The general idea of information demand patterns (IDP) is similar to most pattern developments in computer science: to capture knowledge about proven solutions in order to facilitate reuse of this knowledge. In this paper, the term information demand pattern is defined as follows: *An information demand pattern addresses a recurring information flow problem that arises for specific roles and work situations in an enterprise, and presents a conceptual solution to it.*

An information demand pattern consists of a number of essential parts used for describing the pattern: pattern name, organisational context, problems addressed, conceptual solution (consisting of information demand, quality criteria and timeline), and effects. These parts will be described in the following. An example for an actual pattern is presented in section 5.

- The *pattern name* usually is the name of the role the pattern addresses.
- The *organisational context* explains where the pattern is useful. This context description identifies the application domain or the specific departments or functions in an organisation forming the context for pattern definition.
- The *problems* of a role are identified. The tasks and responsibilities a certain role has are described in order to identify and discuss the challenges and problems, which this role usually faces in the defined organisational context.
- The *conceptual solution* describes how to solve the addressed problem. This includes the *information demand* of the role, which is related to the tasks and responsibilities, a *timeline* indicating the points in time when the information should be available, and q*uality criteria* for the different elements of the information demand. These criteria include the general importance of the information, the importance of receiving the information completely and with high accuracy, and the importance of timely or real-time information supply.
- The *effects* that play in using the proposed solution are described. If the needed information should arrive too late or is not available at all, this might affect the possibility of the role to complete its task and responsibilities. Information demand patterns include several kinds of effects: potential economic consequences; time/efficiency effects; effects on increasing or reducing the quality of the work results; effects on the motivation of the role responsible; learning and experience effects; effects from a customer perspective.

The above parts of a pattern are described in much detail in the *textual description* of the pattern. Additionally, a pattern can also be represented as a *visual model*, e.g. a kind of enterprise model. This model representation is supposed to support communication with potential users of the pattern and solution development based on the pattern.

5   Information Demand Pattern "Quote Responsible"

5.1   The Pattern

In order to contribute to PM and to illustrate the approach presented in section 4, the information demand pattern "quote responsible" was selected. The pattern was developed in the context of the industrial case introduced in section 3, a second case from the same project infoFLOW and work from improving information flow in preparing research proposals in academia. Since there was a high similarity between the information demand of the responsible for quote preparation and this previously analysed case in preparing proposals for project funding in academic institutions, results from this previous case were also integrated. The enterprise knowledge models from the theses cases were analysed starting from the roles and their relations to processes and infrastructure resources.

When looking for recurring roles in the different models we had to observe that some roles were named differently in different organisations. Hence, the focus of the analysis was enlarged to find reoccurring tasks and responsibilities in the different models, which would indicate a specific information demand. The information demand of what in the following will be called the role "quote responsible" was derived from the textual descriptions accompanying the enterprise models and the descriptions developed in the modelling process. The information demand pattern is presented with the textual representation only. The textual description follows the structure introduced in section 4.2. The first element is the context where the pattern is useful:

Context:
The context for this pattern is manufacturing industries, in particular for built-to-order products. When preparing a quote based on a customer request, usually a team of different competences and disciplines is involved. This team commonly has to produce a quote in a relatively short time frame, i.e. many experiences, best practices and sometimes even "qualified guesses" have to coordinated in a process with high time pressure. One role in this team is the responsible person for the overall quote. This role requires experience and accurate information about the technical and quality specification for a product, the envisioned logistics and the price levels, which usually originate from different information sources and actors. The pattern describes the information demand typically experienced by the quote responsible for coordinating preparation of a quote.

The pattern is supposed to be useful for manufacturing enterprises producing built-to-order products with high demands and short preparation times of quotes developed in a teams of engineers.

The next part is the problem addressed by the pattern:

Problem:

The pattern addresses the general problem of submitting quotes of unnecessary low quality, which basically either is reducing the probability of getting the order or creating economic risks for the company. This includes the following problems, which were often observed when preparing quotes:

- *the technical and quality specifications which are basis for the quote are incomplete or incorrect*
- *the requirements regarding the logistic questions are unclear − including material flow and administrative processes (EDI)*
- *wrong price levels are anticipated for a certain customer or the overall market. [...]*

It follows the information demand, which is based on the tasks and responsibilities of the role under consideration:

Information Demand

The information demand is based on the tasks and responsibilities of the role. The tasks of the role responsible for a proposal include

- *The preparation of the a competitive, complete and high quality technical content of the quote (technical specification, quality characteristics, physical logistic solution, administrative logistics)*
- *The preparation of an accurate, complete and consistent economic part of the quote*
- *Team management, i.e. coordination of all contributions from participating team members*
- *On-time submission of the quote including all required attachments, information and signatures*

The information demand of the role responsible for a proposal consists of:

- *Call for tender / terms and conditions from the customer side*
- *Technical specification of the requested product from customer side*
- *Available capacity, production resources (e.g. machinery) and competences / human resources at the own enterprise*
- *market information*
- *own records about customer relation (previous orders, quotes, complaints, financial issues)*
- *applicable standards and norms in the domain*
- *[...]*

The quality criteria for the above information demand information uses three levels:

- Decisive: you can't manage without this information
- High: it is very important to have, but in worst case you could complete the task without
- Nice to have: you will manage without this information, but this will affect the result

For each pattern, the quality criteria are summarized in a table, which includes the information demand (left column), the general importance of this information, and the importance to get the information accurately, as soon as possible and completely. Below is an extract of the table for the example pattern:

Table 1. Quality criteria for example pattern

	General importance	Accurate	as early as possible	complete
Call for tender / terms and conditions	Decisive	decisive	decisive	decisive[1]
Technical specification	Decisive	decisive	decisive	decisive
Own capacity, resources, competences	High	decisive[2]	Nice to have	Nice to have
Market information	Nice to have[3]	high	Nice to have	Nice to have
Own customer records	Nice to have	Nice to have	Nice to have	Nice to have
Domain standards	decisive	decisive	decisive	decisive

The effects of not receiving the needed information or of receiving it too late are described in a short text and in a table. We will only include an excerpt of this text and table (table 2) due to space limitations:

Effects
- *Economic effect: economic consequences can be expected, which could be*
- *The quote is not selected, as the company is considered not qualified to deliver*
- *The capacity of machine is insufficient to deliver the quote; the production has to be outsourced*
- *Time/efficiency of the task: the preparation of the quote will need much more time and will be less efficient. An example is*
- *If the technical specification should be incomplete, inaccurate or available too late, the quote preparation work will produce content which might not be needed*
- *Quality improvement or reduction: the quality of the submitted quote is positively or negatively affected by this information. Examples are:*
  - *If the call for tender or the technical specification are incomplete or not accurate, the quote might fail to address specific aspects of the specification, which are part of the selection criteria on the customer side*
  - *Quotes have to be based on existing agreements with a certain customer regarding special discounts or logistics solutions. If this information is not considered, there is the risk of asking for cost rates which the customer will not accept.*
- *[...]*

---

[1] Possible that customer leaves this to supplier.
[2] E.g. capacity of machinery and equipment.
[3] Depends on the domain.

Table 2. Summary of effects for example pattern

	Economic effect	*Time efficiency*	*Quality effect*	*[...]*
Call for tender / terms and conditions	*high*	*moderate*	*high*	*[...]*
Technical specification	*high*	*moderate*	*high*	*[...]*
[...]	*[...]*	*[...]*	*[...]*	*[...]*

The above matrix shows the relations between information and effects. The following categories were used in the table:

- Low: The impact of any missing/inaccurate/late information is low.
- Moderate: The impact of any missing/inaccurate/late information is limited.
- High: the impact of any missing/inaccurate/late information may be considerable.

The timeline and the visual model of the information demand pattern are not included in the paper due to space restrictions.

5.2   Pattern Validation

The validation of the information demand pattern approach has to be divided into validation of the approach as such (including the structure of information demand patterns and the utility of the approach) and validation of the actual pattern presented as an example in the previous section. The validation task was so far mainly performed in a group of domain experts with five industrial representatives and four researchers.

The pattern structure and definition presented in section 4.2 was discussed and refined in so far 3 iterations. Each iteration included the improvement of the approach as such and the development of one new pattern with the improved approach. The developed patterns include, for example, the roles "responsible for proposal writing" in academic organizations, "change administrator" and "material specification responsible" in manufacturing enterprises, "responsible for branding" in a service organization, and the pattern for "quote responsible" introduced in this paper. The different iterative development steps did not change the structure of patterns significantly, but mainly contributed to a refinement of the level used for describing the quality criteria, the effects and the timeline.

The pattern "quote responsible" as such was validated in three steps:

- The first version was presented, discussed and refined during an infoFLOW-2 project meeting. This included a walkthrough the visual model and a in detail discussion of the textual description

- The revised version was presented to an industrial expert in the field who proposed changes and improvements, primarily regarding the effects to be expected and the required information quality.
- This refined version was again discussed in a project meeting.

5.3   Related Work

Project management has been subject of many research activities during the last decade, which are manifested in proposals for standardization, such as PMBOK [2] or in work addressing deployment and implementation of selected aspects of PM, such as [1]. Information flow problems and communication problems in PM, stakeholder management, customer interaction or production planning have been observed before (see, e.g. [19]). Most solution proposals in this area use process improvement or work re-organization as their main element.

Concepts, methods and technologies for identifying, capturing and reusing organizational knowledge have been subject of research in organizational sciences and industrial engineering since more than two decades. Patterns of organizational knowledge are contributing to this area. Selected recent developments are:

Work from van der Aalst and colleagues [20] in the field of workflow patterns. Van der Aalst et al. proposed patterns of workflow including different perspectives like control, data flow, resources or operational aspects. These patterns focus on the flow of work but do not represent the information flow or information demand perspective.

The Patterns4Groupware project maintains a comprehensive online catalogue of patterns for groupware. Each pattern provides proven solutions for a specific groupware problem, and is expressed independently from the underlying technology [21]. These patterns cover general tasks of cooperation and communication in the collaboration process, but not the specific information demand aspects of roles involved.

The Liberating Voices! Project [22] uses patterns and a pattern language to provide a "knowledge structure" that represents the collective knowledge and wisdom of the community. The goal is to develop pattern languages supporting the community members to design, develop, manage and use information and communication systems. The project selected approx. 240 patterns published on the project website and organized in themes and categories. Information demand is not a subject of these patterns.

Furthermore, in the context of our own work, we proposed the use of task patterns for capturing knowledge about best practices in executable knowledge models. The term "task patterns" was introduced for these adaptable models, as they are not only applicable in a specific company, but are also considered relevant for other enterprises [23].

6   Summary and Future Work

Starting from work on information demand modelling and from an industrial case in automotive supplier industries, the paper proposes an information demand pattern for the role of a quote responsible in an enterprise's project management process. The quote responsible role is responsible for coordinating all change requests in his area of responsibility, in order to avoid the general problem of submitting quotes of unnecessary low quality, which basically either is reducing the probability of getting the order or creating economic risks for the company. This paper aims at contributing to the area by proposing information demand patterns as a means to capture organizational knowledge about the desired information flow in project management. This approach differs from all approaches using process optimization or definition of best practice standards by putting the information demand into focus, not the activities to be implemented. The approach of using information demand patterns was found useful for processes with many different roles involved and at the same time many exceptions and ad-hoc decisions.

The main limit of the research presented here is the missing evaluation of the approach in an industrial setting. The information demand pattern has been implemented in an adapted version in the industrial case considered in section 3, but this implementation has not yet been thoroughly evaluated. It would be worthwhile and interesting to both test the proposed information demand approach in more real-world cases and to compare different industrial domains, in particular aiming at non-domain specific support for information flow. However, this would also require a different research design with preferably an additional focus on organizational learning. A more thorough evaluation was performed for the tightly related "proposal writing responsible" including 6 different academic institutions and in total 20 informants. This evaluation confirmed adequacy and pertinence of the pattern.

Furthermore, the "quote responsible" pattern currently is directed to the context of manufacturing industries. There is reason to believe that it also will be useful for other industrial areas, but the transfer to other areas was not done yet. Thus, further work should be spent on understanding whether and how the transfer between domains is possible, and what adaptations in the patterns might be necessary.

Acknowledgements. Part of the work presented in this paper was supported by the Swedish KK-Foundation, project infoFLOW-2 (grant # 2009/0257), and by the Swedish Foundation for Internationalisation in Higher Education and Research, project DEON (grant # IG 2008-2011).

References

1. Bentley, C.: Practical PRINCE2, 3rd edn., TSO (The Stationery Office) (2005) ISBN 0-11-703544-0
2. Project Management Institute: A guide to the project management body of knowledge (PMBOK Guide), 3rd edn. Project Management Institute, Newton Square (2004)
3. Billig, A., Blomqvist, E., Lin, F.: Semantic Matching Based on Enterprise Ontologies. In: Meersman, R., Tari, Z. (eds.) OTM 2007, Part I. LNCS, vol. 4803, pp. 1161–1168. Springer, Heidelberg (2007)
4. Sandkuhl, K.: Information Logistics Support for Collaborative Engineering. In: Proceedings DDECS 2003, Workshop CCE 2003, Poznan, Poland, pp. 60–67 (April 2003)
5. Lin, F., Sandkuhl, K.: A New Expanding Tree Ontology Matching Method. In: Meersman, R., Tari, Z., Herrero, P. (eds.) OTM-WS 2007, Part II. LNCS, vol. 4806, pp. 1329–1337. Springer, Heidelberg (2007)
6. Sandkuhl, K.: Supporting Collaborative Engineering with Information Supply Patterns. Euromicro PDP. Pisa, Italy (February 2009)

7. Lundqvist, M., Holmquist, E., Sandkuhl, K., Seigerroth, U., Strandesjö, J.: Information Demand Context Modelling for Improved Information Flow: Experiences and Practices. In: Persson, A., Stirna, J. (eds.) PoEM 2009. LNBIP, vol. 39, pp. 8–22. Springer, Heidelberg (2009)
8. Öhgren, A., Sandkuhl, K.: Information Overload in Industrial Enterprises - Results of an Empirical Investigation. In: Proceedings ECIME 2008, London, UK (2008)
9. Vernadat, F.B.: Enterprise Modelling and Integration. Chapman & Hall (1996)
10. Lillehagen, F., Krogstie, J.: Active Knowledge Modelling of Enterprises. Springer (2009) ISBN: 978-3-540-79415-8
11. Lundqvist, M.: Handbook for Information Demand Analysis. Version 1.0, Deliverable 4 of the infoFLOW project. Jönköping University, School of Engineering (April 2010)
12. Lillehagen, F., Karlsen, D.: Visual Extended Enterprise Engineering embedding Knowledge Management, Systems Engineering and Work Execution. In: IEMC 1999 - IFIP International Enterprise Modelling Conference, Verdal, Norway (1999)
13. Krogstie, J., Jørgensen, H.D.: Interactive Models for Supporting Networked Organisations. In: Persson, A., Stirna, J. (eds.) CAiSE 2004. LNCS, vol. 3084, pp. 550–563. Springer, Heidelberg (2004)
14. Lundqvist, M.: Information Demand and Use: Improving Information Flow within Small-scale Business Contexts. Licentiate Thesis, Dept. of Computer and Information Science. Linköping University, Linköping, Sweden (2007) ISSN 0280-7971
15. Bubenko Jr, J.A., Brash, D., Stirna, J.: EKD User Guide. Dept. of Computer and Systems Science, Royal Institute of Technology (KTH), Stockholm, Sweden (1998)
16. Frank, U.: The MEMO Meta Modelling Language (MML) and Language Architecture. Research Report, University Duisburg-Essen (April 2010)
17. Stroh, F., Winter, R., Wortmann, F.: Method support of information requirements analysis for analytical information systems. Wirtschaftsinformatik (1) (2011)
18. Lundqvist, M., Sandkuhl, K., Seigerroth, U.: Modelling Information Demand in an Enterprise Context: Method, Notation and Lessons Learned. Accepted for publication in: International Journal Systems Modeling and Design 3(1) (2011) (to be appear)
19. Hölttä, V., Eisto, T., Nieminen, M.: Impacts of Poor Communication of Design Information and Factors Leading to it. In: 7th International Conference on Product Lifecycle Management. Inderscience Enterprises Ltd., Bremen (2010)
20. Van der Aalst, W.M.P., ter Hofstede, A.H.M., Kiepuszewski, B., Barros, A.P.: Workflow Patterns. Distributed and Parallel Databases 14, 5–51 (2003)
21. Schümmer, T., Lukosch, S.: Patterns for Computer-Mediated Interaction. Wiley & Sons (2007) ISBN: 978-0-470-02561-1
22. Schuler, D., et al.: Liberating Voices! Pattern Language Project (2008), http://trout.cpsr.org/program/sphere/patterns (accessed May 16, 2008)
23. Sandkuhl, K.: Capturing Product Development Knowledge with Task Patterns: Evaluation of Economic Effects. Quarterly Journal of Control & Cybernetics (1) (2010)
24. Sandkuhl, K.: Improving Engineering Change Management with Information Demand Patterns. In: 8th International Conference on Product Lifecycle Management, July 12-14. Inderscience Enterprises, Eindhoven (2011)

On the Suitability of Activity Diagrams and ConcurTaskTrees for Complex Event Modeling

Jens Brüning, Peter Forbrig, Enrico Seib, and Michael Zaki

University of Rostock, Department of Computer Science,
Albert-Einstein-Str.22,
18059 Rostock, Germany
{Jens.Bruening,Peter.Forbrig,Enrico.Seib,
Michael.Zaki}@uni-rostock.de

Abstract. In this paper, we analyze and extend modeling possibilities for complex events in the semiformal business process modeling languages UML activity diagrams and ConcurTaskTrees (CTT). The goal of this paper is to provide an intuitive abstract starting point for complex event specifications in a model-based approach. The resulting models should increase the understandability of the models themselves and the discussion taking place with the developers and the stakeholders. A hierarchy concept for advanced visual event modeling is introduced to activity diagrams. In these models time, data and cardinality aspects can be expressed. A different approach for complex event modeling is proposed using hierarchical task models with CTT. We transform given temporal operators from CTT that are based on process algebra to event algebra. Some extensions for CTT-operators are used to express specific complex event models in a semiformal way.

Keywords: Business Process Modeling, Complex Event Modeling, Unified Modeling Language (UML), Task Modeling, Requirements Engineering.

1 Introduction

Event modelling is getting more and more important for business process models. Since Event-driven Process Chains (EPC) [6], events have become a first class modelling element in business process models. Nowadays, the field of Complex Event Processing (CEP) is connected to the one of business process modelling. Up to now there is no accepted standard for integrating complex event models in business process models. This paper analyzes two existing modelling standards to be used in the field of complex event modelling. This evaluation might help to express complex events in business process diagrams modelled with activity diagrams or ConcurTaskTrees (CTT).

Events are frequently used in business process models to specify passive elements in contrast to activities. Each event occurs at an instant in time and can mark a state change of data or environment [22]. Events can be generated or consumed by processes. If they are consumed they normally have effects on the control flow.

N. Aseeva, E. Babkin, and O. Kozyrev (Eds.): BIR 2012, LNBIP 128, pp. 54–69, 2012.
© Springer-Verlag Berlin Heidelberg 2012

For this purpose, out of the workflow patterns [25], we particularly mention the *Deferred Choice Pattern* that represents an event-based decision in process models. This pattern can be expressed by most of the popular process modeling languages like EPCs, UML activity diagrams (see Figure 3) [28] or BPMN [19]. Thus, event modeling is an integral part of all of those languages.

In EPCs, events invoke activities and they can themselves produce events. In [16] events are categorized into internal and external events for EPCs. Furthermore, events can be used to specify conditions for decisions and pre- and postconditions for activities [13]. A declaration for a state change of the data or the environmental model can be specified using events. Thus, information from model types other than pure activity specifications is additionally weaved with events into EPCs. Compared to other business process modeling languages, EPCs use events in a broader sense and with different meanings. Other process modeling languages have a more focused view on events with the concept of event production and consumption like for example in UML activity diagrams or BPMN.

UML activity diagrams distinguish between *AcceptEvent* for event consumption and *SendSignal* action for event production [20]. The Business Process Model and Notation language (BPMN) [19] has a similar distinction between event types and adds many further types on top. Figure 1 gives a short overview of several types of events in the listed different process modeling languages.

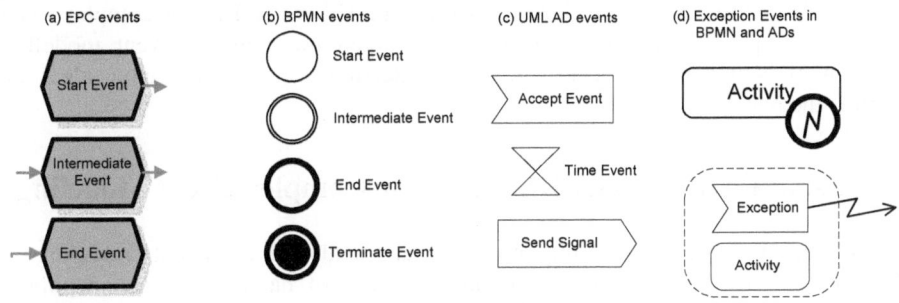

Fig. 1. Different syntaxes for modeling events in different modeling languages

In [14] a visual event modeling language named BEMN is introduced based on event patterns that are identified in [1]. The language is close to the syntax of BPMN and extends it for complex event modeling. E.g. time and data can be expressed in the context of event models. Joining and selection rules can be defined. In contrast to BEMN, we use activity diagrams as a modeling language for complex events in this paper. They already provide a wide set of possibilities for complex event modeling. Only small extensions have to be introduced.

A different approach to express complex events in a hierarchical way is feasible using trees. The task tree modeling language CTT [18] may be convenient for that purpose. Using task trees, it is possible to express several abstraction levels of an activity in one model. Thus, they can be used to create easy-to-use, goal-oriented and stakeholder-centered activity models [7]. Moreover, CTT models are widely used in the HCI domain in combination with model-based user interface development and usability tests [18]. They integrate process algebra terms from the language LOTOS [3] in a tree model to specify the control flow within the hierarchical structure. The process models can be simulated within the modeling environment CTTE. Thus, dynamic properties of the models can be easily tested. This is an advantage compared to activity diagrams and BPMN or BEMN languages. However, CTT models are not as expressive as flow-oriented languages, e.g. activity diagrams. Moreover, it will be discussed how event algebra terms [9] can be expressed in CTT models using LOTOS process algebra [3] terms.

Considering the events at runtime, their correlation to running processes is a big issue [11]. This is done by a process engine and a service bus at runtime. The process engine listens to the service bus and correlates the events to processes. Additionally, the process engine can generate events from running process instances. The focus of this paper is not on the technical part of correlation and process execution at runtime. It rather discusses modeling events in process models at design time in the context of non-executable languages like EPCs, activity diagrams or BPMN with BEMN. In general, modeling languages should enhance visualization, be intuitive and easy to understand in order to increase the discussion for requirements analysis.

The remainder of the paper is structured as follows: In section 2, event modeling concepts focus on activity diagrams. Semantics of event specifications of activity diagrams are compared to EPCs and BPMN. A hierarchy concept is introduced for complex events and we discuss how some event patterns are expressed in activity diagrams. In section 3 we introduce the ConcurTaskTrees (CTT) for complex event models. The approach of task modeling is adapted for complex event modeling. Related work is presented in section 4, while in section 5 we summarize our ideas and conclude the paper.

2   Using UML Activity Diagrams for Complex Event Modeling

In this section different modeling concepts are analyzed for event modeling. In subsection 2.1 we introduce the different semantics of handling events in popular process modeling languages. In subsection 2.2 we discuss a concept to specify complex events using activity diagrams. Events are divided into transient and buffered types in subsection 2.3. Modeling time and cardinality for events are introduced to activity diagrams in subsection 2.4. We present data modeling for events using UML and also the possibilities to access this data for event modeling in subsection 2.5.

2.1   Comparing Event Semantics of UML Activity Diagrams, EPCs and BPMN

Within EPCs events are used to identify circumstances to instantiate a process. Events with no incoming arcs can be identified as start events [13]. If these start events occur, the process is instantiated. In Figure 2a) *Instantiation Event 1* and *2* have to occur to instantiate the process. These semantics are adapted and improved in BPMN by giving a different syntax for those various event types listed in Figure 1b).

Slightly different semantics concerning process instantiation exist in activity diagrams. Process instantiation does not depend on events and has to be explicitly done. The *AcceptEvent* nodes are not enabled for event acceptance until the bearing activity, structured node (a node comprising subnodes) or *Interruptable Activity Region* (see section 2.4) is active. Thus, the events cannot instantiate the process itself. This circumstance is visualized in Figure 2b). A further discussion concerning this subject is given in [13].

The simple syntax and the few language elements provided for modeling are specific characteristics of EPCs. This fact makes it easier for domain experts to understand the models. Consequently, events are used for different purposes in EPCs whereas we have different modeling elements in activity diagrams and BPMN. For example, in EPCs events are used in combination with decisions to specify the conditions to choose the right path in the process model [6]. Activity diagrams use guards notated after the choice node instead. In BPMN the criteria is notated directly to the edges after the choice. Thus, conditions (also pre- and postconditions) are expressed by events in EPCs whereas this is specified by explicit modeling elements in activity diagrams and BPMN.

Activity diagrams distinguish between event acceptance and signal sending modeling elements in process models. Signals are sent to an exclusive target. They are not broadcasted to several or all process instances by default. Broadcasting information can be emulated by object flows labeled with the stereotype <<multicast>> and involved participants modeled with swimlanes [20, p.392]. However, this concept is not sufficient to be used in complex event modeling with activity diagrams.

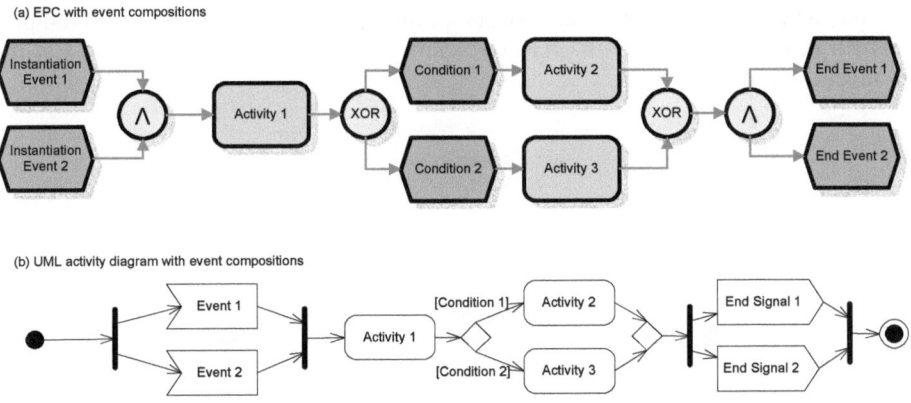

Fig. 2. Different instantiation semantics for process models (a) EPCs use events (b) UML activity diagrams must be instantiated explicitly

If a process instance accepts an event, it is directly consumed [20]. Event acceptance and sending as well as the event consumption concepts are the same in BPMN. Thus, both modeling languages support the *Consume Once* event pattern (pattern 12) from [1]. The consumption of an event by multiple process instances (pattern 13) is normally not supported by activity diagrams although extensions (e.g., by profiles) are allowed to realize this pattern [20, sec.18].

Moreover, some event types which are unspecified in EPCs or activity diagrams are added in BPMN with an explicit syntax. For instance, message or exception events are modeling elements of BPMN. By connecting message send or receive events with a message flow, organizational unit information can be added to event specifications. The pool where the message flow starts indicates the sending organizational unit, whereas the pool in which the message flow ends declares the receiving organizational unit. The connection of event sending and receiving with organizational modeling does not exist in activity diagrams or EPCs.

2.2   Modeling Complex Events in UML Activity Diagrams

In activity diagrams events are matched and directly consumed by event acceptance nodes [20]. After a process instance has consumed an event, this event becomes unavailable for other process instances. However, for complex event processing we need to analyze the events before consuming them. Thus, we introduce a new semantics that distinguish between event accepting or matching and event consumption or releasing.

In Figure 3, we illustrate a hierarchical concept that we added to activity diagrams for modeling complex events. Structured event nodes are identified by the UML hierarchy symbol that similarly marks structured activities. Within structured event models, low level events can be detected and matched by event acceptance nodes. On this level, matched events are not yet consumed. The structured event node ends by reaching the final node. In the same way structured activities are ended [20]. After reaching this node, all the needed low level events are consumed. Other events are released again. This is the proposed non-formal semantics for low level event matching and analysis before event consumption. In section 2.4, we discuss examples in which matched events can be released again after they have been analyzed at the low level event model.

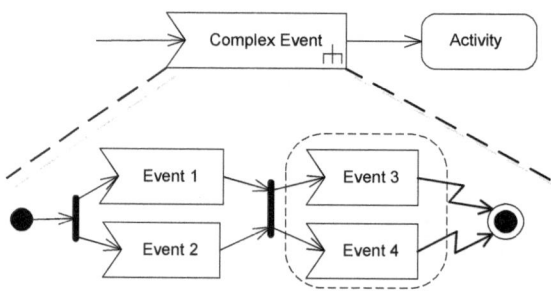

Fig. 3. Specifying complex events in UML activity diagrams

After reaching the final node, the control flow continues at the higher level activity model. This simple semantics may lead to ambiguities in situations in which events are sent to several process instances. However, that is not the default situation in activity diagrams. Normally signals are sent to exclusive targets. Thus, concurrent consumption of several process instances of one specific event may not occur too often with this semantics. The proposed semantics fit into the semi-formal and non-executable semantics of activity diagrams.

An example model for this approach is given in Figure 3. The UML hierarchy symbol for complex activities is adapted for events. In contrast to complex activities, complex events do not allow to contain user-defined activities. Flow operators like fork, join and exceptions are allowed. In the same category, we also add complex flow operators for object flows. In subsection 2.3, they are discussed in more details.

In the model of Figure 3, the events *Event 1* and *2* have to occur before *3* or *4* can be matched. The last two events compete in racing conditions. Thus, the first one of them will be matched. This is the activity diagram model for the deferred choice pattern [28].

Introducing structured event nodes is semantically required. The complex event can be denoted as an event in this node. If we use a structured activity node instead, we would have to denote the structured event as an activity. This would produce a semantical problem in the model.

2.3   Introducing Transient and Buffered Event Types

In this subsection we analyze and differentiate event acceptance types based on the modeling possibilities that activity diagrams provide.

In Figure 4 (a) a transient event type is used. If an event sequence A_1,A_2,B_1 arrives, the events A_2 and B_1 are consumed by the model. A_2 overwrites A_1 before B_1 occurs in this specification.

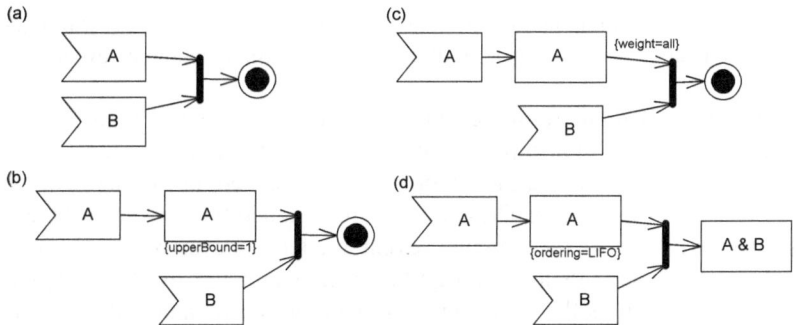

Fig. 4. (a) Specifying transient events (b) Specifying event A as buffered event (c) using a weighted edge to consume several buffered events (d) selecting buffered events in special order

For a model that matches the events A_1 and B_1 for the above event sequence we use the activity diagram specified in Figure 4 (b). The first event A_1 is buffered in the object node. The upper bound of the object node is one. Thus, the second event A_2 does not fit into the object node and that event gets lost.

Using no upper bound for the object node, we can buffer all the events of type A that occur before the process continues after an event B has arrived. All events can be consumed in one step using a weighted edge with the specification *{weight=all}*. This situation is modeled in Figure 4 (c).

Events buffered in an object node can be handled one by one for example in a LIFO or FIFO principle which is modeled in Figure 4 (d). After joining the events of type A and B, they are buffered in the object node *A&B*.

2.4   Modeling Inhibiting Events, Time and Cardinality

In [1] different event patterns are identified and categorized. Among others, the categories *time* and *cardinality* are introduced. These categories can be modeled by activity diagrams with already existing language elements. Figure 5 illustrates different possibilities to model time and event cardinality in complex event models. An example of an alarm device is used, where a complex alarm event is generated following the illustrated event specifications.

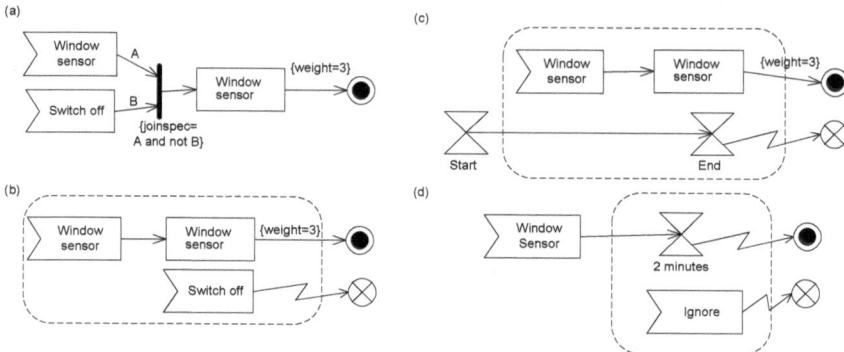

Fig. 5. (a) Specification of an inhibiting event (b) inhibiting event expressed with interruptible region (c) specification of a time interval (d) 2 minutes time for an inhibiting event

In Figure 5 (a) *Window sensor* events are accepted as long as no *Swicht off* event has occurred. This relationship is similar to an inhibition relationship that was introduced in BEMN [14]. If a *Switch off* event is matched, no further occurrences of *Window sensor* are forwarded. These events are matched but will never be consumed because the end node of the complex event model is never reached. Figure 5 (b) models this situation with an interruptible region and the event acceptance node *Switch off* that interrupts the acceptance of *Window sensor* and ends in a flow final node. Reaching that node means that the matched events are not consumed. Thus, the semantics of the models of Figure 5 (a) and (b) are the same.

Cardinality specifications of event occurrences are expressed by weighted edges connected to the object flows. Examples are given in the Figures 5 (a)-(c), where three times *Window sensor* events have to occur until the end node is reached and all needed events are consumed consequently.

We integrate time specification in Figure 5 (c) in the event model. Within a period of time which is specified by *Start* and *Finish* events, three events of the type *Window sensor* have to occur. Event acceptance nodes in interruptible regions are enabled after a token has entered the region [20, sec.12.3.13]. Thus, in the model of Figure 5 (c) *Window sensor* events that occur before the start event are not matched. If three *Window sensor* events are matched within the specified period of time, the end node is reached and the matched events are consumed. If the *Finish* event occurs before, the final flow node is reached by using the interrupting edge. In that case all the event tokens stored in the object node waiting to reach the end node are destroyed and the events are released again.

In Figure 5 (d) we present another event model, where a complex alarm event is generated after a *Window sensor* event has occurred and a time delay of 2 minutes is temporized. If no *ignore* event is sent within this period of time, the end node is reached by the interrupting edge. The complex event for an alarm signal is created then. If the *ignore* event has occurred in the specified period of time, the flow final node is reached by the interrupting edge instead and the complex event is not created.

For creating the complex event, the situation modeled does not need any explicit event occurrence within the specified period of time while in the situation modeled in Figure 5 (c) three events have to arrive in a given time interval. Thus, in those two figures, we modeled contrasting situations.

2.5   Modeling Data, Data-Based Choices and Filtering of Events

In this subsection, we introduce data related analysis and data modeling of events with UML. Events normally hold data. At least a timestamp is related to events.

In Figure 6 (a) event or environmental data can be used for that choice specification. Guards represent conditions that are assigned to the outgoing edges for specifying the relevant path related to that choice.

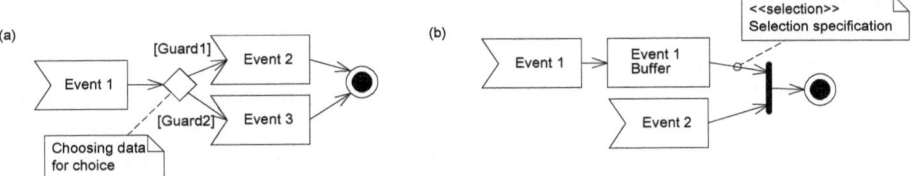

Fig. 6. (a) A data related choice. (b) A selection specification in combination with object flow

In Figure 6 (b) the buffering of events in the object node is used. To the outgoing edge of the object node we have notated a selection specification. In the selection clause, data can be used to choose the right event that should be synchronized with *Event 2*. After reaching the end node, the relevant events are consumed and the complex event is created.

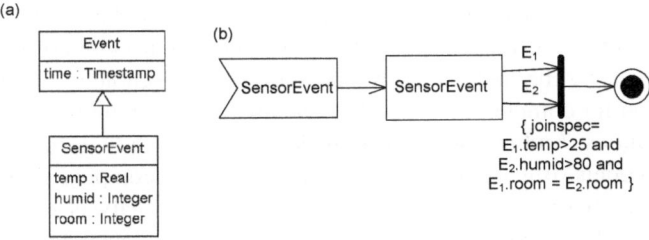

Fig. 7. (a) Datamodel for an event type. (b) A selection specification in combination with two object flows.

An example of a data model for an event is given in Figure 7 (a). Every event has a timestamp which is expressed with the attribute *time* in the class *Event*. Specific event types can be defined using inheritance. In the example of Figure 7 an event of a house control system is modeled.

The sensors of that system measure the temperature and the humidity of specific rooms in the house. They are modeled by attributes of the class *SensorEvent*. The example of Figure 7 (b) is derived from a process algebra term introduced by Seib et.al. [23] saying that a composite event is created when a given event holds a temperature higher than 25° C and the other event is having a humidity value higher than 80. Moreover, these two events must be generated in the same room.

3   Modeling Composed Complex Events Using CTT

In this section we present a concept for modeling composed complex events using tree structure. The main disadvantage of composed event models with activity diagrams or BPEM [14] is the expression of different abstraction levels in different models. Having different levels means handling and understanding several models, where each model corresponds to a level. Adding another abstraction level means adding another model and managing it afterwards. In contrast, we can use trees where different levels can be expressed within one model.

For activity specifications, the concept of having several hierarchical levels existing in one model gives end-users the opportunity to better understand complex workflow models [30]. Task modeling is a semiformal modeling paradigm that expresses activities in an abstract way and adds goal modeling aspects to these diagrams. This modeling approach is useful to do usability analysis or develop analysis models for user interface development [18]. A problem oriented top-down modeling concept is followed in task models. Depth-first modeling can be followed in the case of trees, in contrast to flowchart-like languages where only a breadth-first approach is supported.

Having a tree-like structure means that we get structured models. Structured program code is necessary to get understandable programs written in programming languages [15]. This advantage is adapted to business process models [27, 26], where spaghetti-code-like similarly to the goto-statements used in old programming languages models are not understandable.

Similar to hierarchical workflow specifications [7] it is probably also promising to model complex events using trees and thus get models in a more abstract, structured way that are better to be understood by modelers and stakeholders. Using this semi-formal approach for complex event models, we obviously get ambiguities in the event detection semantics. Ambiguities of task models also exist in their original domain of HCI activity models. But we get a more abstract view on complex events that might be a promising approach to develop first requirements analysis event models for Complex Event Processing. However, CTT was not developed for complex event specifications and thus, some shortcomings can be detected.

In the following, event algebra operators are analyzed to CTT-operators in subsection 3.1. We introduce complex event specifications using CTT in subsection 3.2. An evaluation of those models by simulation is shown in subsection 3.3.

3.1   Comparing Temporal CTT Operators with Event Algebra Operators

In process algebras, processes are seen as a set of events [2]. Process algebra languages like CCS, CSP or LOTOS (Language Of Temporal Ordering Specification) are event-based reactive languages. CTT is based on the process algebra LOTOS [3] and adds a hierarchical concept for task modeling.

In Table 1, event algebra operators are listed and compared to temporal operators of CTT (LOTOS-operators). We use this comparison to elaborate the possibility to adapt the CTT-models and the LOTOS-operators to event algebra specifications. The CTT models can be translated to textual LOTOS algebra terms within the CTTE tool (at least in older CTTE versions like 1.5.9). These specifications may be useful to be further refined and adapted to event algebra terms. In this way the LOTOS specification may be used in a development process and a tool chain where the adapted specifications can serve as input for further tools in model-driven approaches for complex event processing.

Table 1. Comparison of event algebra operators with temporal CTT-operators

Operator	Event algebra notation	CTT notation
Sequence	A ; B	$A \gg B$
Conjunction	E_1 and E_2	$E_1 \parallel\parallel E_2$
Disjunction	E_1 or E_2	E_1 [] E_2
Any	$any(m,E_1,E_2,\ldots,E_n)$	Not available
Iteration	$E_1^{*}(t_i)$	E_1^{*}
Times	$x(n,E_1,t_i)$	Not available
Not	$not(E_1,t_i)$	Not available

Both languages, event algebra [10] used by [23] as well as process algebra LOTOS (see [3]) provide the operators sequence, conjunction, disjunction and iteration. All of those operators are shown in the complex event models discussed in the following.

The equivalent *Disjunction* operator in CTT is the *choice* operator which is notated with "E_1 [] E_2". This CTT operator is event-based. If an enabled event of the left subtree occurs, the right subtree is disabled [18] and vice versa. The events of the two subtrees compete in racing conditions which situation is similar to the deferred choice pattern [25]. For complex event modeling, this behavior is the exact one we need. For workflow modeling we need a further *choice* that represents explicit decisions. Deterministic and non-deterministic choices for CTT are proposed in [24] and a user-based choice is introduced in [7].

However, some temporal operators provided by event algebra are not included in the CTT notation (see Table 1). The operators *Any, Times* and *Not* are only provided by event algebras. The operators *not* and *Times* can be informally emulated. This is further elaborated in subsection 3.2 and 3.3. *Any* is left unspecified in this paper.

Time restrictions are not considered in CTT. Thus, CTT models cannot be used for modeling timeouts or similar models that we have discussed in subsection 2.4. They can only be expressed by events that are denoted as time events. However, they are not automatically evaluated by observing the time in CTTE. The events have to be explicitly generated by the user. The problem of missing temporal information is getting relevant if we consider an event model based on time intervals instead of a time point semantic. This would imply that we have to tackle 13 different temporal relationships [4].

Furthermore, the data modeling part for events is not considered in CTT models. Task modeling comprises the data and resource aspects similar to business process modeling but lacks explicit visual modeling elements for those aspects. Models for the data parts of subsection 2.5 (i.e. formulating constraints on the properties of event attributes and modeling attributes of the partial and composite events) cannot be expressed using CTT.

A general and not CTT-related problem that becomes evident for complex event modeling is the unclear semantics of different composition operators. As an example we consider the *disjunction* operator, e.g. "E_1 or E_2". This operator could be interpreted as an exclusive or inclusive *or*. An even more complicated example is the *sequence* operator "$E_1 ; E_2$". It is obvious that E_1 has to occur temporally earlier than E_2. According to the question if and/or which events are allowed to happen during the occurrence of E_1 and E_2, [29] presents four different semantics for this operator. This example shows that the ambiguity problems do not exist only for event models expressed in CTT. There are more general ambiguities problems for complex event modeling.

3.2   Complex Event Models Modeled in CTT

In Figure 8 two complex event models are presented as examples. Only the leaf nodes represent simple events that are matched in an event stream. An alarm device that observes the garden, the house and the safe is modeled. The inner nodes in the tree of Figure 8 (a) represent complex compound events. A complex *Alarm* event is for example created by the following event sequence *Tactile, Visual, Door, Safe*.

Events are labeled according to sensor events based on things they observe like *Garden*, *House* and *Safe*. Moreover, the subnodes of *Garden* describe the sensor types. The complex event *Garden* is for example created by the event sequence *Tactile, Visual*. Because of the interleaving operator which represents the conjunction operator (see Table 1) also the subsequence *Visual, Tactile* would have been accepted.

After the garden sensors have created events, the house sensors are enabled. A choice node is modeled between *Window* and *Door*. In the example sequence above, a *Door* event is matched. Afterwards, the last simple event *Safe* is needed to consequently create the complex *Alarm* event.

In the example of Figure 9 this model is enriched with iterations. The two complex events *Garden* and *House* have to occur twice in iteration. This is informally specified by the explicit finishing events *2 times*. By this specification the event algebra operator *Times* of Table 1 is emulated.

As listed in Table 1, event modeling needs several further operators. In event algebra in addition to the *Times* operator, the *not* operator is prominent. It has a counterpart with inhibition relationships in BEMN and special join specifications or exception events in activity diagrams that are presented in subsection 2.4. To emulate the semantics of the *not* operator in CTT we can use the *stop* operator that was introduced in [24]. Similar to the emulation of the *Times* operator, this emulation is also informal.

The *Stop* operator indicates that the model execution is stopped and the scenario is unsuccessfully finished. For the complex event modeling this means: After reaching that operator the event matching is canceled and the already matched events are released. In contrast, if the matched events reach the end of the model, then all of those events are consumed following the proposed semantics for activity diagrams in subsection 2.2.

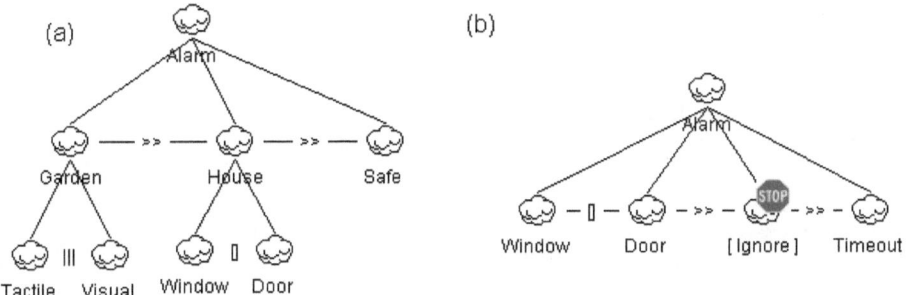

Fig. 8. (a) A complex event model using 3 hierarchy levels (b) A *stop* operator introduced for CTT in [24] emulating the *not* operator of event algebras

In Figure 8 (b) a similar model to the one of Figure 5 (d) is specified. The stop operator is combined with the event *Ignore*. In CTT, the brackets around the *Ignore* node indicate that the event is optional. Thus, the execution can stop if *Ignore* occurs at that point of execution. Otherwise the execution can proceed with the next event *Timeout*. The complex event *Alarm* is for example created by the following event sequence: *Window, Timeout*. In contrast, the event matching is unsuccessfully stopped with the following event sequence *Window, Ignore* or *Door, Ignore*.

3.3   Simulating Composed Hierarchical Event Models Using CTTE

Within the modeling environment CTTE the hierarchical models can be simulated and interactively tested to validate the dynamic flow properties of the models. The animation of those models is necessary due to the big number of temporal operators in CTT. There are more operators than the ones listed in Table 1 (e.g., example *Disabling* or *OrderIndependence*). A full listing of those operators is given in [18]. The big number of operators does not provide a clear interpretation of the semantics of the control flow in some models. For example an enabling or sequence operator is not allowed to be used after iteration. The model simulation is a mandatory step to test the control flow of the models and thus detect problems or soundness errors in a semi-formal way.

In Figure 9 the validation environment for the CTT model is pictured. The developer has to interactively create the event stream based on the model execution. Events that can occur are marked with the green color in the tree model and they are considered as *enabled tasks* on the right side in the middle of Figure 9. For event models, tasks are seen as events.

It is not possible to predefine several event streams, to provide them to the simulation or validation tool as input and test the event model. Only interactive validation is possible. During this process the developer can notice if the model is weakly or strictly specified. Event traces are logged by CTTE and can be analyzed after scenario execution. This analysis takes place in the *scenario performed* window, pictured at the bottom in the middle of Figure 9.

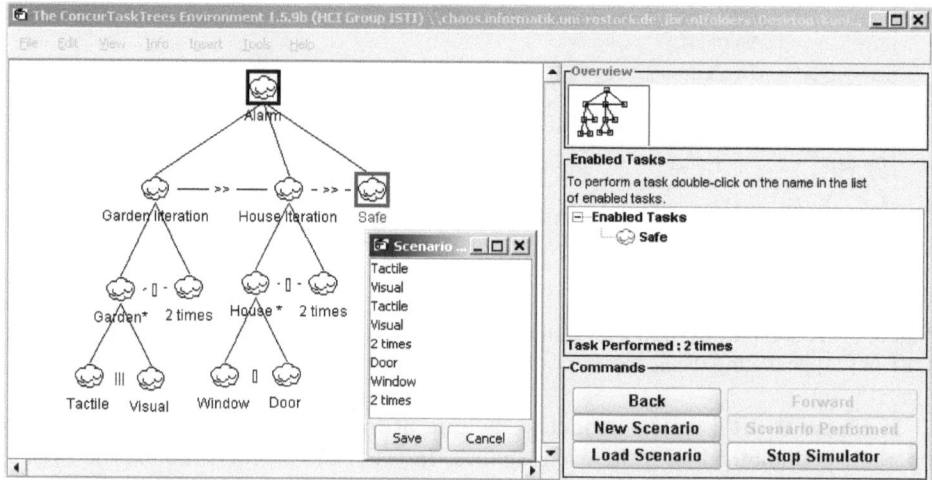

Fig. 9. A composed complex event model in execution presented in the CTTE tool

4   Related Work

Complex event modeling in EPCs is done in [12, p.275]. There, only hierarchical event modeling was considered and no temporal relations between events can be specified. [21] has introduced temporal relations between events in EPCs. Events are classified as external and internal events in [16] with the aim to derive BPEL process models from EPCs. In [6] complex events are used in the context of decision modeling with decision processes in EPCs. Similar to the BPMN syntax, [14] introduced the BEMN language for visual complex event modeling.

Event correlation for process execution at runtime is treated in [11]. Process instantiation semantics for process models based on events taken out of an event pool is proposed in [13].

The usage of event algebra for modeling complex events is mentioned in [22] and is developed in [9] and [17]. There, temporal relations are specified in a way similar to process algebras like CCS and CSP [2] using binary und unary operators. However, some operators of the algebra differ from process algebra to event algebra. This article has identified them by comparing event algebra operators with LOTOS algebra terms that are used for ConcurTaskTrees [18].

In the context of task and activity modeling the CTT language is compared to activity diagrams in [8] by defining transformation rules. In this paper the object flow concept of activity diagrams is frequently used in combination with event modeling. [5] analyzed the object flow concept in activity diagram, its flow operators and the UML action semantics.

5   Summary

In this paper, the suitability of activity diagrams and ConcurTaskTrees for complex event modeling was analyzed. By choosing these languages, an intuitive, visual and semi-formal way for modeling complex events is feasible.

Activity diagrams are widely accepted for technical as well as business process modeling. They provide several opportunities to express complex event models. A structured event node was introduced with non-formal and simple semantics to create complex event models within business process models. To give the context to other business process modeling languages, the different event semantics of activity diagrams concerning EPCs and BPMN were elaborated. Several complex event models were introduced. Time, cardinality, data and inhibiting events can be expressed in activity diagrams.

A different promising approach for complex event modeling was introduced thereafter employing ConcurTaskTrees. This language uses a hierarchical modeling technique where several abstraction levels are expressed in one structured tree model. Within this hierarchy, the LOTOS process algebra operators are used to define the control flow. With this approach, complex events are expressed in a more abstract way that might guarantee a better understandability to modelers and stakeholders as it is the case with CTT-activity models in the HCI domain.

To adapt this language for complex event modeling, event algebra operators are compared to process algebra operators that are provided by CTT. Several event algebra operators already exist in CTT. However, other important ones are still missing. An already proposed extension for CTT was suggested to emulate the *Not* and *Times*-operator. Other operators (e.g. concerning the data) are left unspecified.

References

1. Barros, A., Decker, G., Großkopf, A.: Complex Events in Business Processes. In: Abramowicz, W. (ed.) BIS 2007. LNCS, vol. 4439, pp. 29–40. Springer, Heidelberg (2007)
2. Baeten, J.C.M.: A Brief History of Process Algebra. Theoretical Computer Science 138(2), 243–271 (1995)

3. Bolognesi, T., Brinksma, E.: Introduction to the ISO Specification Language LOTOS. In: van Eijk, P.H.J., Vissers, C.A., Diaz, M. (eds.) The Formal Description Technique LOTOS. Elsevier Science Publishers B. V., North-Holland (1989)

4. Allen, J.F.: Maintaining knowledge about temporal intervals. Communications of the ACM 26(11), 832–843 (1983)

5. Brüning, J., Forbrig, P.: Behaviour of flow operators connected with object flows in workflow specifications. In: BIR 2008. University of Gdansk (2008)

6. Brüning, J., Forbrig, P.: Modellierung von Entscheidungen und Interpretation von Entscheidungsoperatoren in einem WfMS. In: EPK 2009. CEUR-WS, vol. 554 (2009)

7. Brüning, J., Forbrig, P.: TTMS: A Task Tree Based Workflow Management System. In: Halpin, T., Nurcan, S., Krogstie, J., Soffer, P., Proper, E., Schmidt, R., Bider, I. (eds.) BPMDS 2011 and EMMSAD 2011. LNBIP, vol. 81, pp. 186–200. Springer, Heidelberg (2011)

8. Brüning, J., Dittmar, A., Forbrig, P., Reichart, D.: Getting SW Engineers on Board: Task Modelling with Activity Diagrams. In: Gulliksen, J., Harning, M.B., van der Veer, G.C., Wesson, J. (eds.) EIS 2007. LNCS, vol. 4940, Springer, Heidelberg (2008)

9. Carlson, J., Lisper, B.: A resource-efficient event algebra. Science of Computer Programming 75(12), 1215–1234 (2010)

10. Charavarthy, S., Krishnaprasad, V., Anwar, E., Kim, S.K.: Composite Events for Active databases: Semantics, Contexts and Dtetection. In: VLDB 1994, Santiago, Chile (1994)

11. Chen, S.-K., Jeng, J.-J., Chang, H.: Complex Event Processing using Simple Rule-based Event Correlation Engines for Business Performance Management. In: CEC/EEE 2006, Palo Alto (2006)

12. Davis, R.: Business process modelling with ARIS: A Practical Guide. Springer (2009)

13. Decker, G., Mendling, J.: Process Instantiation. Data & Knowledge Engineering 68(9), 777–792 (2009)

14. Decker, G., Großkopf, A., Barros, A.: A Graphical Notation for Modeling Complex Events in Business Processes. In: EDOC 2007. IEEE Computer Society (2007)

15. Dijkstra, E.: Go To Statement Considered Harmful. Communications of the ACM 11(3), 147–148, doi:10.1145/362929.362947

16. Kopp, O., Wieland, M., Leymann, F.: External and Internal Events in EPCs: e^2EPCs. In: Rinderle-Ma, S., Sadiq, S., Leymann, F. (eds.) BPM 2009. LNBIP, vol. 43, pp. 381–392. Springer, Heidelberg (2010)

17. Luckham, D.: The Power of Events. Addison-Wesley Longman, Amsterdam (2002)

18. Mori, G., Paterno, F., Santoro, C.: CTTE: Support for Developing and Analyzing Task Models for Interactive System Design. IEEE Transactions on Software Engineering, 797–813 (2002)

19. Object Management Group: Business Process Model and Notation (BPMN) specification vers. 2.0, http://www.omg.org/spec/BPMN/2.0/PDF (accessed: May 05, 2011)

20. Object Management Group: Unified Modeling Language (UML) version 2.3. OMG document formal/2010-05-05 (2010),
http://www.omg.org/spec/UML/2.3/Superstructure/PDF
(accessed: May 05, 2011)

21. Rommelspacher, J.: Modelling Complex Events with Event-Driven Process Chains. In: SIGSAND-EUROPE 2008. LNI, vol. 129 (2008)

22. Scheer, A.-W.: ARIS – Modellierungsmethoden, Metamodelle, Anwendungen. Springer (2001)

23. Seib, E., Parzyjegla, H., Mühl, G.: Distributed Composite Event Detection in Publish/Subscribe Networks - A Case for Self-Organization. ECEASST 37 (2011)

24. Sinnig, D., Wurdel, M., Forbrig, P., Chalin, P., Khendek, F.: Practical Extensions for Task Models. In: Winckler, M., Johnson, H. (eds.) TAMODIA 2007. LNCS, vol. 4849, pp. 42–55. Springer, Heidelberg (2007)
25. van der Aalst, W., ter Hofstede, A., Kiepuszewski, B., Barros, A.: Workflow Patterns. Distributed and Parallel Databases 14(3), 5–51 (2003)
26. Vanhatalo, J., Völzer, H., Koehler, J.: The Refined Process Structure Tree. In: Dumas, M., Reichert, M., Shan, M.-C. (eds.) BPM 2008. LNCS, vol. 5240, pp. 100–115. Springer, Heidelberg (2008)
27. Laue, R., Mendling, J.: Structuredness and its significance for correctness of process models. Inf. Syst. E-Business Management 8(3), 287–307 (2010)
28. Russell, N., van der Aalst, W.M.P., ter Hofstede, A.H.M., Wohed, P.: On the Suitability of UML 2.0 Activity Diagrams for Business Process Modelling. In: APCCM 2006, Australia, Hobart, CRPIT, vol. 53 (2006)
29. Zhu, D., Sethi, A.: SEL, A New Event Pattern Specification Language for Event Correlation. In: Proc. Int. Conf. on Computer Communications and Networks, pp. 586–589. IEEE (2001)
30. Kolb, J., Reichert, M., Weber, B.: Using Concurrent Task Trees for Stakeholder-centered Modeling and Visualization of Business Processes. In: Oppl, S., Fleischmann, A. (eds.) S-BPM ONE 2012. CCIS, vol. 284, pp. 237–251. Springer, Heidelberg (2012)

Architecture and Language for Semantic Reduction of Domain-Specific Models in BPMS

Lelde Lace[*], Renārs Liepiņš[**], and Edgars Rencis[***]

Institute of Mathematics and Computer Science, University of Latvia
{Lelde.Lace,Renars.Liepins,Edgars.Rencis}@lumii.lv

Abstract. Nowadays each business process management system (BPMS) supports either an industry standard or its own specific modeling language. But no BPMS supports a specific language for each organization. We propose an architecture for building BPMS that allows creating a domain-specific modeling language for every client easily. The main problem is to bridge the gap between the domain-specific language and the executable language. We show that we can look at this problem as a classification of the domain-specific language constructs in the terms of the executable language. To solve this problem we present a novel model transformation language, with which this type of problem can be solved more naturally than with existing transformation languages.

Keywords: Tool-building Platforms, Model Transformations, BPMS, DSL.

1   Introduction

Currently there is a wide array of business process management systems (BPMS) available in the market. Each system is built for one particular process definition language. In most cases the language is either an industry standard like UML Activity Diagrams [1] or BPMN [2], or a tool-specific language. However, it has been shown that using a domain-specific language (DSL) that is tailored to particular needs of a specific client has many advantages [3], namely, less redundancy in specifications, increased readability, less technical symbols and enhanced learnability. Nevertheless, current systems do not fully support the use of custom modeling languages, because there is no easy way to provide such a feature. In this paper we will show, how to build a BPMS that can easily support a custom modeling language for each organization.

The proposed solution consists of two parts. In the first part we separate the process Modeling Environment and modeling language from the Execution Environment. In the second part we propose a new transformation language, in which to specify, how to execute the domain-specific language in the Execution Environment.

---

[*] Partially supported by European Union via European Regional Development Fund project 2010/0325/2DP/2.1.1.1.0/10/APIA/VIAA/109.

[**] Partially supported by the European Social Fund within the project «Support for Doctoral Studies at University of Latvia».

[***] Partially supported by Latvian 2010.-2013. National Research Program Nr.2 project Nr.5.

N. Aseeva, E. Babkin, and O. Kozyrev (Eds.): BIR 2012, LNBIP 128, pp. 70–84, 2012.

A new process modeling tool for each domain-specific language replaces the existing Modeling Environment. Such tools can be built easily using the so-called meta-case tools [4, 5]. The Execution Environment can remain the same, because it supports all the standard control structures and patterns that are needed for all organizations. The only problem then is to transform the models created in the domain-specific language to a language understood by the Execution Environment. The transformation must preserve the semantics of the domain-specific language. A standard solution [6] for this problem would be to describe each language with a metamodel and use some of the existing model transformation languages to specify the correspondence. However, because the existing transformation languages are built for transforming any metamodel type to any other, they cannot exploit all the constraints that are present in this type of problem. The most important constraint is that both models are used for process definition and thus contain execution semantics; therefore the two process definition instance graphs of the same process will be structurally similar.

Since the domain-specific language will also describe a working system, we can look at this problem as a classification of the domain-specific language constructs in terms of the executable language. Then we can solve this problem more simply and compactly using a new transformation language that is based on a classification approach. In a way the new language is "pull-based", i.e. it pulls the source metamodel data into the target metamodel, as opposed to the standard transformation languages that "push" the source data to the target metamodel. The definition of such a transformation language is one of the main results of this paper.

The rest of the paper is structured as follows. In Section 2 we propose a new architectonic solution to building BPMS. Section 3 describes the feasibly of the proposed solution. In Section 4 we propose a new transformation language for the implementation of the domain-specific BPMS. Section 5 discusses related work. Finally, we describe the conclusions in Section 6.

2   Towards a Domain-Specific BPMS

BPMS support many tasks, such as, process definition, data modeling, form design, process execution, etc. However, only process definition task is domain-specific. Therefore we will focus on the two main components that are directly involved in process definition – Modeling environment and Execution environment.

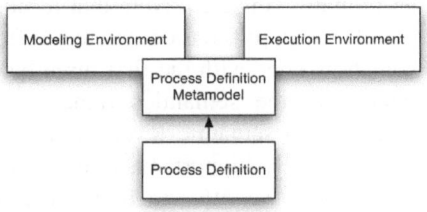

Fig. 2.1. Architecture of classic BPMS

Every BMPS has exactly one process definition language that is used to specify processes. This language is described with a metamodel (Fig. 2.1). Both the Modeling environment and the Execution environment use the same metamodel. Modeling environment is used to develop process definitions graphically; therefore each metamodel element has a graphical notation. Execution environment performs accordingly to the process definitions developed in the Modeling environment. Thus the Execution environment implements the semantics for the process definition language. For an end user the implemented semantics is explained on some process definition example by showing how it will be executed. The explanation is based not only on a singe graphical element but also on a bit larger graphical patterns. Such an explanation that covers all types of semantic patterns we will call **Intuitive semantics**.

The process definition is done by a **Domain expert** using the Modeling environment with the provided process definition language. Thus the Domain expert has to use both – the provided graphical notation and the fixed Execution semantics. However, because the process definitions are developed for a concrete domain, its graphical syntax and Intuitive semantics may differ from the provided process definition language. The most common types of differences are: 1) Domain expert uses different names of the concepts, e.g., „Task" instead of „Activity"; 2) different sets of class attributes; 3) different graphical representation of concepts; 4) the same graphical pattern has a different semantics.

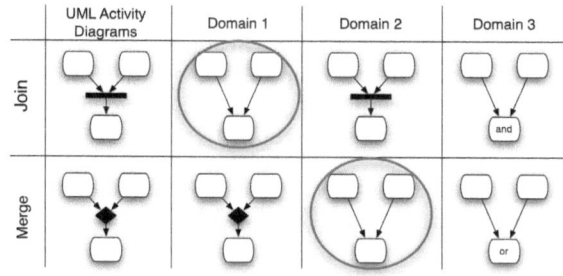

Fig. 2.2. Examples of domain-specific graphical pattern semantics

To better understand the 4th type of distinction let us look at how two semantic concepts, namely, "Join" and "Merge", are depicted in four notations – UML Activity diagrams and three other domains (Fig.2.2). Note that in domain 1 and domain 2 the same graphical pattern (circled with red) has completely different semantic meaning.

Current BPMS can somehow cope with the first three types of differences because they change only graphics but the semantics remain the same. But the fourth difference requires a change on a semantic level. As a result it is not possible for Domain expert to get a tool that fully supports his domain-specific language.

As a solution to this problem we offer to more strictly separate the Modeling environment by creating a metamodel for it (**Domain metamodel**). Architecture of this solution is depicted in Fig. 2.3. Within the Domain metamodel Domain expert can define his own process modeling language consisting of concepts used in his particular domain. Metamodel of the Execution environment is the same that is seen in Fig. 2.1, we call it the **Semantic metamodel**, and it is implemented in the Execution environment.

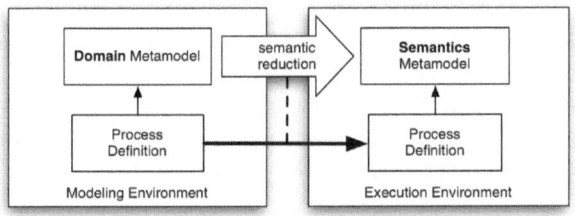

Fig. 2.3. Overview of the proposed solution

If we inspect the Domain metamodel, we must be aware of the Intuitive semantics attached to it. In a general case there are two possible solutions, how to obtain the implementation for some metamodel. One solution is to implement the Intuitive semantics for this metamodel from scratch. The other option is to transform the metamodel instances into another one that already has an implementation. Since the Execution environments implement the Semantic metamodel, we chose the second solution – the Domain metamodel instances are transformed into the Semantic metamodel instances. We call this step the **Semantic reduction** of a domain metamodel.

In order to correctly understand our goal let us state the task more precisely. A new tool that conforms to the architecture seen in Fig. 2.3 is made for every domain. The Domain metamodel is different for each tool, and it contains concepts of that domain. On the other hand, the Semantic metamodel is the same for all tools. Since each tool has its own Domain metamodel, we would have to create a different semantic reduction for each tool. We offer a new language and a methodology, how to cope with this task. It is described in more detail in Section 4.

3   Architecture of Modeling Environment

Before outlining the proposed language let us show its place in the overall architecture and inspect other necessary components. Let us look at the newly proposed architecture of BPMS seen in Fig. 2.3. It consists of two main components – the Modeling environment and the Execution environment. One of the main requirements is that implementations of both components are based on metamodels and that the metamodels and their data must be accessible. It is required for the implementation of transformations. If we want to implement only a one-way functionality (i.e. first define a process definition and then execute it), then there are little requirements for cooperation between the components. If, on the other hand, we want to also assure a graphical run-time monitoring, then a closer cooperation between the two components is needed. We will start by inspecting only the first case thus maximizing the possibility to reuse existing components by adding only a part that is necessary for specifying and implementing the transformations.

Since in our approach we offer to separate the Modeling environment, a question arises, whether the Modeling environment needs to be built completely from scratch or is there some existing solution on which it can be based. To make it clear let us analyze the BPMS Modeling environment. It must satisfy three main requirements: 1) domain metamodel and its instances must be explicit; 2) there must be a way to easily specify a concrete domain-specific process modeling language; 3) there must be a convenient way to graphically edit domain-specific process definitions. So what we actually need is a domain-specific modeling tool.

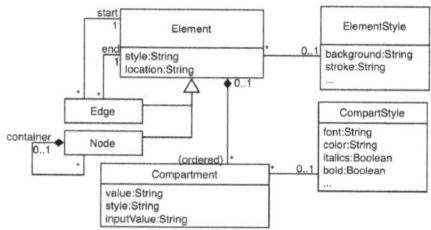

Fig. 3.1. Metamodel fragment for a Universal Graphical Editor

Since the base functionality of the tool is to provide graphics, it is natural for its metamodel to contain such concepts as "Edge" and "Node" being the graphical primitives. A small universal core, on which any graphical editor can be based, is seen in Fig. 3.1. A very natural wish is to define the particular domain as subclasses of this graphical core because then we get a domain metamodel and a graphical notation for each concept. This approach is also used in [7], so this tool-building platform could be one of implementations of the Modeling environment. We will base our explanation on this particular tool building idea, but we will simplify some details in order not to lose the basic ideas of our solution in technical details.

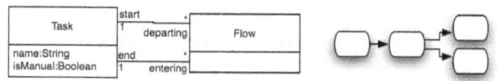

Fig. 3.2. Domain metamodel and a graphical instance example

Let us use a simple domain as an example. Metamodel of this domain together with a small example is seen in Fig. 3.2. From the Modeling environment point of view it is not essential, what the Intuitive semantics of that Domain metamodel is – only concepts and their graphical representations are defined here. In order to make the Domain metamodel *graphical*, it is rewritten as subclasses of the graphical core. Metamodel of Fig. 3.3 is the Domain metamodel of the Modeling environment.

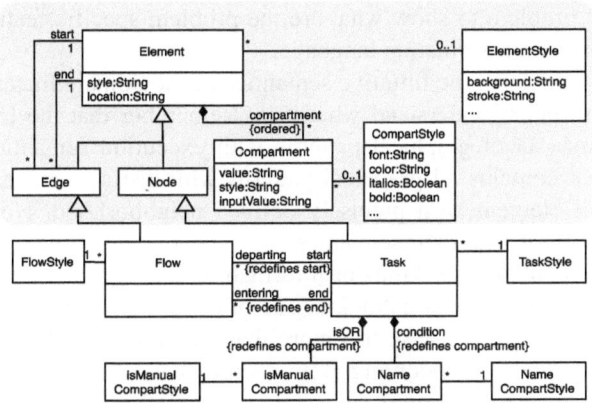

Fig. 3.3. Universal graphical core metamodel specialized for the domain-specific notation

4   Pull-Based Transformation Language

To build a tool we would use the metamodel seen in Fig. 3.3 as a Domain metamodel of the Modeling environment. However, to avoid technical details, for the examples in this Section we will use the metamodel from Fig. 3.2. We can do this because all the information that is needed for transformations, i.e. elements containing the semantic information, is included in that metamodel. In this particular domain-specific language we can do that, but we need to keep in mind that in some cases style elements (like color) can also contain semantics, and in that case they cannot be omitted. Also, in this metamodel, graphical elements of type "Compartment" have been moved to classes as attributes. This is a simpler notation for writing transformations.

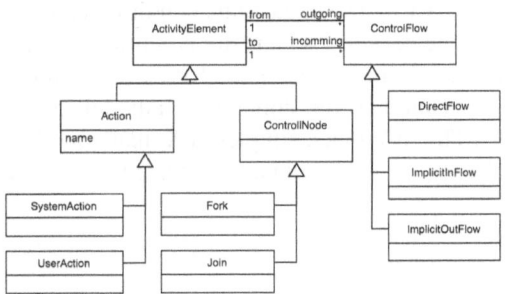

Fig. 4.1. Simplified Semantics metamodel

So, our goal is to define a semantic reduction (transformation) of the Domain metamodel instances (Fig. 3.3) into instances of the Semantics metamodel. In our example we will use a simplified version of UML Activity diagram metamodel as the Semantic metamodel (Fig. 4.1). Because both metamodels contain process execution semantics the transformation problem is not general but specific. We will start by an analysis of the problem to show what are the problem specific features on which we base our proposed transformation language.

We need to transform the Intuitive semantics of the domain metamodel. To do that we first need to better understand what it is. Remember that the Intuitive semantics was defined as a set of graphical patterns with execution semantics. The set is the smallest set that contains all graphical patterns with distinct semantics. Each pattern has one central element with precisely defined neighborhood. Now we will try to formalize the patterns and their semantics.

Each pattern contains two kinds of information, namely, the graphical context and the semantic explanation. Let us look at one of the patterns in more detail. Its textual form is the following "If a Task has more than one incoming flow, then it will start executing when all of its incoming flow sources have finished executing". For the Domain expert this explanation is sufficient, but to define a transformation we need a more formal notation. The previous example in this notation will look as follows:

```
If an Element is a Task and has more than one incoming flow,
     then it corresponds to a Join
and
If an Element is a Task,
     then it corresponds to an Action.
```

All other patterns have the same structure – one or more assertions (joined with an "and"). Each assertion consists of two parts – condition and conclusion. Condition is based on the Domain metamodel pattern and the conclusion contains the corresponding semantic term. Now we will try to understand what is the correspondence between these patterns and the concepts of the Semantic metamodel.

When we look more closely at the patterns written in the formal notation we can see that the semantic concepts occur in the conclusion part of each assertion. This correspondence is shown graphically in Fig. 4.2. If we analyze the formal patterns and correspondences further we can see that some condition assertions are the same, when there is a link to the same concept. As a result condition becomes a definition for how the concept should find its instances. Therefore we can look at the transformation problem as a reclassification of the domain metamodel instances into the Semantic metamodel concepts. That is a much simpler task than a model transformation written in the opposite direction (from domain patterns to semantic concepts).

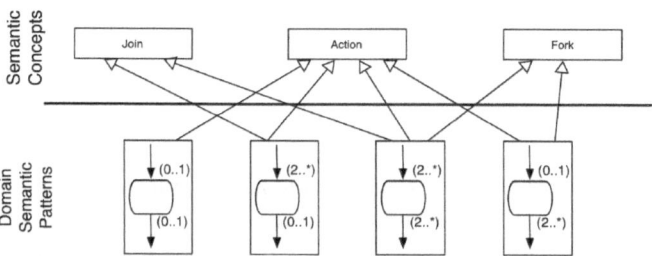

Fig. 4.2. Correspondence between Domain Semantic Patterns and Semantic Concepts

So the transformation is defined by looking at the Semantics (target) metamodel and stating, how instances of that metamodel will be created based on instances of the Domain (source) metamodel. Note that here the direction of transformation definition is opposite of the usual "Push" direction. Since we define transformation in the "Pull" direction, we cannot directly use ideas of previous transformation languages. We have to think a little differently instead. This task reminds a classification, and this type of thinking is closer to the way humans typically thinks of the world by explaining, what each concept means or how to recognize individuals belonging to the class of that concept and how to create the corresponding instances.

In order to explain the mechanism better and to create the necessary associations let us step aside and look at this process more generally and outside the current domain. We start by a class "Person" (Fig 4.3, the Definition phase), to which a recognition rule is attached – "Tool using". In the next phase – the Classification phase – real world individuals are selected that satisfy the given recognition rule. Part of individuals conforms to this rule, other part does not and maybe there are some individuals left on the border. Lastly, in the Instantiation phase a representation (an instance) is made for each recognized individual (a decision must be made here about partly recognized individuals). In order to not lose the connection between the generated instances and individuals, a mapping link is "created". Now the attached individual is called the **source** of the instance.

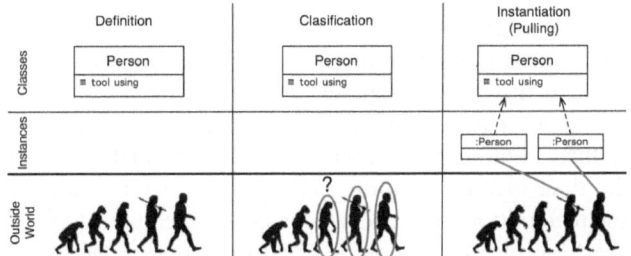

Fig. 4.3.[1] Illustration of intuitive classification process

Example demonstrated in Fig. 4.3 is only an illustration though the main steps of the recognition process are described there. If we use a formalized world instead of the "Outside world" (in our case – the Domain metamodel and its instances), then it becomes self-evident that we thus obtain a possibility to formalize and automate this process. In this case a precise description appears in the class recognition rule. It can be used to automatically select the right set of instances out of the whole set of domain instances. It can be done unambiguously. Also the Instantiation phase can be automated, so the mapping links made in the example can now be really created between instances of both metamodels for later use.

---

[1] Picture taken `http://challenge2.wordpress.com/2011/03/24/` `another-move-to-make-evolution-mandatory/`

Let us now return to the initial task – the transformation definition. As was mentioned before, it will be performed by looking from the Semantic (target) metamodel to the Domain (source) metamodel.

1. Transformation Specification

For every element of the Semantic (target) metamodel (class, association and attribute) a separate recognition rule is defined (the Definition phase). Since metamodel elements differ greatly, every one of them (class, association and attribute) has a recognition rule of different type.

Class type recognition rule states, how to recognize the potential set of source instances for that class among all Domain (source) instances, or in other words – what will be the result of the classification step. Recognition rules for associations and attributes employs the fact that exactly one instance of the Domain (source) metamodel is mapped through a link to each instance of the Semantic (target) metamodel. **Attribute type** recognition rule states, what will be the value for that attribute. **Association type** recognition rule generally performs the same way as the class type recognition rule stating the set of association link seeds. However, it is specified in different form, and there is a condition – whether a link conforming to that association needs to be created between the two given instances of the Semantic (target) metamodel or not. It must be mentioned that, when writing recognition rules, one may refer only to information found in the data of Domain (source) metamodel.

2. Transformation Execution

Transformation execution is an algorithm working in certain sequence and performing the Classification and Instantiation phases for each element of the metamodel based on its recognition rule. The algorithm starts with processing all the classes of the metamodel and then continues to process associations and attributes. If there are superclasses with their own recognition rules in the Semantic (target) metamodel, the inheritance of the recognition rules takes place before the algorithm.

As we can see from the description of transformation execution, its superstructure is very simple. The main question is what to use for writing and executing recognition rules. We propose using a transformation language lQuery [8] for this purpose. The transformation language lQuery is directly oriented towards selecting collections of instances of metamodel classes using filtration and navigation. Operations are performed with collections (sets) of metamodel instances applying the given selector for each of them thus getting another instance collection. Usually only part of the full lQuery functionality is needed when writing recognition rules, so they come out simple and intuitively understandable. However, in the next examples we will show an insight into syntax and semantics of recognition rules written within lQuery.

Table 1 shows all the necessary information needed for performing the semantic reduction of the Domain metamodel seen in Fig. 3.2. The table is organized as follows. The Domain metamodel is put in the upper left corner. Remember that the transformation is specified from the Semantic metamodel, so recognition rules need to be written for elements of the Semantic metamodel. In the right part of Table 1 there is the Semantic metamodel, whose classes and attributes have reduction rules attached (they follow the "≡" sign). We will come back to class recognition rules. Now let us look at the table section "Domain markings". If we look at "JoinTask", we can notice it has several incoming arrows in the Domain part that need to be recognized, as well as the element "Join" is attached in the Semantic part. On one hand name describes the semantics, but on the other – "Task [/entering.count() > 1]" is an lQuery selector describing the detection of such Tasks, which have more than one incoming arrow.

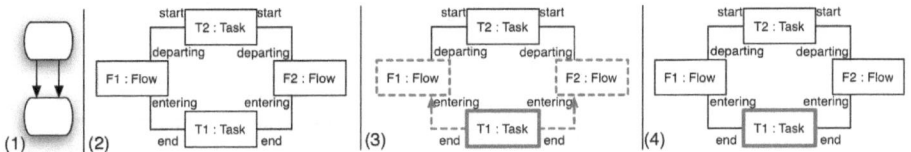

Fig 4.4. Example of the selector „Task [/entering:count() > 1]" execution

Graphical representation of a small example Domain process is depicted in Fig. 4.4 (1). Since transformations occur in the level of Domain metamodel instances, in (2) the same example is depicted, only as instance diagram. It has four instances, because flows are also described as classes.

The lQuery selector „Task [/entering:count() > 1]" consists of a chain of two selectors ("Task" and „[/entering:count() > 1]"), i.e. they are executed sequentially. The selection process starts with a collection containing all the instances of the metamodel – the four instances (T1, T2, F1, F2) in the example of Fig. 4.4. The first selector "Task" is a simple selector describing a filter by the given class name. After this selector has executed only instances of that class are left in the collection, so the collection is now {T1, T2}. The selector "[expr]" means that only those instances are left, for which the value of "expr" is true. Every instance of the set is evaluated. In order to understand, what will be checked, we need to analyze the expression found in the square brackets. It is inspected in the context of every instance of the set. Let us first take the instance T1. We can think we have a new collection {T1}, for which the selector "/entering.count() > 1" is executed. The first part of the selector "/entering" denotes navigation from existing collection by the link "entering". In (3) we can see that the obtained navigation result is {E1, E2}. Calculating the count of collection instances (operation ":count()"), we get the value 2. It is greater than one; therefore the obtained expression value for the instance T1 is *true*. Likewise, we can check that for the instance T2 the value of the selector is *false*, because we get an empty collection when navigating through the link "entering". So after the evaluation (T1 has the value *true*, T2 has the value *false*), thus the result of the original selector is {T1} (4). If the diagram where be larger and more complicated, then we would have selected all those tasks, for which there are more than one incoming flow.

In this detailed analysis of the lQuery selector we saw all the basic elements used in further examples, such as filtration by class name ("Task"), navigation ("/entering") and filtration by condition ("[expr]"). The previously analyzed selector is defined in section "Domain markings" in Table1. It is used for describing the domain marking "#JoinTask". In all recognition rules where #JoinTask appears; actually that selector definition is used. On the other hand we can imagine that a new subclass "JoinTask" of the Domain metamodel class "Task" is defined using this selector.

Table 1. Definition of the transformation between the Domain metamodel and the Semantics metamodel

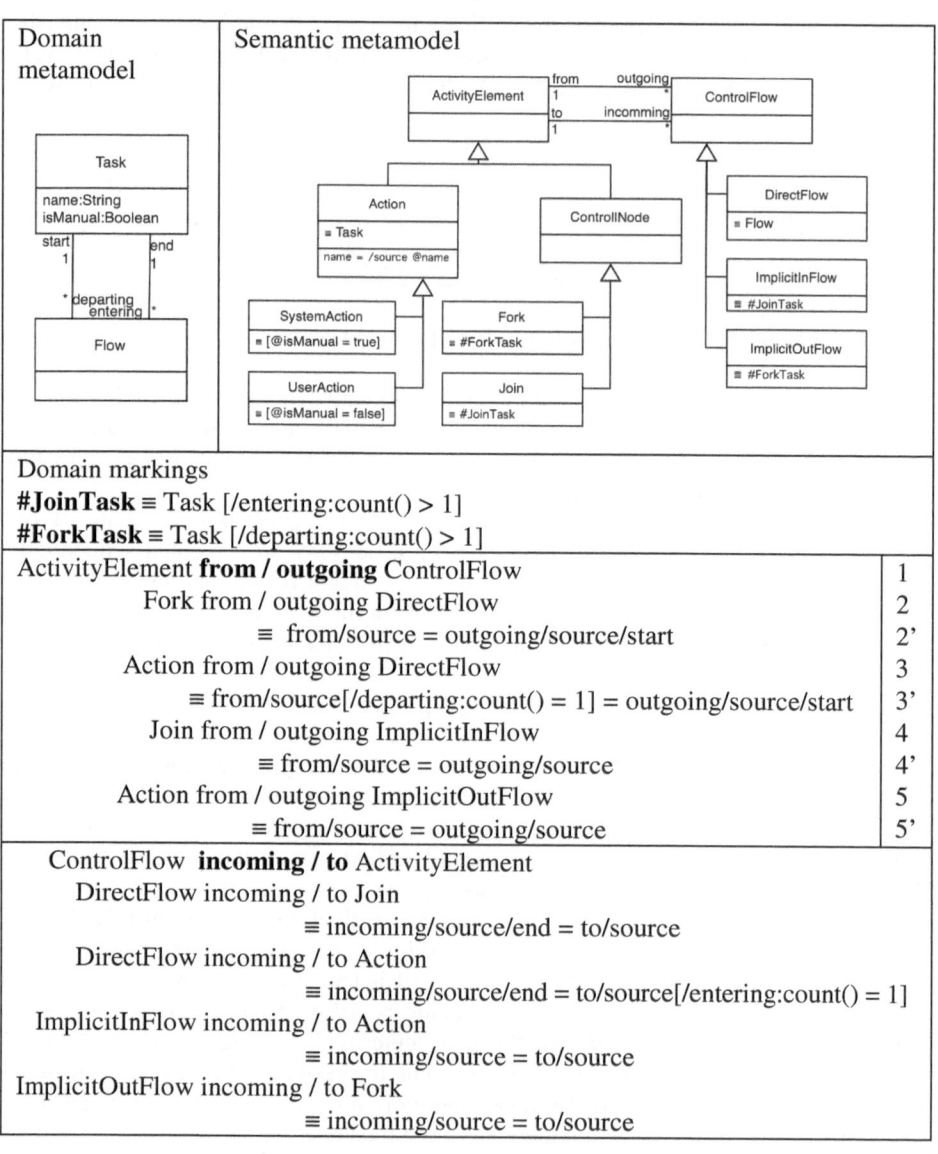

Domain markings
#JoinTask ≡ Task [/entering:count() > 1]
#ForkTask ≡ Task [/departing:count() > 1]

ActivityElement **from / outgoing** ControlFlow	1
Fork from / outgoing DirectFlow	2
≡ from/source = outgoing/source/start	2'
Action from / outgoing DirectFlow	3
≡ from/source[/departing:count() = 1] = outgoing/source/start	3'
Join from / outgoing ImplicitInFlow	4
≡ from/source = outgoing/source	4'
Action from / outgoing ImplicitOutFlow	5
≡ from/source = outgoing/source	5'

ControlFlow **incoming / to** ActivityElement
DirectFlow incoming / to Join
≡ incoming/source/end = to/source
DirectFlow incoming / to Action
≡ incoming/source/end = to/source[/entering:count() = 1]
ImplicitInFlow incoming / to Action
≡ incoming/source = to/source
ImplicitOutFlow incoming / to Fork
≡ incoming/source = to/source

Let us look at a small example and see, how the transformation is executed. The situation described in the previous example corresponds to the Classification phase, i.e. the instance set is found in the Domain metamodel that will be used when creating instances of the Semantic metamodel in the Instantiation step. In Fig. 4.5, part (1) the graphical representation of the Domain process example is shown. Part (2) of the figure contains instances of the Domain metamodel conforming to that graphical example. Also, we can see instances of the Semantic metamodel here that are created when executing class recognition rules "DirectFlow(≡Flow)", "ImplicitInFlow (≡#JoinTask)" and "ImplicitOutFlow(≡#ForkTask)". For the first class its recognition rule is an elementary lQuery selector, which finds all instances of the class "Flow" – {F1, F2}.

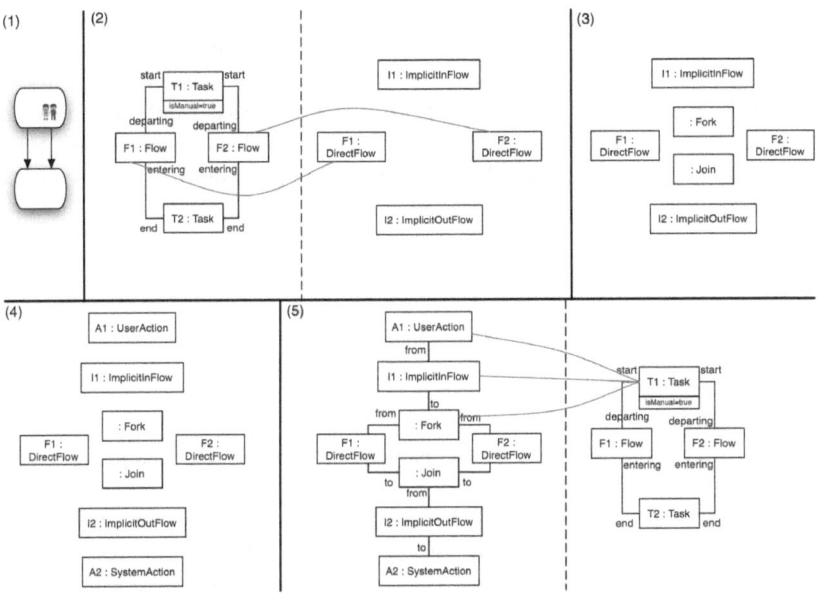

Fig 4.5. Transformation execution example

Then two instances of the metamodel class "DirectFlow" are created and connected with a mapping link to their source instances in the Domain metamodel. For the other two classes domain markings are used in their recognition rules. Therefore lQuery selectors attached to them are also executed thus creating two more instances. After the recognition rules of classes "Fork" and "Join" are executed, we have the situation in (3).

Let us see the class "Action(≡Task)" and two of its subclasses – "SystemAction (≡[@isManual=true])" and "UserAction(≡[@isManual=true])" from Fig 4.1. Since in this case a recognition rule is attached also to superclass, the first step is to add this rule to both subclasses. As a result we get the following set of classes – Action(), SystemAction(≡Task [@isManual=true]) and UserAction(≡Task [@isManual=true]). A new lQuery symbol "@" appears in these selectors, it denotes an attribute value. After applying the corresponding recognition rules we get the situation (4). The situation (5) is obtained after applying recognition rules of all associations.

Association cases need to be inspected in more detail, because their implementation differs from the case of classes. Moreover, we must remember that execution of association recognition rules occurs only after the class recognition rules are already executed. Let us go a little deeper into the notation of association recognition rules. Association is characterized by its role names (e.g. from/outgoing) and the classes the association connects (ActivityElement and ControlFlow). Since association end classes (in Table 1 (1)) have subclasses, recognition rules are attached only to those pairs of subclasses, between which a link is possible. Table 1 (2) is a subassociation between the corresponding classes, and (2') is the recognition rule for this association.

Generally a recognition rule of an association works in the following way. Two collections of instances are made – one consists of instances of the association start class, and the other consists of instances of the end class. For example, the association (5) shown in Table 1 has a start class Action and an end class ImplicitOutFlow. In the process example shown in part (4) of Fig 4.5 the start class instances are {A1, A2} and the end class instance is {I1}. Now for each pair of instances of these collections the value of the recognition rule is checked.

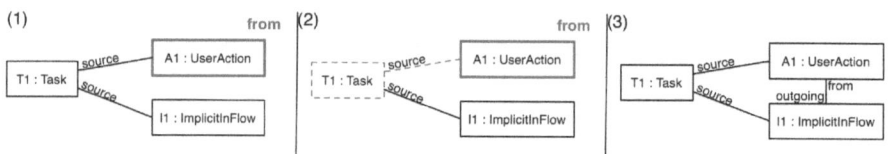

Fig 4.6. Example of the association recognition rule „from/source = outgoing/source"

Let us assume we have a pair {A1, I1}. In Fig. 4.6 we can see fragment of instances of both metamodels for this pair. The association recognition rule „from/source = outgoing/source" consists of the left hand side selector "from/source", applied to the first instance A1, and the right hand side selector "outgoing/source", applied to the second instance I1. If we look at the first selector "from/source", we can see that the first word "from" matches the role name of association (5) from Table1. The first instance is identified by this word in this selector (Fig. 4.6 (1)). Next the usual selector application takes place (the navigation "/source") and a source for the instance A1 is searched in the Domain metamodel. The result is {T1} (Fig. 4.6 (2)). Likewise, we can find the value of selector "outgoing/source" being {T1}. Then both of these collections are compared and, if they are equal, then an association link is created between the initial instances (Fig. 4.6 (3)). For the other pair of instances {A2, I1} the results are „from/source = {T1}", "outgoing/source" = { }. Thus no link is created between these instances.

Association recognition rules are not always as simple as in the previous case. For example, the recognition rule (3') of association (3) (in Table 1) is more complicated – it contains longer navigation expressions and filtration. However, the working principles are the same.

If we look at the Semantic metamodel, we can see that several subclasses have appeared for class "ControlFlow". Such a construction is necessary for coding information about what has been the instance creation condition. Our approach allows freely supplementing the Semantic metamodel with subclasses, because it does not affect the execution, but it allows correctly performing the further classification.

5   Related Work

Since the main contribution of this paper is a new model transformation language, in this Section we will make comparison with some of the existing model transformation languages that are in some way related to ours.

The existing model transformation languages can characterized by a number of features, e.g., those offered by Czarnecki [9]. The feature selection closest to the approach proposed in this paper are rule based languages with implicit (declarative) concurrent rule application in the exogenous (source model to target model) context. The most relevant rule definition features would be declarative patterns syntactically separated into the source (the left) part and target (right) part. Certainly, many transformation languages have these mentioned features but some other ones as well, but we are interested here only in these features. Typical such languages are AGG [10] and AToM3 [11] using simple graphical pattern definition facilities. The declarative subset of Viatra [12] has advanced textual pattern definition facilities including recursive patterns. The declarative subset of the most used in practice transformation language ATL [13] also has similar features with pattern definition based on OCL expressions and functional style elements such as helper functions. An element common to all these (and other similar) languages is that we think of rule application from left to right – find an instance of the source pattern in the source model and create an appropriate instance (fragment) in the target model. Such an approach in this paper is named the push approach. While it is initially the most intuitive approach to define a model transformation, it has some drawbacks as well. For example, some sort of source-target traceability has implicitly to be supported in order to avoid creating multiple copies in the target from the same source model fragment.

Another relevant subset of transformation languages are the explicit mapping languages defining the source to target correspondences explicitly, such as e.g. R2RML language [14] for mapping RDB to RDF and especially MALA4MDSD [15] for simple MDSD transformations. For such languages a typical task is a hierarchical model structure mapping, therefore some mapping execution order has to be defined; the push approach is typically used as well.

6   Conclusions

In this paper we proposed a solution for building BPMS that can support a domain-specific modeling language for each organization. The proposed solution consisted of two parts, namely, the separation of Modeling Environment from the Execution Environment. The separation allowed us to replace the Modeling Environment with a specific tool for each domain-specific language (such tools are easy to create with the so called meta-case tools). Then the remaining problem was to transform the domain-specific process model to the model that is understood by the Execution Environment. We noticed that this transformation task can be looked at as a classification problem and proposed a novel transformation language that is specifically designed for such types of problems. In the future we plan to explore, how this approach can be combined with elements of "push-based" approach to transformations.

References

1. UML, http://www.uml.org
2. BPMN, http://www.bpmn.org
3. Barzdins, J., Cerans, K., Grasmanis, M., Kalnins, A., Kozlovics, S., Lace, L., Liepins, R., Rencis, E., Sprogis, A., Zarins, A.: Domain Specific Languages for Business Process Management: a Case Study. In: Proceedings of the 9th OOPSLA Workshop on Domain-Specific Modeling (2009)
4. Barzdins, J., Kozlovics, S., Rencis, E.: The Transformation- Driven Architecture. In: Proceedings of DSM 2008 Workshop of OOPSLA 2008, Nashville, USA, pp. 60–63 (2008)
5. MetaEdit+, http://www.metacase.com
6. Doux, G., Jouault, F., Bézivin, J.: Transforming BPMN process models to BPEL process definitions with ATL. In: GraBaTs 2009: 5th International Workshop on Graph-Based Tools, Zurich (2009)
7. Rencis, E., Barzdins, J., Kozlovics, S.: Towards Open Graphical Tool-Building Framework. Scientific Journal of Riga Technical University, "Computer Science", 80–87 (2011); special issue for the Grabis, J., Kirikova, M. (eds.): BIR 2011. LNBIP, vol. 90. Springer, Heidelberg (2011)
8. Liepins, R.: lQuery: A Model Query and Transformation Library. Scientific Papers, vol. 770, pp. 27–45. University of Latvia (2011)
9. Czarnecki, K., Helsen, S.: Feature-based survey of model transformation approaches. IBM Systems Journal 45(3) (2006)
10. Taentzer, G.: AGG: A Tool Environment for Algebraic Graph Transformation. In: Nagl, M., Schürr, A., Münch, M. (eds.) AGTIVE 1999. LNCS, vol. 1779, pp. 481–488. Springer, Heidelberg (2000)
11. de Lara, J., Vangheluwe, H.: AToM^3: A Tool for Multi-formalism and Meta-modelling. In: Kutsche, R.-D., Weber, H. (eds.) FASE 2002. LNCS, vol. 2306, pp. 174–188. Springer, Heidelberg (2002)
12. Csertán, G., Huszerl, G., Majzik, I., Pap, Z., Pataricza, A., Varró, D.: VIATRA: Visual automated transformations for formal verification and validation of UML models. In: Proceedings of the 17th IEEE International Conference on Automated Software Engineering, ASE 2002, pp. 267–270. IEEE Computer Society, Washington, DC (2002)
13. Jouault, F., Kurtev, I.: Transforming Models with ATL. In: Bruel, J.-M. (ed.) MoDELS 2005. LNCS, vol. 3844, pp. 128–138. Springer, Heidelberg (2006)
14. W3C: R2RML: RDB to RDF Mapping Language, W3C working draft edn. (September 2011)
15. Kalnina, E., Kalnins, A., Sostaks, A., Celms, E., Iraids, J.: Tree Based Domain-Specific Mapping Languages. In: Bieliková, M., Friedrich, G., Gottlob, G., Katzenbeisser, S., Turán, G. (eds.) SOFSEM 2012. LNCS, vol. 7147, pp. 492–504. Springer, Heidelberg (2012)

Characterizing Trustworthy Digital Rights Exporting

Wenhui Lu, Zheying Zhang, and Jyrki Nummenmaa

School of Information Sciences, University of Tampere
FIN-33014 Tampere, Finland
{wenhui.lu,zheying.zhang,jyrki.nummenmaa}@uta.fi

Abstract. Digital Rights Management (DRM) is an important business enabler for digital content industry. Rights exporting is one of the crucial tasks in providing the interoperability of DRM. Trustworthy rights exporting is required by both the end users and the DRM systems. We propose a set of principles for trustworthy rights exporting by analysing the characteristic of rights exporting. Based on the principles, we provide some suggestions on how trustworthy rights exporting should be performed.

Keywords: Digital Rights Management (DRM), rights exporting, DRM interoperability.

1   Introduction

Digital contents, such as music and video, have been increasingly welcomed on the consumer market. According to the shipment statistics of RIAA [1], the U.S. total digital music market grew to $3.2 billion in 2010, while digital downloads continued double digit annual growth reaching $2.2 billion. Overall, digital formats comprised a record 47% of the total music shipments in the United States. For comparison, digital shipments only accounted for 9% of the market back in 2005. On the other hand, the shipments in physical formats declined 20% by value in 2010.

The popularity of digital contents has attracted business interests. Meanwhile, digital contents by nature are more vulnerable to piracy than physical copies from the content distribution point of view. Therefore, Digital Rights Management (DRM) [2], as an essential part of a business enabler, was introduced to the digital content industry, and has been continuously evolving. In this paper, DRM refers to a system to protect high value digital assets and to control their distribution and usage. A few mature and sophisticated DRM standards have been generated and well adopted by industry, such as Windows Media DRM [3], and Open Mobile Alliance (OMA) DRM version 2 [4].

As Carlisle and Navin mentioned [5], in the digital music market (and accompanying digital players), use of different DRM systems, have effectively locked-in consumers to proprietary technologies of respective companies. The lack of interoperability becomes increasingly problematic. For example, the end user has to purchase the rights to play same music file more than once simply because the devices he or she has are based on different DRM systems and not interoperable to each other. The key question in DRM interoperability is how to deal with distinctions among DRM systems and to export rights from one system to another in a trustworthy way.

N. Aseeva, E. Babkin, and O. Kozyrev (Eds.): BIR 2012, LNBIP 128, pp. 85–95, 2012.

Many authors have addressed the issue of DRM interoperability in general [5, 6, 7, 8, 9, 10, 11, 12, 13, and 16]. Koenen et al. [6] proposed three approaches to interoperability in DRM systems. Those approaches are full format interoperability, connected interoperability, and configuration-driven interoperability.

Full format interoperability is regarded as the ideal approach. However, it is not practical in the short term as it requires consolidation among all existing standards and an effort to build a standard that covers all the requirements that come from various environments. Configuration-driven interoperability is especially suitable for solutions between two specific systems since it forces the target DRM systems to change by way of installing tools. When dealing with interoperability between many systems, this approach shows its limitation, as installations are required on all the DRM systems concerned. Also, tool installation implies the potential risk of security compromise. The connected interoperability approach centralizes the effort of interoperability among DRM systems and it is relatively secure as the service is provided remotely. However, it requires connection between the service providers of interoperability and the targeted DRM systems.

On the standardization track for DRM interoperability, Coral Consortium [14] and Marlin developer community [15] have been trying to standardize DRM interoperability. In the Coral approach, different licenses for different DRM systems are generated from a common token in accordance with a common ecosystem. In the Marlin approach, licenses are expressed programmatically in the form of control objects to prevent dependence on any one particular rights expression languages (REL) [12]. Besides, the Digital Media Project group proposed their interoperable DRM standard in 2007 [9]. Doncel et al [11] discussed the potential of MPEG Extensible Middleware to serve DRM interoperability in the MPEG-21 standard. According to these studies, researchers argue that full format interoperability seems unlikely achieved across the broader DRM market [8]. Coral Consortium [14] have been taking the initiative to standardize DRM interoperability but not aiming at a generic DRM standard. Marlin developer community [15] attempts to provide truly interoperable and open digital content sharing platform and the industrial impacts are yet to be seen. In such situation of lacking the universal and widely-adopted DRM standard, if we accept the differences between DRM systems, how to deal with the distinctions among DRM systems forms the key question to DRM interoperability.

Schmidt et al. [7] expanded the idea of connected interoperability from Koenen et al. [6], and introduced the concept of intermediated DRM. Moreover, they listed four general tasks for the intermediary DRM: Content and rights reformatting, data management, condition evaluation, and dynamical state evaluation.

Except for the full format interoperability, these four tasks are generic to the solutions of DRM interoperability. According to Schmidt et al. [7], the reformatting of rights and content is a relatively simple task. Meanwhile, data management is not only a task for interoperability but also a mandatory task for rights purchasing of the DRM system. The technical aspects related to data management have been well studied and matured as compared to other tasks. However, condition evaluation is a pre-condition to fulfilling a trustworthy rights exporting process. Decisions shall be made according to the diversity of DRM systems and the constraints of devices. Safavi-Naini et al. [16] have proposed some strategies for condition evaluation, but there are still unresolved issues such as lack of principles to define criteria for trustworthy rights evaluation. Therefore the task to evaluate rights to be exported is one of the key tasks which require further elaboration.

2   Rights Exporting

Safavi-Naini et al. [16] discussed the import and export concept among the DRM systems. Based on it, we define rights exporting as a task to provide the usage rights governed by a domestic DRM system to a target DRM system. Rights exporting shall be trustworthy, which can be explained from the perspectives of both end users and the DRM systems. From an end user point of view, his or her usage rights granted on the domestic system should not be deprived in the process of exporting the rights to a target system. From the system point of view, a trustworthy process of rights exporting should not break the integrity of the DRM system by granting the end user extra usage rights.

In order to export a rights instance from a system to another, we firstly check if a system level support exists for rights exporting. It can be formulated as a statement *IsExportable(A, B)*, where *A* represents the domestic system that rights are exported from, and *B* represents the target system that rights are exported to. When the statement is *true*, i.e. *IsExportable(A, B)==true*, it means such a support exists. Secondly, we check whether a specific rights instance can be exported from A to B or not. Given a rights instance R_x, if R_x is governed by a system A, this can be expressed as $R_x(A)$. Once it is possible to export a rights instance $R_x(A)$ from A to B (*IsExportable(A, B)==true*), the actual exporting task can be formulated as a function *Export(R_x(A),B)*. Ideally the output of rights exporting should be the equivalent rights in the target system, which can be expressed as *Export(R_x(A),B)$\Rightarrow R_x$(B)*. However, due to the difference between A and B, it is hard to have an equivalent rights exporting. Some part of the rights instance needs to remain on the domestic system, while the other part is exported to the target system. For example, if some part of the rights instance cannot be translated by the target system [16], then we need to extract the part from the rights instances. Also if we want to keep the rights available on both systems, we need to store the original rights instance on the target system. The exporting result shall include one part of R_x remaining in system A and the other part of R_x exporting to system B. We define $R_{x'}$ as the remaining part and $R_{x''}$ as exporting part when exporting R_x from one system to another. Therefore, the exporting function shall be formed as *Export(R_x(A),B) $\Rightarrow R_{x'}$(A)+$R_{x''}$(B)*. The process of rights exporting can be defined as follows:

```
Input: A set of rights instances (R₁(A),R₂(A),...Rₙ(A)) to be
exported from DRM system A to DRM system B
Output: A set of exported rights instances
(R₁''(B),R₂''(B),...Rₙ''(B)) on B, and a set of remaining rights
instances (R₁'(A),R₂'(A),...Rₙ'(A)) on A after exporting
if IsExportable(A, B)==true, then{
  for each Rₓ (x=1,2,...n){
    Export(Rₓ(A),B) ⇒ Rₓ'(A)+Rₓ''(B)
  }
}
```

As the formalized process represents, the rights exporting is defined with respect to an original system and a target system for rights exporting. The direction of rights exporting and the rights instance to be exported are the input of rights exporting. Once the inputs are determined, various approaches can be applied to achieve rights exporting. Those approaches can be categorized into different modes according to where the rights instance is stored and governed. Once an approach is selected, then the results of rights exporting needs to be assured, which lead to the principles of rights exporting. The direction, modes, and results form the essential characteristics of the rights exporting. We can discuss these three aspects of rights exporting in a more organized manner by using the formalized process.

2.1 Directions of Rights Exporting

When talking about rights exporting, the only direction is from the domestic system to the target system. However, a specific DRM system can be the domestic system in one case of rights exporting, and be the target system in another case. The directions of rights exporting between two specific DRM systems are illustrated into three cases, as shown in Figure 1.

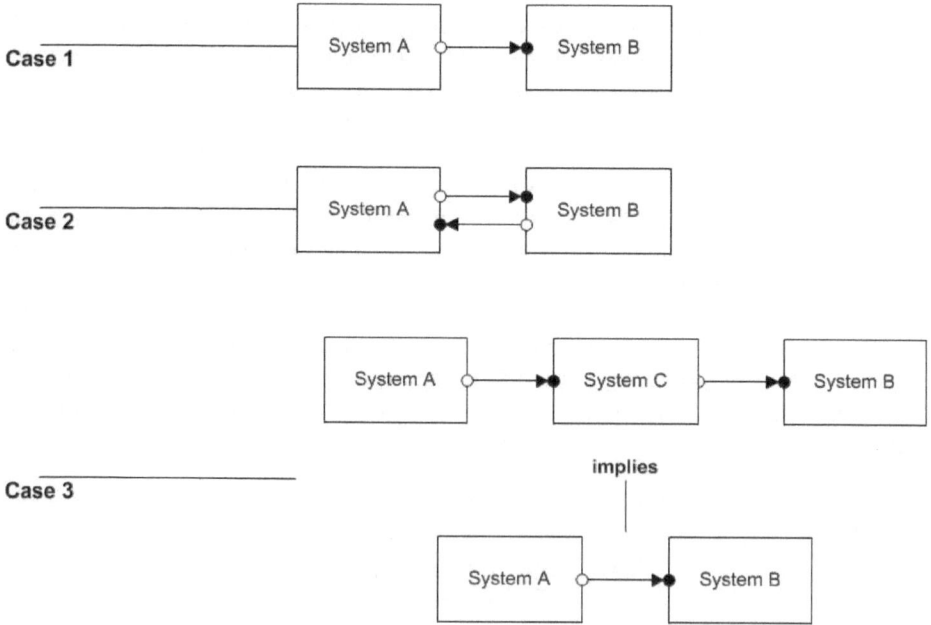

Fig. 1. Directions of rights exporting

In Case 1, a rights instance is only allowed to export from system A to system B, which means *IsExportable(A, B)==true* and *IsExportable(B,A)==false*;

In Case 2, a rights instance is allowed to export in both directions between system A and B, which means *IsExportable(A, B)== true* and *IsExportable(B, A)==true*;

In Case 3, a rights instance can be exported from system A to system C as well as from C to B. But there is no support for rights exporting between system A and system B directly, which means *IsExportable(A,C)==true and IsExportable(C,B)==true and IsExportable(A,B)==false*. This is considered as an indirect rights exporting between A and B. In this case, a rights instance can still be exported from system A to system B via system C, although there might be rights reinterpretation during the process of rights exporting.

From a rights exporting point of view, both Case 1 and Case 3 have a one-directional rights exporting between system A and system B, while Case 2 has a mutual rights exporting between system A and system B.

The direction of rights exporting between two systems may cause potential risk to system integrity. If the rights exporting between system A and system B is a mutual rights exporting, and some rights may be reinterpreted to grant looser usage rules than the original does, then by proceeding via the rights exporting back and forth between the two systems, the end user could obtain free rights other than the rights originally granted to him or her. The selection for the direction of rights exporting between two systems is also sensitive to business competition. In order to retain the customers in system A while attracting customers from system B, system A may restrict right exporting from A to B while granting rights exporting from B to A.

2.2   Modes of Rights Exporting

OMA DRM 2 has defined two modes for rights exporting: copy mode and move mode [4]. The modes determine the storage and governance of rights between two systems, as illustrated in Figure 2.

- Copy mode retains the original rights instances on the domestic system and makes a copied rights instance on the target system
- Move mode makes a copied rights instance on the target system and removes the original rights instance from the domestic system.

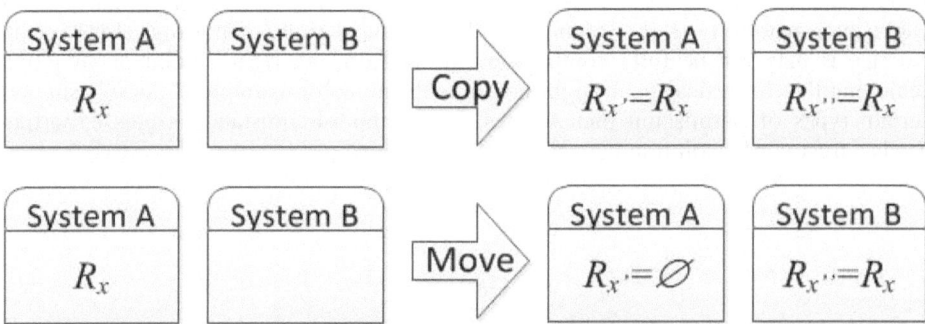

Fig. 2. Modes of rights exporting

Different modes result in a variety of outputs in rights exporting. In an ideal situation, they can be expressed as follows:

- In the copy mode, theoretically the exported rights instances on B should be equivalent as the original rights instances on A and the rights instance that remains on A, which can be expressed as: $R_x == R_{x'} == R_{x''}$;
- In the move mode, ideally the exported rights instance on B should be identical as the original rights instance on A and no remaining part of the original rights should be on A after rights exporting, which can be expressed as: $R_x == R_{x''}$ and $R_{x'} == \varnothing$;

The modes meet different needs. The copy mode allows an end user to use a rights instance on different systems at the same time. However, it is only suitable for rights with only stateless conditions, such as absolute time based condition. When a rights instance with only stateful conditions, such as count based condition, is exported from system A to system B with the copy mode, the internal state in the rights instance on system A cannot be updated according to the usage on system B. That is to say, the end user receives two instances of rights with the same stateful condition, and the usage rights are expanded. It implies that the end user may retrieve the rights freely by exporting the rights instance between system A and system B. It is obviously an untrusted process. The move mode allows an end user to use a rights instance on different systems but the rights can be assigned on only one system each time. That is to say when an end user exports a rights instance from system A to system B, if he later wants to render the content on system A, the end user has to export the rights from system B back to system A, or purchase another rights instance for system A, which obviously causes inconvenience to the end user.

In addition, selection of a mode is not only a technical issue, but also a decision with respect to the business strategy. Usually, systems using different DRM technologies are rivals from a market share point of view.

2.3   Results of Rights Exporting

In theory, the level of DRM interoperability varies from access denial to free access if measured by the rights upon protected content outside of the domestic system. Ideally the rights should not be reinterpreted differently than they are in the domestic system. Theoretically if system A accepts rights exporting from A to B, B should grant the same rights to the end user as A does, which means $R_x == R_{x''}$. This is the goal of DRM interoperability in theory and the ideal result of rights exporting. However, in practice B may not be fully compatible with A from the right's point of view and achieving the theoretical goal might not be realistic, if for example B doesn't support certain types of permission that A does. Under this circumstance, rights exporting needs a trustworthy solution between the two systems.

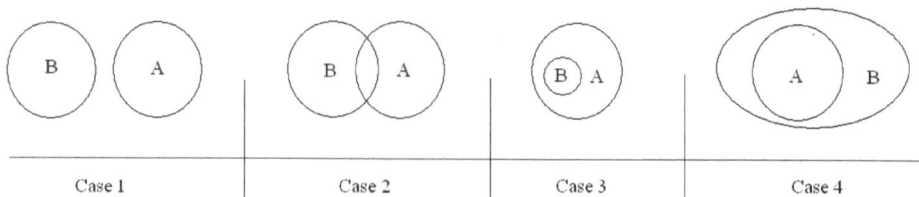

| Case 1 | Case 2 | Case 3 | Case 4 |

Fig. 3. Results of rights exporting

There are four types of results when a rights instance is exported from system A to system B. They are illustrated in Figure 3, where rights are represented as circles inside which are the system names. Area A represents the rights allowed by the domestic DRM system, while area B represents the rights in the target DRM system. The overlapping area represents the rights available on both systems.

Case 1 describes an extreme situation where totally different rights are granted to target system B when the end user exports the rights instance from system A to system B, which can be expressed as $R_x \cap R_{x''} == \varnothing$. For example, Jack has rights to play an MP3 file on his smart phone. If he transfers the song to his PC, the DRM system on his PC grants him rights to burn the song into a CD instead of the rights to play. The permission type changes from "play a song" to "burn a song onto a CD". Since the rights are reinterpreted, Case 1 can hardly be accepted in rights exporting. However, under certain circumstances, the case can be used to realize special features. For example, it may allow end users to exchange some rights instances for content on system A into rights instances for other content on system B.

Case 2 indicates that after rights exporting from system A to system B, part of the usage rules will be reinterpreted differently for the end user on system B, which can be expressed as $R_x \cap R_{x''} \supset \varnothing$, $R_x \cap R_{x''} \subset R_x$, and $R_x \cap R_{x''} \subset R_{x''}$. For example, our imaginary actor Jack London has rights to edit a document file and to send out the text within the document via a short message service on his phone. Then, after he transfers the rights to his PC, the DRM system on his PC allows him to edit and to print the document. Compared with Case 1, this case at least exports some part of the rights precisely from system A to system B, although it still reinterprets differently some part of the rights from system A. The case may be used, for example, to handle differences between devices, like the rights to transfer data through infrared or the rights to transfer data through Bluetooth.

Case 3 represents the case where system B makes the usage rules more restrictive when rights are exported from system A to system B, which can be expressed as $\varnothing \subset R_{x''} \subset R_x$. For example, Jane has the rights to print and view a picture on her PC. If she exports the rights to her phone, then she could only view the picture on her phone. The case is quite common when some types of permission or constraints supported by system A are not supported by system B.

Case 4 indicates that system B not only grants the rights that system A does to the end user, but also offers some extra rights that system A does not, which can be expressed as $\varnothing \subset R_x \subset R_{x''}$. For example, Jack has rights to play a music file. If he exports the rights to his PC, he could then play the file and burn it onto a CD as well. The case could be caused by differences of interpretation for permissions or rights between DRM systems. For example, the interpretation of full rights for content on a PC grants end users more permission than the interpretation of full rights on a mobile phone does.

Not all the cases can be accepted as a trustworthy result of rights exporting. Except for Case 3, all other cases lead to extra rights in the target system. If some extra rights can be directly or indirectly transferred back to the original system or other systems, then it means that some DRM systems could obtain extra rights without payment or with less payment, which implies that the system integrity might be jeopardized.

Therefore, we choose Case 3 and combine it with the ideal goal as a practical goal for DRM interoperability: $\emptyset \subset R_{x''} \subseteq R_x$, which means we aim at enforcing that the exported rights on the target device are no less restrictive than the exporting rights on the domestic device.

Different modes lead to different practical results of rights exporting. In copy mode, the ideal result is $R_x == R_{x'} == R_{x''}$ as discussed on the modes of rights exporting. We can easily keep R_x unchanged to be $R_{x'}$ in order to achieve $R_x == R_{x'}$. However, achieving $R_x == R_{x''}$ seems much more challenging when dealing with system differences, and the practical goal for DRM interoperability can be applied. Then the practical result of copy mode can be formulated as $R_{x'} == R_x$ and $\emptyset \subset R_{x''} \subseteq R_x$.

Similarly, in move mode, the ideal result, $R_{x'} == \emptyset$ and $R_{x''} == R_x$, needs to be revised given the potential differences between two systems. If some part of the rights instance cannot be interpreted by the target system, then the incompatible part has to be extracted from the original rights instance if possible and stored on the domestic system, which means $R_{x'} \supseteq \emptyset$. On the other hand, $R_{x''}$ need to be in line with the practical goal for DRM interoperability $\emptyset \subset R_{x''} \subseteq R_x$. then the practical result of move mode can be formulated as $R_{x'} \supseteq \emptyset$ and $\emptyset \subset R_{x''} \subseteq R_x$.

3   Principles for Rights Exporting

By analyzing the factors of rights exporting, we noticed that in some cases rights exporting could lead to extra rights than those an end user pays for. This may happen in the copy mode if a stateful condition is exported to the target system. Also the result of rights exporting may bring extra rights. If extra rights are generated in one-direction rights exporting between two systems, the consequences are limited since it cannot be repeated for a rights instance. However, if a mutual rights exporting could bring extra rights, then the end user could gain endless extra rights by simply repeating rights exporting between the two systems. Therefore, creating extra rights should be strictly forbidden during rights exporting. On the other hand, although the end users may accept the fact that not all rights from the domestic system can be exported to the target system, they still want to export as many rights as possible. So the principles of a trustworthy rights exporting can be summarized to maximize the amount of rights to be exported and to prevent generating extra rights.

Preventing generation of extra rights can be formulated as $R_{x'} \cup R_{x''} \subseteq R_x$, while maximizing the amount of rights to be exported can be formulated as an intention to $R_{x''} \rightarrow R_x$. By combing these principle conditions with the results of rights exporting, we can reason out the formulated principles of rights exporting.

In copy mode, combining the practical results $R_{x'} == R_x$ and $\emptyset \subset R_{x''} \subseteq R_x$, and the principle conditions $R_{x'} \cup R_{x''} \subseteq R_x$ and $R_{x''} \rightarrow R_x$, we get $R_{x''} \rightarrow R_x$ where $\emptyset \subset R_{x''} \subseteq R_x$ and $R_{x'} == R_x$.

In move mode, combining the practical results $R_{x'} \supseteq \emptyset$ and $\emptyset \subset R_{x''} \subseteq R_x$, and the principle conditions $R_{x'} \cup R_{x''} \subseteq R_x$ and $R_{x''} \rightarrow R_x$, we get $R_{x''} \rightarrow R_x$ where $\emptyset \subset R_{x''} \subseteq R_x$, and $R_{x'} \rightarrow \emptyset$, where $\emptyset \subseteq R_{x'} \subset R_x$, and $R_{x'} \cup R_{x''} \subseteq R_x$.

To conclude, the formulated principle of trustworthy rights exporting is as follows:

- In copy mode: $R_{x''} \rightarrow R_x$ where $\emptyset \subset R_{x''} \subseteq R_x$; and $R_{x'} == R_x$.
- In move mode: $R_{x''} \rightarrow R_x$ where $\emptyset \subset R_{x''} \subseteq R_x$; and $R_{x'} \rightarrow \emptyset$ where $\emptyset \subseteq R_{x'} \subset R_x$; and $R_{x'} \cup R_{x''} \subseteq R_x$.

4   Discussion

The principles for trustworthy rights exporting can facilitate rights exporting in two aspects. Firstly, before exporting rights to a target system, an exporting strategy needs to be determined based on evaluation of rights to be exported and differences between two DRM systems. The strategy should define which part of usage rights will be exported, and what is the required adaptation. The principles should be enforced in the process of forming the strategy. Secondly, depending on the different strategy, the result of rights exporting may vary. The principles can be used as a benchmark to measure the performance of rights exporting.

In order to enforce the principles, the principles need to be taken into consideration in every decision making step of rights exporting. Thus, they can be regarded as part of design principles during the system design phase. Each time when the process of rights exporting is utilized, the output $R_{x''}(B)$ needs to be checked to ensure $\emptyset \subset R_{x''} \subseteq R_x$. If additional rights are generated due to the rights exporting, the process needs to be cancelled, or at least an alternative approach needs to be applied in order to rectify the output. Even more proactively, algorithms can be developed to reflect the principles in the implementation. For example, the algorithm of rights decomposition we developed in the previous research [17, 18] can be an example to proactively enforce the principles.

In order to benchmark the performance of rights exporting based on the principles, a comprehensive set of rights can be pre-defined for two given systems. Then by examining the results of rights exporting upon different solutions, we can measure the performance how different solutions perform in maximizing the amount of rights to be exported. Given two approaches $Export1(R_x(A),B)$ and $Export2(R_x(A),B)$ to export the same set of $R_x(A)$ on A to B, if the output $R_{x1''}(B)$ from $Export1$ and the output $R_{x2''}(B)$ from $Export2$ relates in the manner $\emptyset \subset R_{x2''} \subset R_{x1''} \subseteq R_x$, then we prefer $Export1$ over $Export2$ for the $R_x(A)$ exporting from A to B, as Export1 provides more rights as an output compared with what $Export2$ does. Another approach is to perform mutual rights exporting with a given amount of iterations and then examine the results of rights exporting, if mutual rights exporting is in place between A and B.

5   Conclusion and Future Work

The paper has reviewed the importance of DRM interoperability and the related research for rights exporting. By analyzing the different aspects in rights exporting, we concluded the principles of rights exporting and discussed how to apply the principles to enhance the solution of rights exporting.

The contributions of this paper start from firstly establishing a formulation of rights exporting. By using the formulation, we examine and categorize the essential aspects of rights exporting: directions, modes, and results; although the modes of rights exporting are derived from OMA DRM 2[4]. Especially, we provide the relation between modes and results. The key contribution of this paper is that according to the essential aspects of rights exporting we concluded the principles of trustworthy rights exporting via the formulation we established. In the end of paper, we discuss how to utilize the principles in various occasions.

In the future, we will take into account the difference of rights exporting modes, the possible rights flows between two systems, etc. in the empirical studies of rights exporting and propose an integrated process to support the decision-making in the rights exporting process. Using the principles as a benchmark, we can further measure the performance of the process and try to enhance the performance of the solution.

References

1. RIAA 2010, 2010 Year-End Shipment Statistics,
   http://www.riaa.com/keystatistics.php (accessed September 25, 2011)
2. Liu, Q., Safavi-Naini, R., Sheppard, N.P.: Digital rights management for content distribution. In: Proc. Australasian Information Security Workshop Conference on ACSW Frontiers, vol. 21, pp. 49–58 (2003)
3. Microsoft WMDRM, Licensing Windows Media DRM Technologies,
   http://www.microsoft.com/windows/windowsmedia/licensing/drmlicensing.aspx (accessed September 25, 2011)
4. OMA DRM v2, OMA Digital Rights Management V2.0.2 (July 23, 2008),
   http://www.openmobilealliance.org/Technical/release_program/drm_v2_0.aspx (accessed September 25, 2011)
5. Carlisle, G., Navin, C.: Issues and challenges in securing interoperability of DRM systems in the digital music market. International Review of Law, Computers & Technology 20(3), 271–285 (2006)
6. Koenen, R.H., Lacy, J., MacKay, Mitchell, S.: The long march to interoperable digital rights management. Proc. IEEE 92, 883–897 (2004)
7. Schmidt, A.U., Tafreschi, O., Wolf, R.: Interoperability challenges for DRM systems. In: Proc. IFIP/GI Workshop on Virtual Goods, Ilmenau, Germany (2004)
8. Heileman, G.L., Jamkhedar, P.A.: DRM interoperability analysis from the perspective of a layered framework. In: Proc. of the 5th ACM Workshop on Digital Rights Management, Architectures, pp. 17–26 (2005)
9. Chen, X., Huang, T.: Interoperability issues in DRM and DMP solutions. In: IEEE on Multimedia and Expo., pp. 907–910 (2007)
10. Serrão, C., Torres, V., Delgado, J., Dias, M.: Interoperability Mechanisms for registration and authentication on different open DRM platforms. International Journal of Computer Science and Network Security 6(12), 291–303 (2006)
11. Doncel, V.R., Delgado, J., Chiariglione, F., Preda, M., Timmerer, C.: Interoperable digital rights management based on the MPEG Extensible Middleware. Multimedia Tools and Applications 53(1), 303–318 (2010)
12. Jamkhedkar, P.A., Heileman, G.L., Lamb, C.C.: An interoperable usage management framework. In: Proc. of the Tenth Annual ACM Workshop on Digital Rights Management (2010)

13. Serrão, C., Rodriguez, E., Delgado, J.: Approaching the rights management interoperability problem using intelligent brokerage mechanisms. Computer Communications 34(2) (February 2011)
14. Coral consortium, Coral consortium whitepaper (February 2006), http://www.coral-interop.org (accessed September 25, 2011)
15. Marlin: Marlin architecture overview (2006), http://www.marlin-community.com (accessed September 25, 2011)
16. Safavi-Naini, R., Sheppard, N.P., Uehara, P.: Import/export in digital rights management. In: Proc. 4th ACM Workshop on Digital Rights Management, pp. 99–110 (2004)
17. Lu, W., Zhang, Z., Nummenmaa, J.: A Generic Data Model with a Decomposition Operation for DRM Interoperability. In: Proc. IEEE International Conference Wireless Communications, Networking and Information Security (WCNIS), pp. 630–634 (2010)
18. Lu, W., Zhang, Z., Nummenmaa, J.: Rights Decomposition for DRM Interoperability. International Journal of Wireless Communications and Networking 2(2) (December 2010)

How to Design and Deliver Process Context Sensitive Information: Concept and Prototype

Armin Stein[1] and Robin Fischer[2]

[1] ERCIS, University of Münster, Münster, Germany
[2] KIT – Karlsruhe Institute of Technology, Karlsruhe, Germany

Abstract. Providing employees with relevant, context-specific information is crucial to achieve productivity and efficiency while executing business processes. Today, tools exist to model various aspects of organizations such as processes, organization structures, services, and their descriptions. However, there still exists a gap between information modeling on a conceptual level and information provision on a runtime level that hinders information dissemination and retrieval while employees execute processes. In daily business life, information workers demand for unstructured content to fulfill well-defined process steps. In this paper, we adapt an existing conceptual approach of process-driven information requirements engineering and present its prototypical implementation based on an industry-developed BPM product. Our solution therefore introduces "information objects" and integrates these with process activities to model the users' information requirements at process runtime. In doing so, users are empowered to leverage context information such as documents, reports, or emails, while executing human steps in a process.

Keywords: Information Delivery, Business Process Management, Process Context Sensitivity.

1 Introduction

Today, huge quantities of data are created, transformed, and searched in every millisecond. Knowledge workers are thus required to deal with information overflow and high complexity in information processing. That is, companies have become overwhelmed by ubiquitously available information such as documents, data records, reports, Web pages, emails, or other digital assets. In fact, only through the close alignment of information systems and business processes can organizations gain competitive advantages over others [22]. This alignment has to deliver the right information to the right users at the right time. We claim that this information has to be modeled on a conceptual level and then requires an integrated dissemination in process execution environments. We propose an approach to delivery relevant information based on explicitly modeled context information to bridge the gap between information management and business process management. In particular, the paper at-hand will answer the following research questions:

N. Aseeva, E. Babkin, and O. Kozyrev (Eds.): BIR 2012, LNBIP 128, pp. 96–110, 2012.
© Springer-Verlag Berlin Heidelberg 2012

Question 1: How can business process modeling languages be extended to model information that knowledge workers require in a given process context at the time of process execution?

Question 2: What changes to process design and execution environments are required to model and deploy contextual information into process runtime environments?

In the sense of [13], we employ a design science-based approach to answer these questions. In design science, the constructed result should be an artifact like a method, a modeling language, or a software tool (requirement 1). Furthermore, research needs to prove that the artifact covers an area that is relevant to the Information Systems (IS) research discipline (2). Additionally, the artifact has to extend and enrich the existing knowledge base of the area covered, ensuring that no similar artifacts already exist, thus substantiating its innovative character (3). Finally, to prove the achievement of the research goals formulated, the artifact has to be evaluated (4).

As will be shown, in accordance to these considerations, a gap exists in the area of BPM that leaves the provisioning of process context sensitive information for business participants such as employees uncovered (see req. 2). The software that is being constructed during our research is an artifact in the sense of the design science approach (1). The implementation of our approach presented at the end of this paper in conjunction with the motivating example proves the feasibility of our approach and can be regarded as first evaluation of our initial research iteration (4). Since our software prototype builds-upon earlier results of conceptually integrating information and process modeling at design time [3], the breaking down into deployable and executable processes can be seen as the immediate consequence in the initial iteration step of the research life-cycle. To the best of our knowledge, no equal artifacts exist; therefore we see our solution as innovative (3).

The remainder of this work is structured as follows: We introduce our approach by a motivating example in the Section 2. In Section 3 we introduce the foundational terminology and concepts as well as related work. Subsequently, we provide a detailed overview of our model-driven solution approach to develop our software prototype that integrates information and process modeling features both at design time and runtime in Section 4. Finally, we outline the architecture of our prototype (Section 5), before we reflect our findings in Section 6.

2   Motivating Example

To illustrate the approach of delivering process context sensitive information, we assume the setting of a medium sized company that sells software and software related services. Each project team documents its work and publishes these documents on a collaboration platform such as Microsoft Office SharePoint Server (MOSS). A major customer of this fictive company is MG, a finance company that mainly demands CRM software and services. Paul, our company's junior sales representative, just received a request for a software service from Sophia, an employee of MG. To create a service quote, Paul starts a new "create quote process" and immediately starts working on the first process step "create quote". Paul logs onto the human task user interface (UI) and brings up the initial task execution screen that is pre-completed with default values such as customer id, customer discount, or risk assessment values. Since Paul is new to the company, he is not sure whether he needs to change the risk assessment, a surcharge, or to discount the calculated quotation price. Paul is therefore skimming through the huge database of past quotations documents on MOSS. Paul requires about 15 minutes to retrieve the last three quotations for MG from the collaboration platform, assuming Paul is aware of the collaboration platform and is been granted access.

Easing and speeding-up this kind of information retrieval processes is the scope of our approach, which is delivering information that is process context sensitive. For this purpose, process designer are empowered to model anticipated, but abstract contextual information needs at design time by means of information objects. Obviously, abstract information has to be mapped to available documents at process runtime. We will illustrate this process by continuing in our example.

After the latest BPM system upgrade that now handles contextual process information, Max, our example company's process designer, has redesigned the "create quote process" to include an information object. In doing so, Max models an abstract information object that defines all documents that deal with quotations for companies of the same branch to be relevant for the "create quote" activity. The next time Paul executes this activity, the process execution environment will show all past documents that deal with quotations for the finance customers. Paul will review relevant information that has been associated to the task while process modeling. However, after checking the initial set of documents, Paul decides to further narrow the search space of the information object. Consequently he reconfigures the information object at runtime to only consider the information that is specific for the given company. To his surprise, reconfiguring the information object also reduced the amount of shown documents to only the past quotations for MG. Paul instantly finds a calculation of another quote for MG and copies the risk and discount levels to the new quotation. Finally, Paul reconfigures the IO again, to see further information that is related to best practices in finance.

3   Foundations

The following sections will introduce basic foundations, our approach of process context sensitive information delivery, and a running prototype making the motivating example reality.

Research on information systems has adapted to the changes in requirements of information systems development and provides concepts such as Information Management [7] and Business Process Management [11, 27] to address the required alignment of information systems to business processes and information needs. Lately emerging research on topics such as service composition or ubiquitous computing focuses on leveraging contextual information to compose situational services or provided situational information.

3.1   Information Management

In brief, Information Management (IM) – a subtype of business management – ensures optimal use of "information" as a resource with regard to corporate goals [15]. Information is data that has been put into a form that is meaningful and useful to human beings [16]. IM realizes the performance potential – strategic corporate goals – by establishing and maintaining suitable information architectures, while meeting the formal target – operational efficiency – in all tasks that support achieving the performance potential [12]. Hence, IM aims at configuring a company's adequate information supply, i. e. matching information supply and information need. The identification and dissemination of relevant information, however, is one of the major problems in modern organizations [5]. Szyperski's model of information subsets distinguishes four sets of information [24]: (1) Objective information need, i. e., information a person objectively requires for taking decisions or performing tasks. (2) Subjective information need, i. e., individually demanded information to complete a task. (3) Information supply, i. e. information that corporate information systems can deliver. The intersection of this information needs results in (4) relevant, requested and deliverable information. Based on this classification, we formulate the goal of IM as the establishment of the best possible congruency between all information subsets (1–3).

3.2   Business Process Management

Characterizations of Business Process Management vary and are most of the time subjective in nature, i. e. depend on the interest that motivates the author or the vendor of Business Process Management Systems (BPMS). The focal objects of BPM are processes. We define a process as a completely closed, timely and logical sequence of activities that are required to work on a process-oriented business object [4]. An activity represents work that needs to be done manually (human activity) or work that is done automatically (automated activity; [9]). As a management philosophy, BPM in its core plans, controls, and monitors intra- and inter-organizational processes using methods, techniques, and software to design, enact, control, and analyze operational processes involving humans, organizations, applications, documents and other sources of information [26,27]. In doing so, BPM capitalizes on business user involvement to align business process and information infrastructures as they carry valuable process knowledge that was formerly only considered during requirements analysis phases of information systems development, if at all. The tasks of BPM to holistically manage business process over time fall into the categories of Business Process Modeling (BPMO), Business Process Enactment (BPE), Business Activity Monitoring (BAM), and Business Operations Management (BOM): BPMO introduces capabilities to meet the needs of expressing business processes in process models. BPE, i. e. automating process execution, requires formal process models to route documents, information and tasks within and between organizations. BAM allows for the diagnosis of operational processes based on data logged by information systems. Finally, BOM collaborates with BPMO, BPE, and BAM to enable efficient use of resources, to include operational intelligence (e. g., sales prediction services), or enable production planning. BPMS are designed to support effective BPM.

3.3   Related Work

In the domain of context-aware process design and context-ware computing, information is used to improve system flexibility. The idea behind applying context information to business processes is to instantiate a modified version of a process model in process runtime environments [19, 21]). This work differs by using context information to supply relevant information (e. g., emails or documents) while executing human process steps.

In the KnowMore approach, [1] integrate contextual information with workflow data to ease information retrieval for knowledge workers. They employ information agents and ontologies to provide information for knowledge intensive tasks by means of extended workflow variables. We build-upon their idea of using agents to capture, classify and filter information when developing our architecture for context sensitive information delivery and extend the approach by providing conceptually integrated, explicit ways to model information needs at process design time. In addition, knowledge workers are enabled to navigate and configure information needs while executing knowledge intensive tasks.

Our approach to integrate process and information modeling based-on meta models draws on concepts introduced by [3]. There, business process models – modeled as event-driven process chains (EPC) – were connected to information models that depicted information requirements. For this purpose, the modeling languages MetaMIS [2,6], used for describing data warehouse specifications, and EPC, used for describing the process flow, were integrated on a conceptual level by combining their respective meta models [3]. The focus of the integration was on extending the capabilities of information requirements engineering by optimizing methods to conceptually retrieve information needs. Our approach goes beyond, as the goal is to use conceptual information modeling to deliver relevant information (e. g., documents) at process runtime. Hence, the perspective is not to start with process models and then derive adequate data structures for systems such as data warehouses, but to enrich process models with context specific information to support decision makers at process runtime. In doing so, we reuse information that was designed by IS engineers at the level of knowledge worker, who perform a tasks to get the job done.

4   Model-Driven Solution Approach

In this section, we propose a conceptual approach to integrate process and information modeling, addressing research question 1. Following the concept of model-driven software development, our approach to design an information system for process context sensitive information delivery follows a modeling hierarchy with four levels [9, 10]. Putting the solution approach into a goal-driven way, i. e. starting with expected user experiences, concepts and components that display information to task executors are required on the level of process execution (L0 in Fig. 1). To provide this information, existing process models require enrichment with contextual information. Creating these models is the subject of the modeling level (L1 in Fig. 1). The foundations of integrated process and information modeling, i. e. the integration of their respective meta models, must be achieved on the meta model level (L2 in Fig. 1). However, integrating meta models will only be possible, if all meta models share a common modeling language [23]. For this reason, a common meta model that describes the language of both the process modeling notation and the information modeling language has to be defined at the meta-meta level (L3 in Fig. 1).

For the following, we chose to use MetaMIS. This language has been developed as a method to easily model relevant information needs in a hierarchical way and has proven its suitability in many pilot projects that have been conducted with industry partners (for details and examples see [20]). The meta model of MetaMIS is described in a very detailed way, thus easing the integration of its meta model with those of other process modeling languages. As mentioned above, [3] integrate the meta models of MetaMIS and the EPC, which is solely a conceptual modeling language without execution semantics. We integrate the MetaMIS meta model with the BPMN meta model [9] to bring conceptual information models into process runtime environments. The following subsections explain our approach to conceptually integrate information and process modeling in a model-driven way, i. e. will focus on L3 and L2 of our solution approach. More details of L1 and L0 will be given in Section 5.

4.1   Meta-Object Facility

The first step to conceptually integrate MetaMIS and BPMN is to introduce a common modeling language for the creation and integration of information and process meta models. We applied the Meta-Object Facility (MOF – [9]). MOF provides a modeling architecture that consists of four modeling-layers: Information (M0), model (M1), meta model (M2) and meta-meta model (M3), which reflects the layers that we proposed for the solution approach of process context sensitive information delivery (see Fig. 1). MOF, furthermore, is a closed type system. That is, only types that are either defined in the meta meta model or types defined in a specific meta model can be used when creating models. Parent of all MOF elements, however, is the *ModelElement* construct. First order subtypes of *ModelElement* are constructs such as *Package*, *Classifier*, *TypedElement* and *Feature*. These rather abstract elements do not yet allow for the creation of modeling languages such as the Unified Modeling Language. Therefore, *Classifiers* are further classified into *DataType*, *Class* and *Association*. The following sections show how these abstract constructs allow defining more specific meta models.

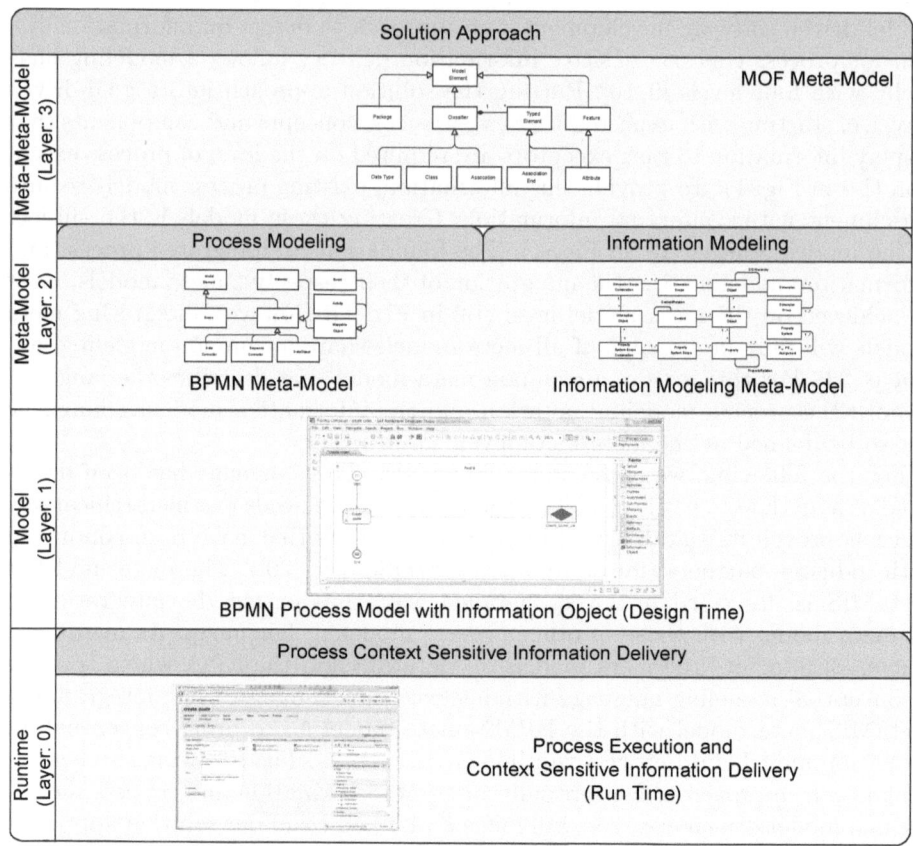

Fig. 1. Layers of the Solution's Approach

4.2 Information Modeling Meta Model

We will now outline the meta models of MetaMIS to further ground our meta model integration. In the following, we provide an overview of relevant modeling elements. Extensive discussions on MetaMIS meta model are given in [2, 6].

The MetaMIS meta model is designed in a hierarchical way (see Fig. 2). Beginning from the top of the created inheritance hierarchy, we introduced the abstract *BaseElement*. The idea behind inserting this abstract super-type is to provide a generic meta model element, which allows for the identification of MetaMIS artifacts (similar to *ModelElement* in MOF). MetaMIS modeling elements are further divided into *DimensionElements*, *PropertyElements* and *ContentElements*. *ReferenceObject* (RO) represents real world entities such as measures, processes, and states of affairs [18] and do not fall under any of these classifications. They are consequently modeled as a subtype of *BaseElement*. The modeling element *InformationObject* (IO) completes the simple hierarchy of MetaMIS.

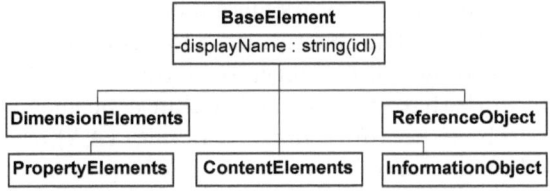

Fig. 2. Hierarchy of MetaMIS Meta Model Elements

For the following, we will focus on explaining the design of the meta model for *DimensionElements*. Meta model elements falling into the types of *PropertyElements* or *ContentElements* are designed in a similar way, we therefore again refer the reader to [2, 6] for further clarification of those meta model elements.

DimensionScopeCombinations (DSC) – being a sub-type of *DimensionElement* – contain one or many *DimensionScopes* (DS), which themselves are sets of *DimensionObjects* (DO; see Fig. 3 in the following). DO always refer to one individual RO and are assigned to only one *Dimension*. *Dimensions* of the same type may be summarized by *DimensionGroups* (DG), but must have at least one DG assigned. A hierarchy of DO is supported by the means of the *DO_Hierarchy* association. Finally, IO are defined by creating an relationship to exactly one DSC for the sake of simplicity in this paper.

Please note that we only introduce an extract of MetaMIS in this paper. For the complete version of MetaMIS, IO are required to have relationships to the equivalents of DSC of packages *PropertyElements* and *ContentElements*, which do not have to be taken into consideration in our case.

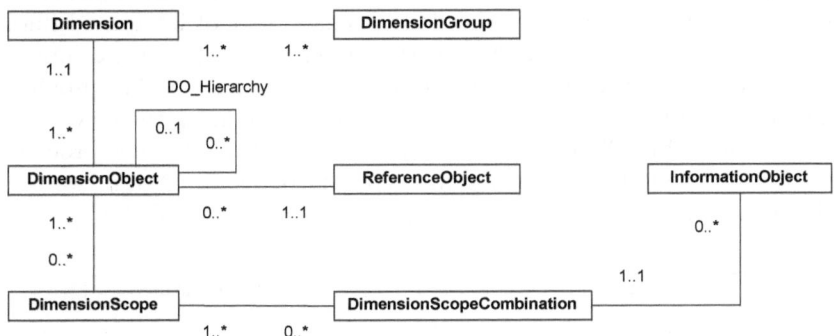

Fig. 3. MetaMIS DimensionElements Meta Model (Simplified Extract)

4.3   Process Modeling Meta Model

With respect to BPMN, BPMN 2.0 introduces a MOF-based meta model [9]. The following outline of BPMN language elements focuses on modeling elements that are relevant for process context sensitive information delivery. Some inheritance constructs are simplified, as intermediate parents may be skipped.

According to [27], a simplified process meta model consist of *Nodes* and *Edges* that always relate two *Nodes*. The generic meta model element *Node* – or *FlowObject* – is further classified into three subtypes: *Activity*, *Event* and *Gateway*. An *Activity* represents work that is performed within a business process. We distinguish *Activities* to be either an *AutomatedActivity* (AA) or a *HumanActivity* (HA). AAs are used to automate individual steps of a process, e. g. calling a web service. HA, on the other hand, require human interaction. Thus, HA must provide features to support the assignment of a process enactment user interface. Events may occur as *StartEvent*, *IntermediateEvent* or *EndEvent*. Obviously, *StartEvents* describe conditions under which a process may start, while *EndEvents* define the termination of a process instance. *IntermediateEvents* may occur at any given time during process execution and therefore enable process modelers to integrate real-world dynamics into their process models. Finally, *Gateways* either refer to a *ParallelGateway*, *InclusiveGateway*, *ExlusiveGateway*, and *ComplexGateway*. All *FlowObjects* may be associated by artifacts. *DataObjects* may be used to assign workflow relevant data to a process or a particular activity. Finally, *FlowObjects* may be related to each other through *ConnectingObjects* such as *SequenceFlow*, *MessageFlow* or *Association*.

4.4   Meta Model Integration

The previous sections set the ground to conceptually integrate MetaMIS and BPMN meta models. Doing so expresses semantic relationships between the partial models, which secure referential integrity between both, models and meta models [14]. The integration of meta models is achieved by defining an IO to be a subtype of the BPMN modeling element *DataObject* (see Fig. 4). Each IO inherits the basic characteristics of the *DataObject* such as attributes of type *DataConnector*. With respect to the desired enactment of integrated information and process models, this allows for reusing process deployment approaches that have already been defined in for *DataObjects* in BPMN. We provide further integration of the respective meta models by introducing the new modeling construct *InformationObjectConnector* (IOC) that allows to link process and information meta models by an unique type of connector. Again, we applied the inheritance pattern by defining IOC to be a subtype of a *DataConnector* in

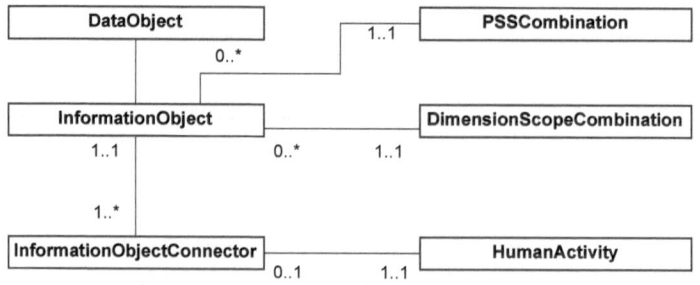

Fig. 4. MetaMIS and BPMN Meta Model Integration

order to benefit from the runtime characteristics of a model type *DataConnector*. An IOC is, finally, defined to have two associations, one to each an IO and an HA. IOC may relate to exactly one IO and exactly one HA. Since information relevant for performing a HA should always be defined by a single IO, a HA is only allowed to have one potential IO assigned.

5   Prototype Development

Up to now we have shown, how information and process modeling can be integrated based on the integration of their meta models. We will now focus on changes to typical BPMS runtime environments that were required to implement a prototype (research question 2).

5.1   Extended BPMS Architecture

To facilitate the outline of our approach, we introduce a software architecture that characterizes the components of a BPMS for process context sensitive information delivery (see Fig. 5). The BPMS architecture is based on studies of available whitepapers of BPMS vendors and related publications on BPMS in general [8, 17, 25].

The architecture is structured into five tiers. Located at the center is the *Process Context Sensitive Information Delivery* tier (PCSID). It comprises a typical *BPM tier* and the newly introduced *Information tier*. The BPM tier provides capabilities for process enactment and the management of rules and arbitrary sequences of events. The information tier is designed to provide the backend functionality that enables integrated modeling, administration and execution of context-sensitive process models.

Autonomous agents such as file crawlers that regularly screen group-directories or file servers for new information can do information capturing. To support the management of information, additional classification, filtering and navigation components are located in the Information tier. Classification is required to integrate newly identified information into the modeled information structures. Filtering components provide features to filter relevant information according to process contexts such as the actual user, requesting context sensitive information. This may incorporate management of user access rights to customize the subset of relevant information. Finally, providing navigational means empowers users to not only view context-specific information, but also to navigate to related information.

Placed at the side of the PCSID tier are both a *Client tier* and a *Web tier*. *Client tier* and *Web tier* differ in terms of the underlying technological principles, e. g. remote method invocation vs. HTTP requests or Eclipse's Rich Client Platform vs. JavaServer Pages. However, the capabilities that each tier supplies for modeling, administration and execution are complementary. In order to incorporate information modeling capabilities, the components to model, administer,

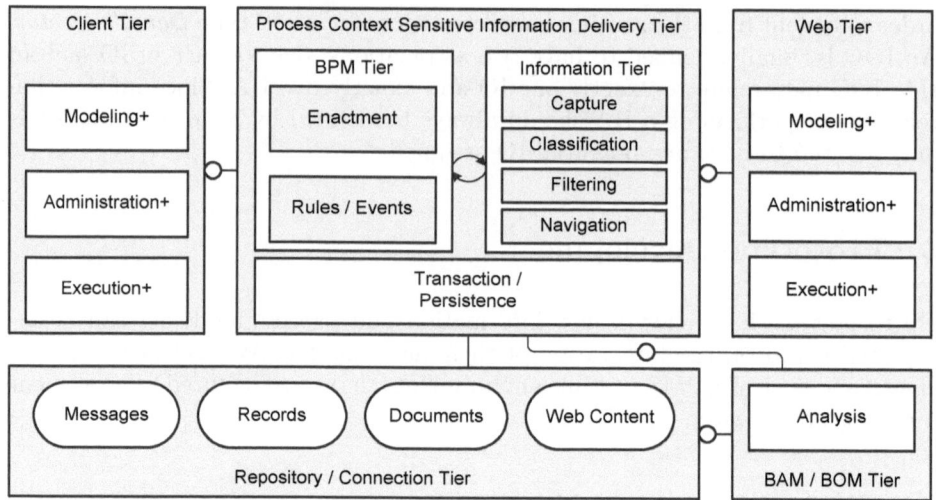

Fig. 5. Extended BPMS Architecture for Context Sensitive Information Delivery

and execute must be adapted to handle the integrated meta model of information and process modeling. Components that require changes when compared to traditional BPMS are denoted by having a "+"-suffix (see again Fig. 5).

The *Repository / Connection tier* supplies features to access application data such as messages, records, documents and web content. Access to this kind of data is complementary to the build-in persistency of control and relevant data of process enactment as required by the *BPM and Information tier*. The architecture of a BPMS is completed by a *BAM / BOM tier*, where functionality to track events that are generated during process enactment and comprehensive analysis features are located.

5.2   Prototype Implementation

The prototype has been implemented as an extension to SAP NetWeaver Business Process Management. SAP NetWeaver BPM consists of three major components: A process composer providing BPMO functionalities, a process server for BPE and a process desk that provides a humans task interface for HA. Our prototype environment uses an instance of Microsoft Office SharePoint Server 2007 (MOSS) as document repository. The integration of the information tier and the MOSS instance is based on Web services. Modelling and displaying context sensitive information at design- and runtime, required extensions to both process composer and process desk. In the following, we briefly depict our prototype's components for the proof-of-concept step of our Design Science approach (see Section 1).

According to the life cycle of creating, deploying and running context sensitive process models, we first focus on the Information Composer component that extends SAP's process composer. The Information Composer allows modeling of business processes including a specification of context sensitive information. To model this information, a process and / or information modeler first adds a new IO shape from the palette of modeling concepts onto the modeling canvas. Context sensitive information, i. e. DSC, Dimension, and DO can then be modeled by using the IO's property editor that is shown below the modeling canvas (see Fig. 6).

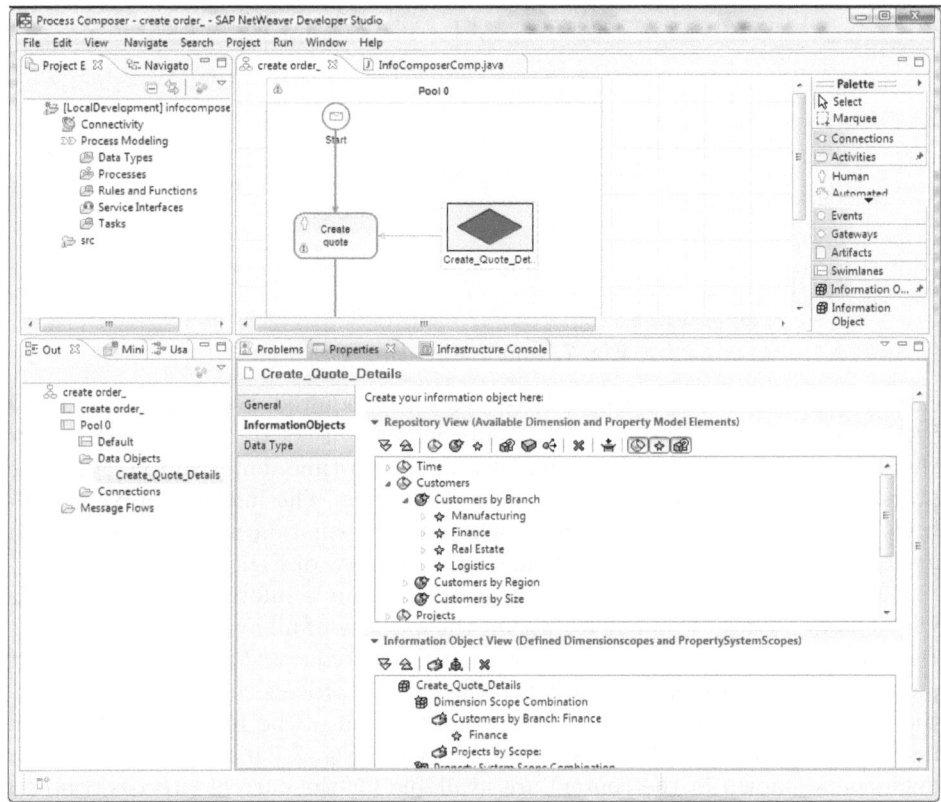

Fig. 6. Information Composer

Note that only dimensions of relevant context information are defined at this point. Files or documents are never assigned directly to a particular process step. Associating an IO to an HA is done through connecting the corresponding IO and activity over a visual link, which instantiates an IOC object. The example given in Fig. 6 illustrates a defined DG "Customers", having a Dimension "Customers by Branch" that contains DO "Manufacturing", "Finance", "Real Estate", and "Logistics" (see "Repository View" in Fig. 6). Out of this defined DG only Customers that fall into the "Finance" category have been selected to be relevant (see "Information Object View" in Fig. 6, bottom right). Assuming the just defined process model has been finalized and deployed onto a BPE environment, e. g. SAP's process server, now a component that displays context

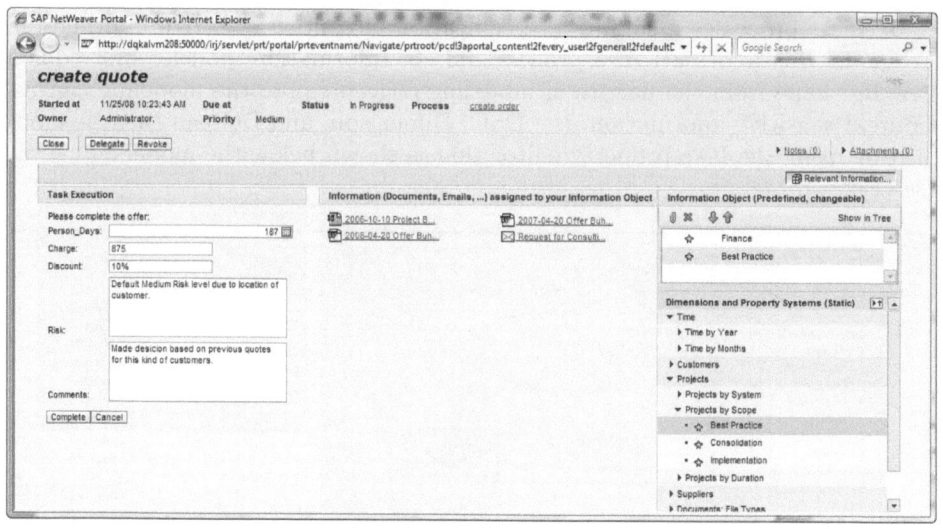

Fig. 7. Information Browser

sensitive information next to the HA-interface is required. We therefore adapted SAP's process desk. Our prototype empowers the users to not only show relevant information that has been modeled at design-time, but also to change the initial context according to their needs at runtime. The initial context will always be the exact representation of what the information modeler has defined at design-time (e. g., compare IO element "Finance" of Fig. 7).

The lower right part of Fig.7 shows a company's information space. This view allows the user to navigate within the entirety of all available information. Particular files, e-mails and documents, are always requested from the underlying data source (e. g. MOSS) according to the current process context as defined by the IO. Users may modify the initial configuration of the IO by removing and adding items into the IO. The example shown in Fig. 7 indicates that only four documents (shown in the center) are available for the current process context, e. g. the given combination of DO "Finance" and "Best Practice".

6   Conclusion and Outlook

In this paper, we provide a conceptual approach to combine existing BPM principles, in particular graphical modeling of business processes, with existing concepts that allow modeling information needs. Based on a review of existing literature on BPM and information modeling, we argue that adding context sensitive information to human process steps improves the users' experience in terms of human computer interaction. Moreover, human decision makers are supported while performing human process steps. Following the given design science approach, we integrated separated meta models and evaluated our concept by a comprehensive proof-of-concept implementation based on commercial, state-of-the-art BPM tools.

Although the prototypical implementation provides a first step to prove the fundamental applicability of the approach, the information capturing, classification, and filtering could not be evaluated. This was mainly due to the enormous technology stack the implementation had to cope with. Furthermore, manual tagging of information elements as performed in this approach is not feasible for the usual amount of data in organizations. Further implementations should focus on automating the assignment of metadata to documents, files or record sets by using semantic technologies like ontologies, as applied in, e.g., [1]. Future studies should moreover focus on lifecycle aspects of process context sensitive information delivery. In doing so, incorporating features provided by BAM or BOM should be examined, since possibilities of providing long term improvements can only be anticipated up to now.

References

1. Abecker, A., Bernardi, A., Maus, H., Sintek, M., Wenzel, C.: Information supply for business processes: Coupling workflow with document analysis and information retrieval. Knowledge-Based Systems 13(5), 271–284 (2000)
2. Becker, J., Dreiling, A., Holten, R., Ribbert, M.: Specifying information systems for business process integration – a management perspective. Information Systems and E-Business Management 1(3), 231–263 (2003)
3. Becker, J., Brelage, C., Dreiling, A., Ribbert, M.: Business process-driven information requirements engineering. In: Proceedings of the 2004 Information Resource Management Association Int. Conference, New Orleans, pp. 352–356 (2004)
4. Becker, J., Kugeler, M., Rosemann, M. (eds.): Process Management: A Guide for the Design of Business Processes. Springer, Berlin (2003)
5. Berthel, J.: Informationsbedarf. In: Handwörterbuch der Organisation, Poeschel, Stuttgart, pp. 872–886 (1992)
6. Brelage, C.: Web Information System Development – Conceptual Modelling of Navigation for Satisfying Information Needs. PhD thesis, University of Münster, Germany (2006)
7. Earl, M.J.: Information Management. The Organizational Dimension. Oxford University Press, Oxford (2001)
8. Fujitsu: Interstage i-flow^{TM} architecture white paper (2002), http://www.fujitsu.com/downloads/SG/fapl/workflow/iflow_whitepaper.pdf
9. O.M. Group. Metaobject facility (March 2011), http://www.omg.org/spec/BPMN/2.0/PDF/
10. Hailpern, B., Tarr, P.: Model-driven development: The good, the bad, and the ugly. IBM Systems Journal 45(3), 451–461 (2006)
11. Harmon, P.: Business Process Change – a Manager's Guide to Improving, Redesigning, and Automating Processes, San Francisco (2003)
12. Heinrich, L.J., Lehner, F.: Informationsmanagement: Planung, Überwachung und Steuerung der Informationsinfrastruktur. Oldenbourg Wissenschaftsverlag, Oldenbourg (2005)
13. Hevner, A.R., March, S.T., Park, J., Ram, S.: Design science in information systems research. Management Information Systems Quarterly 28(1), 75–106 (2004)
14. Höfferer, P.: Achieving business process model interoperability using metamodels and ontologies. In: Proceedings of the 15th European Conference on Information Systems (ECIS), pp. 1620–1631 (2007)

15. Krcmar, H.: Informationsmanagement. Springer, Berlin (2005)
16. Laudon, K.C., Laudon, J.P.: Management Information Systems: Managing the Digital Firm. Prentice Hall, Upper Saddle River (2007)
17. Pyké, J.: BPM in Context: Now and in the Future. In: 2006 Workflow Handbook, pp. 17–28. Future Strategies Inc., Lighthouse Point (2006)
18. Riebel, P.: Gestaltungsprobleme einer zweckneutralen grundrechnung. Zeitschrift für Betriebswirtschaftliche Forschung 31, 863–893 (1979)
19. Rosemann, M., Recker, J.C., Flender, C., Ansell, P.D.: Understanding context-awareness in business process design. In: Proceedings of the 17th Australasian Conference on Information Systems (2006)
20. Rosenkranz, C., Holten, R.: Combining cybernetics and conceptual modeling: The concept of variety in organizational engineering. In: Proceedings of the 2007 ACM Symposium on Applied Computing, Seoul, pp. 1228–1233 (2007)
21. Saidani, O., Nurcan, S.: Towards context aware business process modelling. In: 8th Workshop on Business Process Modeling, Trondheim (2007)
22. Smith, H., Fingar, P.: IT Doesn't Matter – Business Processes Do: A Critical Analysis of Nicholas Carr's I. T. Article in the Harvard Business Review. Meghan-Kiffer Press, Boston (2003)
23. Strahringer, S.: Metamodellierung als Instrument des Methodenvergleichs: Eine Evaluierung am Beispiel objektorientierter Analysemethoden. PhD thesis, Technische Hochschule Darmstadt, Aachen (1996)
24. Szyperski, N.: Informationsbedarf. In: Handwörterbuch der Organisation, Poeschel, pp. 904–913 (1980)
25. Tibco Software Inc. BPM in the federal government, http://forms2.tibco.com/bpmwp_bpm__fed_govt
26. vom Brocke, J., Rosemann, M. (eds.): Handbook on Business Process Management, vol. 1. Springer, Berlin (2012)
27. Weske, M.: Business Process Management: Concepts, Languages, Architectures. Springer, Heidelberg (2007)

Joint Use of SCOR and VRM

Marite Kirikova[1], Robert Buchmann[2,*], and Razvan Aurelian Costin[3]

[1] Riga Technical University, Dpt. of Systems Theory and Design,
Kalku 1, Riga, LV-1658, Latvia
marite.kirikova@cs.rtu.lv
[2] University of Vienna, Faculty of Computer Science, Knowledge Engineering Dpt.,
Brünnerstrasse 72, A-1210, Vienna, Austria
rbuchmann@dke.univie.ac.at
[3] Babes-Bolyai University, Faculty of Economic Sciences and Business Administration,
Business Information Systems Dpt., str. T. Mihali 58-60, 400591 Cluj Napoca, Romania
razvan.costin@econ.ubbcluj.ro

Abstract. Supply Chain Operations Reference (SCOR) and Value Reference Model (VRM) are two popular business process reference models. Practitioners have suggested integrating these frameworks for achieving maximum value from the reference models. However, there are no methods and tools available for the integration of SCOR and VRM. The goal of the research is to find similarities and patterns of differences in the aforementioned reference models. The obtained results are applied to propose blueprint of guidelines for joint use of SCOR and VRM. The paper also presents a comparison between SCOR and VRM from several perspectives, which can support a semantic realignment of processes between the categories proposed by the two management frameworks.

1 Introduction

In Business Process Management reference models facilitate achievement of high-quality design while keeping the necessary resources at an acceptable level [1]. Being generic conceptual models that to a particular extent formalize industrial experience in a special domain, they represent frameworks that serve as representations of best practices, have universal applicability, are reusable, and help to reduce process design time and assure high design quality [1], [2]. As the market of available reference model evolves, the available frameworks must be evaluated and compared [1].

Supply Chain Operations Reference (SCOR) [3] and Value Reference Model (VRM) [4], [5] are two popular business process reference models. Companies and networks of enterprises, which are aiming to use reference models in the development or re-engineering of their business processes, are interested in pros and cons of both frameworks and their degree of compatibility [6], [7]. Currently, few practical observations and opinions are available concerning similarities, differences, and

---

* On leave for the ComVantage EU Project, from Babes Bolyai University, Faculty of Economics and Business Administration, Cluj Napoca, Romania.

N. Aseeva, E. Babkin, and O. Kozyrev (Eds.): BIR 2012, LNBIP 128, pp. 111–125, 2012.

compatibility of these frameworks [7], [8]. However, while the continuing debate on the importance of supply chain management versus the value chain concepts converges into the conclusion that the next level of business performance will be achieved by companies that learn to integrate fully the concurrent flows of value and supply [7], there is no research available that would consider thoroughly similarities and differences of both frameworks and suggest frameworks analysis based guidelines of joint use of SCOR and VRM. Therefore, the purpose of the research reflected in this paper is to investigate both reference models in order to find similarities and/or patterns of differences in the frameworks, which could be used as a basis of guidelines for joint use or, in contrary, as arguments against joint use of SCOR and VRM. We apply multi-perspective analysis as a research method for achieving the research goal. Current findings reflected in this paper can be useful for companies which intend to base their business process development efforts on the aforementioned frameworks as well as for researchers working on development of new or assessment of existing business process reference models.

The paper is structured as follows: Section 2 introduces SCOR and VRM using guidelines for comparison of reference models [2]. In Sections 3 to 6 we analyze SCOR and VRM from the perspectives of framework architectures, business process definitions, conceptual structures and experimental application of reference models respectively. For these perspectives we present our findings concerning (1) similarities and/or patterns of differences of the reference models; (2) possibilities to "translate" particular parts of one model into language of another model, and (3) possibilities to extend one model with the parts of another model or substitute parts of one model with parts of another model. We briefly discuss related work in Section 7 and sum-up guidelines for joint use of the frameworks in as part of our conclusions.

2   Feature-Based Comparison

The role of this section is twofold. First, it introduces SCOR and VRM frameworks and, second, it presents a comparison of the reference models from the first perspective of their analysis, i.e. a perspective of feature analysis of the models.

VRM and SCOR are standardized business process frameworks comprising process models with their inputs and outputs, metrics, and best practices. The frameworks provide common languages and taxonomies for communication purposes.

In the context of SCOR and VRM, the framework concept refers to a set of theories widely accepted and used by value network or supply chain processes practitioners. The theories apply to the composition of common language, metrics, measures and best practices. Therefore, the aforementioned frameworks, in the form of business process reference models, enable supply and value chain practitioners to communicate, benchmark, and compare against other competitors in the industry, or align processes with their partners.

Feature analysis of SCOR and VRM is based on suggestions for comparing reference models available in [1] and [2]. Fettke et al. [2] have developed four categories of criteria for describing process reference models. Altogether these categories include 16 criteria, which are represented in column 2 of Table 1. The categories are represented in Column 1 respectively. Fettke at al. have evaluated SCOR in 2006 [2]. In Table 1the information inherited from [2] is marked by grey font.

Table 1. SCOR and VRM in the light of 16 criteria suggested by [1] (year 2012)

Category	Criterion	SCOR	VRM
Reference Model	Number	n/a	n/a
	Release date of the first version*	November, 1996	September, 2006
	Version analyzed*	10.0	2.2
	Name	Supply Chain Operations Reference Model (SCOR Model)	Value Reference Model (VRM)
	Primary Literature (Secondary literature)	[4], Ref 46, 47, and 48 in [2], [9]	[10]
General Characterization	Origin	Practice	Practice
	Responsibility for Modeling	Supply Chain Inc.	Value-Chain Group
	Access	Limited Member price: companies – 300-5000USD Individuals – not offered	Limited Member price: companies – 600-4800 USD Individuals – 300USD
	Tool Support	Yes	Yes
Construction	Domain	Function, Supply Chain Management	Function, Value Chain Management
	Modeling Language(s)	Graphical and Verbal	Graphical and Verbal
	Modeling Framework	Yes	Yes
	Size	185 the smallest granularity processes	214 the smallest granularity processes
	Construction Method	Similar to data flow diagram	Similar to data flow diagram
	Evaluation	n.s.	n.s.
Application	Application method(s)	Training and Certification [11]	Value-Chain Group's Education and Training [12]
	Reuse and Customization	Specification and configuration tool	Specification and configuration tool
	Use Case (s)	Multiple	Multiple

* not used in [2]

3   Comparison of Framework Architectures

Both frameworks have their specific forms of representation that are well recognizable by their users. SCOR is presented as a leveled structure of processes: four operational processes (their categories) at the second level, the detailed variations of these processes at the third level, leaving the fourth level of models to be designed by the company applying the framework. VRM specifies first three levels of five level pyramid (namely, Strategic, Tactical, and Operational ones) leaving Activities and Actions levels for choice/design of companies. Traditional visualizations of architectures of both frameworks are available at [3] and [4]. In this paper we use different form of architecture representation, which is obtained by analysis of process details of both frameworks.

We start the comparison from the operational core of the models represented in Fig. 1 and then present the frameworks in a two level architecture (one level for operational core, another level for the chain) in Fig 2. At core level, SCOR addresses four process categories, giving for each of them several specific models; VRM addresses nine process categories and provides one process model for each of them (see Fig. 1). The VRM framework refers to the supply chain through the process categories Acquire, Build, and Fulfill. From the point of view of definitions, Source in SCOR maps to Acquire in VRM, Make maps to Build, and Deliver maps to Fulfill (Fig. 1 and Table 2).

Table 2. Examples of process definitions from SCOR and VRM [4]

SCOR	VRM
Source: The processes associated with ordering, delivery, receipt and transfer of raw material items, subassemblies, product and/or services.	**Acquire**: The process of procuring goods and services to forecasted or actual value chain demand.
Make: The process of adding value to products through mixing, separating, forming, machining, and chemical processes.	**Build**: The process of transforming product to a finished state to meet forecasted or actual demand.
Deliver: The processes associated with performing customer-facing order management and order fulfillment activities.	**Fulfill**: Processes that provide finished goods and services to meet planned or actual demand.

However, none of variations of models from SCOR process categories are exactly the same as their corresponding processes in VRM. The fact that SCOR provides specific processes for different production situations makes it more directly applicable for companies than processes of VRM. One more difference is that the supply chain of VRM does not include Return processes. Some return issues can be found in the description of Support process category, which is not denoted as supply chain process in VRM (dashed link in Fig 1).

In Fig. 2 the architecture of the reference models is represented at two levels: (1) the chain level and (2) core level. The Operational Process area corresponds to any SCOR or VRM process represented in Fig. 1. Areas with darker filling are those where process decompositions are available in the framework. Lighter filled areas denote processes that do not have further decomposition in the framework. These are Value Chain and Supply Chain, because they would refer to actual value or supply chains at the company. Govern Information and Govern Finance have no decomposition here, because the architecture in Fig. 2 shows their particular parts that correspond to particular operational process. All these parts together form Govern Information and Govern Finance processes as they are shown originally in VRM.

More formally, at the process level, each VRM operational process P_i (i=1,.., 9) has its decomposition, it is supported with a Govern P_i process, which has its own decomposition, the Plan P_i process, which has its decomposition, and parts of Govern Information and Plan Information processes. For SCOR, at the process level, each operational process P_{ij} (i=1,..,4; j_1=3, j_2=3, j_3=4, j_4=6; see Fig. 1) has its decomposition; it is supported with Enable P_i and Plan P_i process for any j, and Plan and Enable processes have their decompositions.

At the chain level VRM has the same pattern as at the operational level except the Information and Finance are Governed instead of Planned, and these processes have sub-processes. SCOR explicitly defines the process Enable Plan Supply Chain, therefore it is positioned above Plan, not next to the Supply Chain although in its contents it is very similar to Govern Value Chain of VRM.

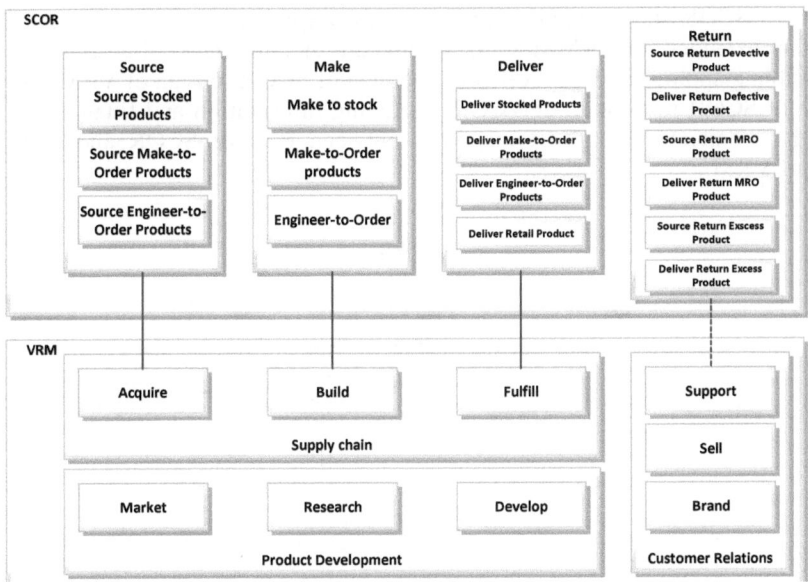

Fig. 1. Operational core of SCOR and VRM (links show correspondence between process classes)

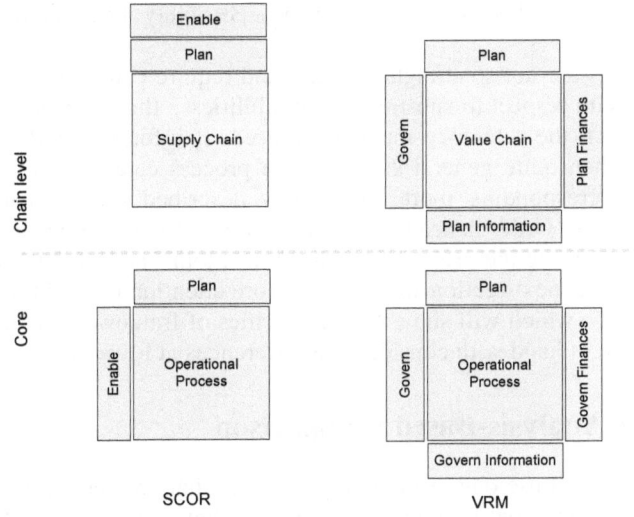

Fig. 2. Comparison of architectures of SCOR and VRM

The architecture in Fig. 1 helps to search for similar processes in SCOR and VRM. Operational processes in SCOR are similar to particular operational processes in VRM as it was described earlier. The VRM framework tries to encapsulate supply chain specific processes into a composite structure comprising product design chain and customer relationship chain as well. Taking into consideration that one of the SCOR goals is to enable practitioners to align their processes with their supply chain partners, a SCOR standard approach for process alignment (Fig. 3, upper part) could be further extended for VRM (Fig. 3, bottom part) at a high level of abstraction.

Possible mappings at core level could be Plan of SCOR to Plan of VRM, as well as Enable of SCOR to Govern of VCOR (including information and finance). At chain level the architectures suggest mappings between Plan of SCOR and Plan Value Chain of VRM.

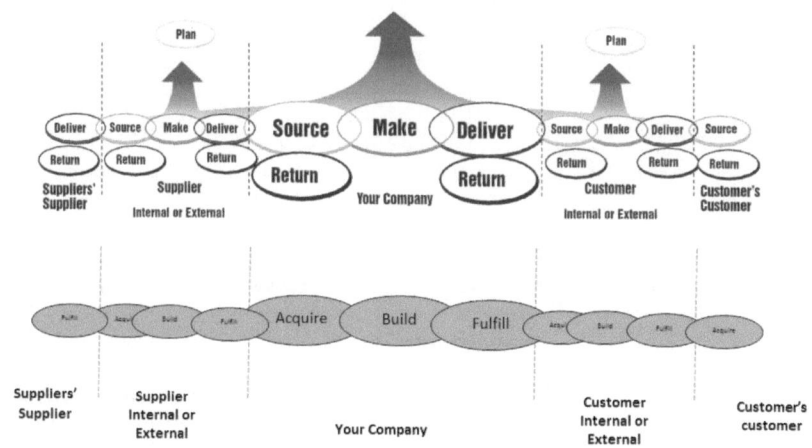

Fig. 3. SCOR [3] and VRM [4] core process alignment possibility at a high level of abstraction

Other mappings are not so straight forward and require careful examination of the sub-processes. With respect to substitution possibilities, - they depend on the abstraction level at which the reference models are used. If information flows are not an actual concern, then quite general supply chain process categories of VRM can be substituted by corresponding more specifically described process categories from SCOR (e.g., Make to Order instead of Build), however there can be cases where it is not feasible to substitute the processes even when it looks appropriate at a high level of abstraction. In the next section we will pay more attention to the information flows and process details, which will show that similarities of frameworks at a high level of abstraction can go in hand with considerable differences at lower levels of abstraction.

4   Process Analysis-Based Comparison

In this section we will use one example of processes that are very similar at the level of definitions to show what problems may arise if they are to be translated one into another. In Table 2, looking at definitions of Plan Source from SCOR and Plan, Acquire from VRM, we can conclude that both processes are similar and could be "translated" one into another. In Table 3, additional information about these processes is represented. Plan Source and Plan, Acquire have four sub-processes, which have almost identical definitions in both frameworks. At this level of abstraction we can assume that the processes can be translated one into another, as well as they could be substituted one with another. Looking more cautiously, we would see that the metrics in frameworks for these processes are bit different and could hinder straight forward translation or substitution of processes. If metrics are not the main focus of use of these frameworks, this issue can be left out of the discussion and so it is done in this paper. In Table 4 one sub-process of Plan Source and the corresponding sub-process of Plan, Acquire are shown with their inputs and outputs.

Table 3. Plan Source and Plan, Acquire [4]

Comparison position	SCOR	VRM
Acronym and title	**P2** Plan Source	**PA** Plan, Acquire
Sub-processes	*P2.1 Identify, Prioritize and Aggregate Product Requirements* The process of identifying, prioritizing, and considering, as a whole with constituent parts, all sources of demand for a product or service in the supply chain. *P2.2 Identify, Assess and Aggregate Product Resources* The process of identifying, evaluating, and considering, as a whole with constituent parts, all material and other resources used to add value in the supply chain for a product or services. *P2.3 Balance Product Resources with Product Requirements* The process of developing a time-phased course of action that commits resources to meet requirements. *P2.4 Establish Sourcing Plans* The establishment of courses of action over specified time periods that represent a projected appropriation of supply resources to meet sourcing plan requirements.	*PA1 - Gather Requirements, Acquire* To collect and structure the external factors and internal strategies so that a plan can be developed. *PA2 - Assess Resources, Acquire* To understand and structure the status of the enterprise assets so that the impact of the requirements can be assessed. *PA3 - Align Resources, Acquire* Harmonization of the current status of the assets with the change from the requirements and identifying the actions to reach equilibrium *PA4 - Create Plan, Acquire* The establishment and communication of courses of action over the appropriate time-defined ... planning horizon and interval, representing a projected appropriation of value-chain resources to meet market requirements.

Table 4. Plan Source and Plan, Acquire (one level down) [4]

Comparison position	SCOR	VRM
Acronym and title	*P2.1 Identify, Prioritize and Aggregate Product Requirements*	*PA1 - Gather Requirements, Acquire*
Inputs	Production Plans from P3.4 Delivery Plans from P4.4 Planning Data from EP.3 Supply Chain Plans from P1.4 Item Master from EP.7 Source Return Requirements from P5.4 Order Signal from sD2.3, from D3.3 Bill Of Materials from EP.7 Product Routings from EP.7	Business Objectives, Acquire from PV4 Schedule, Production from B01 Source Package from D08
Outputs	Product Requirements to to P2.3	Requirements, Acquire to PV1 Requirements, Acquire to PA3

While outputs of both sub-processes are similar, the inputs differ considerably. To better see the differences the inputs of Plan Source and Plan, Acquire are represented graphically (Fig. 4). We can see differences in input contents (e.g., Business objectives is information which is available only to Plan, Acquire. On the other hand, Plan Source receives multiple inputs from two times more sources than Plan, Acquire. For Plan, Acquire the information is much more packaged which shows that both processes internally will have different approaches of information handling. It is possible to do analysis of inputs step by step further. By doing this we will learn that in, this case, SCOR does not suggest any information about how Bill of Materials, Item Master and Product Routings can be obtained, while reasons behind Source Package will be possible to find in VRM. By decomposing information we can discover more commonalities in the frameworks, however, the flows of information are different and cannot be easily translated or substituted in-between the frameworks.

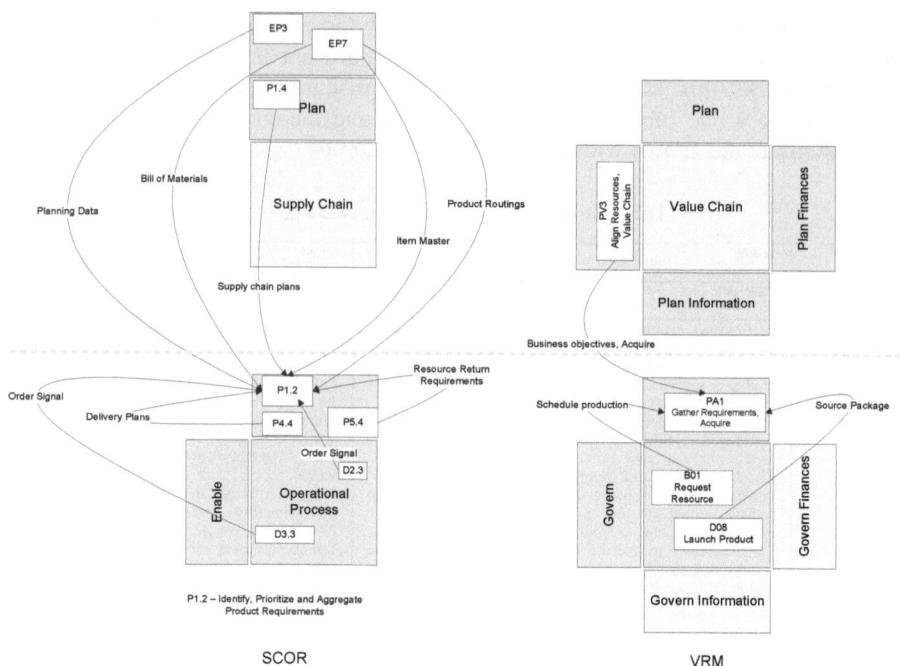

Fig. 4. Graphical Representation of inputs of two similar processes. Legend for SCOR processes is as follows P1.4 - Establish & Communicate Supply-Chain Plans; EP3 - Manage Plan Data Collection; EP7 - Manage Planning Configuration; P4.4- Establish Delivery Plans; P5.4- Establish and Communicate Return Plans; D2.3 - Reserve Inventory and Determine Delivery Date; D3.3 - Enter Order, Commit Resources & Launch Program.

Thus, we can conclude that at lower levels of abstraction any translations and substitutions can be made only after careful analysis of information flows among the processes. Their mapping onto the framework architecture can help to better understand where the sinks on sources of information flow are situated.

5   Conceptual Semantic Structure Mapping

For this approach we employ ontology mapping techniques to mediate between the two different views on value creation. Both frameworks are, at their core, taxonomies of process classes complemented by taxonomies of metrics. This maps directly to the backbone of any OWL ontology [13]: the class subsumption hierarchy (the rdfs:subClassOf taxonomy).

In SCOR, the semantic relations between the framework levels are as follows:

- On level 1 we have the most abstract process classes: Plan, Source, Make, Deliver, Return;
- On level 2, each level 1 class is specialized in disjoint subclasses:
  :Source owl:disjointUnionOf (:S1 :S2 ...).
  :Make owl:disjointUnionOf (:M1 :M2 ...).

OWL inferences triggered by these declarations will generate statements like:
:S1 rdfs:subClassOf :Source.
:M1 rdfs:subClassOf :Make.

- On level 3, again we have subclasses:
:S1 owl:disjointUnionOf (:S1-1 :S1-2 ...).
...which will further build up the taxonomy:
:S1-1 rdfs:subClassOf :S1.
:S1-2 rdfs:subClassOf :S1.

- On level 4, SCOR shifts from the model level to the instance level and integrates actual business processes in the previously established categories. Considering some custom business processes identified by :MyDeliveryProcess and :MyStockSourcingProcess, we can have:
:MyDeliveryProcess rdf:type :D11.
:MyStockSourcingProcess rdf:type :S11.

- Further on, we have the components of these processes which can be semantically modeled with a primitive construct provided by the Semantic Web paradigm, the containers. We consider a generic process for exemplifying the structure, in Fig 5:

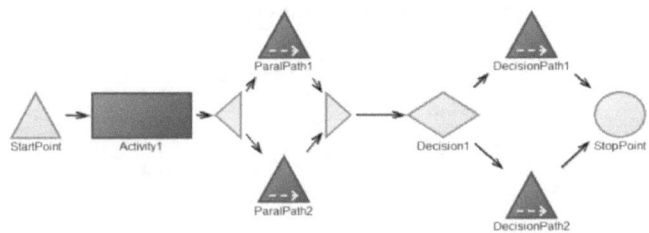

Fig. 5. Generic example of a business process model, represented with [14]

First, a process is an ordered sequence of actions:
:MyDeliveryProcess   rdf:type   rdf:Seq;rdf:_1   :StartPoint;rdf:_2
:Activity1; rdf:_3 :Parallelity; rdf:_4 :Decision1; rdf:_5 :StopPoint.

Each parallelity is a bag of paths that can be considered subprocesses:
:Parallelity   rdf:type rdf:Bag;
rdfs:member   :ParalPath1; rdfs:member   :ParalPath2.

Further on, the same pattern can be used to model decisions, this time using a bag of alternative subprocesses:
:Decision   rdf:type rdf:Alt;
rdfs:member   :DecisionPath1; rdfs:member   :DecisionPath2.

Each of these paths, regardless if they belong to the parallelity or to the decision fork, can be again modelled as sequences, in the same manner as any process.
:DecisionPath1   rdf:type   :Subprocess,   rdf:Seq;   rdf:_1
:StartPointDecisionPath1; ....

Obviously, semantic annotations and more detailed descriptions can be attached to all elements of a process:

:Activity1 :hasCost 100.
:Decision1 :hasCondition "product test passed".
Finally, each instance level process component can be assigned to their node type explicitly...
:Activity1 rdf:type :Activity.
:Decision1 rdf:type :Decision.
...or by rules, based on some key property, such as cost for activity:
:hasCost rdfs:domain :Activity; rdfs:range xsd:integer.

This representation leads to a view on SCOR that can be managed as an ontology. A similar structure can be developed for VRM, then semantic mapping rules can integrate the two views with an alignment ontology. Common mapping techniques rely on equivalence declarations (owl:equivalentClass for process categories considered similar, such as Make and Build) but also partial semantic overlapping is possible using mediating concepts as recommended by ontology term reconciling techniques [15], [16].

In Fig. 6 we emphasize the fact that the classes of Return processes from SCOR and Support from VRM encompass some processes but are not completely overlapped.

Mediating concepts can be added to the ontology:

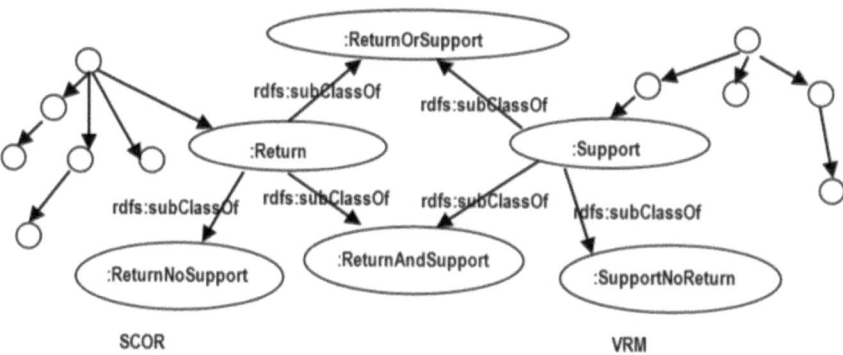

Fig. 6. Mediating concepts used for mapping Return and Support process categories

:ReturnOrSupport will contain all processes from the two categories, while :ReturnAndSupport is a common subsummer to which the user can assign processes that are common. :ReturnNoSupport and SupportNoReturn are designated for processes that fit one framework but not the other (set differences). These can be defined in OWL as follows:
:ReturnOrSupport owl:unionOf (:Return :Support).
:ReturnAndSupport owl:unionOf (:Return :Support).
:ReturnNoSupport owl:intersectionOf (:Return [owl:complementOf :Support]).
:SupportNoReturn owl:intersectionOf (:Support [owl:complementOf :Return]).

This structure will support process type propagation and queries that will cross over boundaries of the frameworks. It can potentially support switching between views such as those provided by Fig. 7 and Fig. 8. Of course, a prerequisite would be to have a modeling tool able to serialize its business process models according to the knowledge structure presented in this section and to query them accordingly.

An example of ontology query that employs the mediation exemplified here and gives us all activities from all processes that fall under both Return (from SCOR) and Support (from VRM) is (using SPARQL [17]):

SELECT ?x WHERE
{?process rdf:type rdf:Seq, :ReturnAndSupport.
?process ?relation ?x.
?x rdf:type :Activity.}

…while the next example would give us Return activities that do not fall under the Support category of VRM:

SELECT ?x WHERE
{?process rdf:type rdf:Seq, :ReturnNoSupport.
?process ?relation ?x.
?x rdf:type :Activity.}

Another usage scenario for the ontological approach is to check flow compliancy in models such as those presented in Fig.4 and Fig.5. For example, SCOR specifies that D1.14 process category (the installation of a product) should take input from D1.13, D2.13, D3.13 (reception of a product at customer site). For compliancy checking, a rule can be added to the ontology:

:D1-14InputSources	*rdf:type*	*owl:Restriction;*
	owl:onProperty	*:InputTo;*
	owl:hasValue	*:D1-14;*
	owl:oneOf	*(:D1-13 :D2-13 :D3-13).*

In this way, the objects that can have the :InputTo relationship with :D1-14 are restricted to the list of the 3 mentioned process categories.

In a system where all process categories have been declared distinct (thus the unique naming assumption holds) and the user generates, using the modeling tool, the following statement…

:S2-2	*:InputTo*	*:D1-14.*

…then the ontology would trigger a SCOR compliancy problem.

Thus we consider ontology mapping as a fitting solution for overcoming discrepancies between these frameworks, with partial semantic overlapping. This research direction can address two of the key problems mentioned in the introduction: the translation of existing models from one framework to another and the extension of one model with process categories from another.

6   Application-Based Comparison

Analyzing Figures 1-3 we can say that the two frameworks have different approaches to the supply chain. Translation at core level would be possible if we consider that both SCOR and VRM define the level1 processes as process types. This means that, by particularization, the processes types of VRM could grasp SCOR processes types details. Thus, to answer the question if the two frameworks can be converted one to another we went deeper into detail at level 2 and level 3 processes for a concrete supply chain example. We applied SCOR and VRM to model the activity, information, and material flow, in the context of a supply chain comprising two suppliers, a t-shirt company, and its clients. The t-shirt company is divided in two parts: a factory and a warehouse. The warehouse receives orders from a client, and based on this order it launches a production program. The clients have specific demands, meaning that they specify what material should be used for the t-shirt and provide the drawing that should be printed on the t-shirts. The t-shirt company supplies the material from Supplier 1, and the printed picture from Supplier 2. The supplies are sent to the factory that assembles the t-shirts. The final product is sent then to the warehouse. The warehouse ships the products to the customers using the services of a transportation company.

We modeled the activity, information and material flow using SCOR (Fig. 7) and VRM (Fig. 8), with a customized version of [14], on the Open Model Initiative platform [18]. Even though by birds view the models seem quite resembling, differences between them are obvious.

A comparison of the two models as graphs showed the results reflected in Table 5.

Table 5. Model element comparison

	SCOR	VRM
Number of nodes	73	49
Activities	55	33
Decisions	3	3
Parallelism	5	4
Merging	2	2
End	3	2

The third level of both SCOR and VRM is the last level of process decomposition based on a common vocabulary. Thus, if a correspondence between the two frameworks at this level would be possible, a dictionary could be written to allow translation between them. As the number of the nodes differs, the only way the translation would work is to suppose that combination of SCOR activities could define a VRM activity (ies) or vice versa. For instance, M3.1 + M3.2 = B01: The two SCOR activities on the right side of the equality, Finalize Production Engineering and Schedule Production Activities can be translated in VRM as Schedule Resources. In this case the further particularization of the activities should have a one to one relation. More than that, VRM does not provide the means to model some aspects that can be modeled in SCOR. An example of such a case is the waste disposal process.

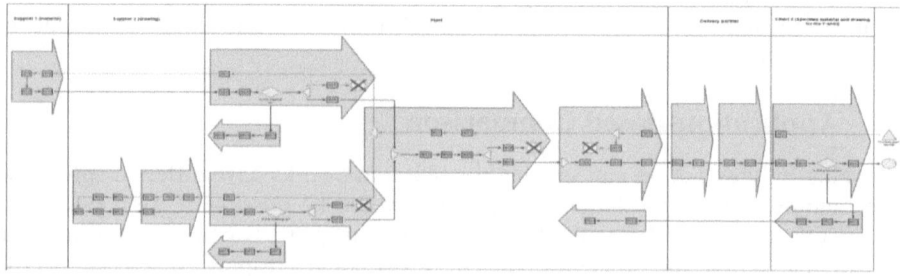

Fig. 7. Activity, Information, and Material Flow (SCOR)

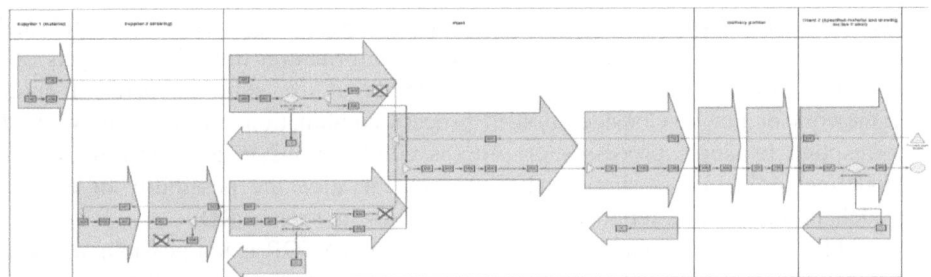

Fig. 8. Activity, Information, and Material Flow (VRM)

7   Related Work

Frameworks or criteria for comparison of business process reference models are provided in [1] and [2]. We have applied them in Section 2. Borros and Julio [19] propose to organize all processes in four macro-processes – collections of processes (1) for production of goods and services, (2) for development of new capabilities, (3) for business planning; and (4) for support of other processes. These groups of processes are used for developing process patterns and are not very handy for comparing several already existing reference models. Rebe et al [20] propose multi-purpose Reference Model for Supply Chain. However, this framework is not appropriate for analysis presented in this paper as it includes such elements as Simulation, TO-BE model description, etc. Additional information, from a practical point of view, about relationships between SCOR and VRM is available in [8]. The popularity of the frameworks and their usability is approved also by implementations of SCOR and VRM in different enterprise and business process modeling tools, e.g. [21] and [22]. Some implementations approach supply chain management frameworks through metamodels. For example, ADOLog [23] [24][25] is such a modeling tool. Visualization issues have been approached in works such as [26]. Efforts regarding identification of commonalities in supply chain frameworks and implementation of supporting modeling tools are being spent in European projects such as ComVantage [27].

8   Conclusions

The analysis of possibilities of joint use of SCOR and VRM from all perspectives described in this paper show that these possibilities depend on the level of abstraction and detail at which the frameworks are used. A blueprint set of recommendations can be helpful for joint use of SCOR and VRM: a. Reference model architecture representations described in Section 2 (Fig 2) help to see the correspondence between process categories in the reference models. b. Representation of processes next to each other in tables (e.g. Table 3) helps to visualize their commonalities and differences. Note that if in tables processes of interest of SCOR have non-identified inputs, - VRM processes – sources of input information for similar processes, are candidates for extending business processes that are based on SCOR with elements from VRM. c.

Representation of process inputs outputs onto architecture patterns (Fig. 3) for analysis of information flows. d. Decomposition of information flows and analysis of related processes to make a decision on whether to use some subparts of another framework or not. e. Consideration of process combinations in one framework that correspond to single processes or process combinations in another framework. f. Modeling tool builders should take into consideration the possibility of exporting models in formats that support ontological alignment, such as RDF.

A direct, one-to-one mapping between VRM and SCOR is not possible, as the two frameworks do not provide a common approach of supply chains. VRM was created for a more general purpose: to model aspects of a value chain, including the supply chain but not focusing on it. SCOR is a more specialized framework, focused on supply chains. However, ontology mapping techniques hold potential in providing a mediating knowledge model that can encompass both visions and render them as different interpretations to the same problem. We demonstrated also other analytical means that help to see how particular parts of the reference models can be translated, mapped, extended or substituted by elements from another framework. Our future work includes analysis of SCOR in combination with other Supply Chain Council's reference models versus VRM using an ontological approach; and we will take into consideration similarity metrics for the ontological approach in order to get a quantitative measure of the semantic overlapping between the frameworks.

Acknowledgment. The research leading to these results was funded by the European Community's Seventh Framework Programme under grant agreement no. FP7-284928 ComVantage.

References

1. Kirchmer, M.: High Performance through Process Excellence. Springer, Heidelberg (2011)
2. Fettke, P., Loos, P., Zwicker, J.: Business Process Reference Models: Survey and Classification. In: Bussler, C.J., Haller, A. (eds.) BPM 2005. LNCS, vol. 3812, pp. 469–483. Springer, Heidelberg (2006)
3. Value Reference Model,
   http://www.value-chain.org/bptf/buildingblocks/vrm/
4. Supply Chain Operations Reference, Supply Chain Council,
   http://supply-chain.org/scor
5. Brown, G.W.: Value Chains, Value Streams, Value Nets, and Value Delivery Chains, BPTrends (April 2009),
   http://www.bptrends.com/publicationfiles/FOUR%2004-009-ART-Value%20Chains-Brown.pdf
6. SCOR vs. the Value Reference Model (VRM),
   http://supplychainadvice.wordpress.com/2010/01/25/scor-vs-the-value-reference-model-vrm/
7. Feller, A., Shunk, D., Callarman, T.: Value Chains Versus Supply Chains,
   http://www.ceibs.edu/knowledge/papers/images/20060317/2847.pdf

8. Harmon, P.: Business Process Change: A Guide for Business Managers and BPM and Six Sigma Professionals, 2nd edn. Morgan Kaufmann (2007)
9. Bolstorff, P., Rosenbaum, R.: Supply Chain Excellence, 3rd edn. AMACOM (2011)
10. Business process library, Value-Chain Group, http://www.value-chain.org/business-process-library/public/
11. Carrier and Education, Supply Chain Council, http://supply-chain.org/career
12. Value-Chain Group's and Education and Training, http://www.value-chain.org/educationandtraining/
13. OWL 2 Web Ontology Language, http://www.w3.org/TR/owl2-syntax
14. ADONIS Community Edition, http://www.adonis-community.com/
15. Euzenat, J., Shvaiko, P.: Ontology Matching. Springer (2007)
16. Allemang, D., Hendler, J.: Semantic Web for the Working Ontologist. Morgan Kaufmann (2011)
17. SPARQL Query Language for RDF, http://www.w3.org/TR/rdf-sparql-query/
18. Open Model Initiative, http://www.openmodels.at
19. Barros, O., Julio, C.: Enterprise and Process Architecture Patterns. Business Process Management Journal 17(4), 598–618 (2011)
20. Rabe, M., Jackel, F.-W., Weinaug, H.: Reference Models for Supply Chain Design and Configuration. In: Perrone, L.F., Wieland, F.P., Liu, J., Lawson, B.G., Nicol, D.M., Fujimoto, R.M. (eds.) Proceedings of the 2006 Winter Simulation Conference, WSC, pp. 1143–1149 (2006)
21. Metastorm Reference Model for Value Chain (VRM), http://www.metastorm.com
22. ARIS SCOR: Do More with SCOR, https://signon.softwareag.com
23. ADOLog, http://www.boc-group.com/products/adolog/
24. Lindemann, M., Junginger, S., Rausch, T., Kühn, H.: ADOLog: An Implementation of the Supply Chain Operations Reference Model. In: Proceedings of the 9th European Concurrent Engineering Conference 2002 (ECEC 2002). Society for Computer Simulation (SCS) (2002)
25. Junginger, S., Karagiannis, D., Lindemann, M.: Prozessorientiertes Supply-Chain-Design. Industrie Management 18(5), 39–42 (2002)
26. Fill, H.G.: Survey of Existing Visualisation Approaches. In: Visualisation for Semantic Information Systems, pp. 39–159. Springer (2009)
27. Comvantage project, http://comvantage.eu

Spin-Off Phenomenon as a Factor of University Clusters Competitiveness Increasing: A Methodological Proposal

Natalia Klimova and Pavel Malyzhenkov

National Research University Higher School of Economics,
25/12 Bolshaja Pecherskaja Ulitsa, Nizhny Novgorod 603155, Russia

Abstract. In the modern economic reality the level of competitiveness of entire countries and national economies highly depends on innovative activity in the industry and technology. The present article analyzes the diffusion of a cluster model in international experience and the spread of spin-offs model as an effective solution for clusters' efficiency increasing and a promising organizational form for successful functioning of ICT industry. The description of new approaches aimed to powering of links between industry and educational bodies in Russia is delivered too. A methodological proposal for evaluating of clusters' competitiveness is formulated.

Keywords: university clusters, spin-offs, innovation.

1   Introduction

Modern Russian economy faces a challenge linked to a transition to innovative way of development. It means not only the growth of innovative activity but the qualitative changes in the major part of spheres of economy. The directions of these changes are represented by forming of groups of the enterprises – clusters consisting of small innovative enterprises. Problems of their functioning and possibilities to form the clusters are an actual topic of research.

The main condition of successful development of business is the open access to resources, information and credits. The number of small enterprises in Russia in 2010 constituted hardly more than 1 million, the contribution to gross national product was equal to 12% (for comparison, in Europe about 20 million small and medium scale enterprises contributed to gross national product by more than 60%). In the USA more than 15 million of small enterprises contributed by 40% to gross national product [13]. Such insignificant number of small enterprises, in comparison to developed countries, is caused by considerable number of unresolved problems of small and medium business. The most important among them are problems of the State control and supervision, consisting in excessive checks and in all kinds of administrative barriers and infrastructural restrictions.

In the conditions of market economy and globalization the necessity to increase the competitiveness of the country's separate regions arises. In this context clusters become a reserve of growth of competitiveness at regional level as the accounting entities connected among themselves by close economic mutual relations and

N. Aseeva, E. Babkin, and O. Kozyrev (Eds.): BIR 2012, LNBIP 128, pp. 126–135, 2012.

supplementing each other. In the course of placing of production and development of regional economy there were various forms of the territorial organization [17]. Industrial areas, agglomerations, industrial knots, territorial and production complexes are traditionally allocated there.

Clusters represent the modern, quickly extending form of the territorial organization of regional economy. Problems of clusters formation and realization of regional competitive advantages as a rule are considered at level of regions. The author's approach to concept determination «regional cluster» is based on theoretical concepts like placing theories. Porter's determination of cluster focuses attention on its three properties: geographical localization, interrelation between the enterprises and technological coherence of industries.

Different authors [1, 5, 11-14, 16] consider the achievement of possible synergetic effect as the consequence of interaction, influence on innovative development of region, long-term alliances in the field of production. The analysis of the basic approaches to determination of clusters has shown that in the scientific literature, as a rule, two moments are reflected: territorial localization of the interconnected companies and their possession of competitive advantages implemented in frameworks of cluster model of the territorial organization of economy.

The international experience shows that namely small innovative enterprises represent the element that links together research and industry [1, 2, 6, 18]. They can assume the risk of transforming of business idea into industrial prototypes realization, without which it is impossible to evaluate how perspective the research idea will be on the market and if it's worth commercial realization. This mechanism is realized by means of spin-offs companies.

2   Clusters Model Description

Under regional cluster we understand group of the interconnected companies localized in a certain region and the organizations cooperating with each other in the course of production and realization of the goods and services within the limits of a uniform chain of creation of cost for achievement of concrete economic effect and implementing competitive advantages of given territory. Unlike other forms of the territorial organization of economy, cluster is distinguished by market interaction between participants of the consolidations, based on a competition and cooperation, capability of adaptation to changing environmental conditions. Clusters are formed in the conditions of market economy when the enterprises are interested in strengthening of the competitive advantages and in reception of profits on joint activity in certain territory.

Thus, regional cluster as a form of the territorial organization of economy is developed not only in the industries, but also in service trade. The cluster approach to the territorial organization of economy of region is directed on studying of operating conditions of the concrete enterprises and the organizations.

International experience witnesses that cluster approach to regional growth assumes character of national strategy of economic policy of competitiveness increasing [5, 12, 14, 15, 18]. In the world practice three main models are known: North American, European and Asian, that are conditioned by traditions of economy development of the different countries, security factorial conditions, branch structure of economy, a reservoir of the national and regional markets and a State role in economy.

The North American model is characterized by small intervention of the federal government in process of regional clusters developments. The European region shows an active role of the federal authority in the course of realization of regional clusters development principles, determining methodical bases, promoting organizational development, performing financial support. It is connected to dependence on external deliveries of strategic kinds of resources, narrowness of national market outlets. If in the USA they are separated from each other, in Europe the state cooperates with businessmen, but without direct penetration into structures of large private industrial firms that distinguishes it from the Asian model of relations "state-business". On the basis of the analysis of the experience the leading role of clusters in stimulation of regional growth, an improvement in employment, growth of budgetary incomes, investment attraction becomes crucial. The companies which form clusters have higher financial indicators, labor efficiency, sales volume.

The main research problems to be discussed consist in the theoretical justification and development of methodical approaches for forming of strategic development for economic clusters for large technology like oil and gas complex in the conditions of forming of national innovative system.

So, the principal factors for universities research parks competitiveness treated as an innovation cluster around the universities should be investigated. In «new economy» the level of competitiveness of any country depends on innovative activity in industry and technology. In particular, the global problem of Russia which slows the development of innovations is the absence of history of success. In the international practice it is widely accepted that before placing investments into realization of new products and technologies the foreign companies analyze not only financial and economic conditions of separate subjects of national economy, but also take into consideration the number of successful innovative enterprises or businessmen grown in a certain country. In 2010 in Russia only 4-5% of industrial organizations developed and implemented innovative developments (in the USA this indicator exceeds 35%) in the activity, in small-scale business the innovative enterprises constitute less than 1% against 4-5% in the USA [3]. Research and technological parks represent the platform which allows initiating innovations, in its frameworks conditions for motivation of the enterprises and people to the creation of innovations, for their transformation into successful products and, hence, successful companies.

3   Spin-Offs as an Efficient Organizational Business Form

Innovative cluster is the localized set of industrial companies, the research centers, individual businessmen, high schools and other organizations with motivated and steady formal communications. From the point of view of the innovative clusters theory founder M. Porter [5, 16], clusters assume various forms depending on the depth and complexity, but the majority include: the companies of a "ready" product or service, suppliers of factors of production, financial institutions, firms in accompanying industries. In a cluster, also, the firms working with sales channels or consumers, manufacturers of by-products, specialized providers of an infrastructure, the governmental and other organizations providing special training, formation, information receipt, carrying out of researches and giving technical support (universities, advanced training structures) often enter. The governmental structures, making essential impact on clusters, can be considered as its part. Many clusters include enterprise consolidations and other joint structures of a private sector, the organization on the cooperation, supporting members of cluster. Character of communications between the enterprises forming a cluster, can be both vertical and horizontal. Cluster can include itself the enterprises of one industry or different industries [5].

The analysis of international experience shows the broad diffusion of spin-offs phenomenon all over the world [6]. So, in Australia the growth of spin-off firms is being verified since the beginning of 80s and the peaks of activity were registered few times since 80s until 2000; the financing of spin-offs in Australia is distributed in the following way: 33% falls onto the research bodies, 23% onto privates and 15% is delivered by venture funds. Less than 15% don't obtain financing and the investing in their activity is limited by the obtaining of technological license.

In Canada, according to the data of National Research Council of Canada in 80s 205 such firms and 444 in 90s were opened on the base of 45 leading universities. The program of new industrial applications sustaining covered with proper financing 40% of opened spin-offs on the universities base. The equity share of research bodies amounted to 50% and large universities can permit themselves to have proper funds to develop such enterprises.

French experience shows that in 80s 387 spin-off firms were opened (including those opened by professors, researchers and students). The peak of spin-offs had fallen onto the end of '80 and beginning of '90, but after that, in the 2000s the reduction of their number was registered. In France the financing of spin-offs is the combination of proper funds of the universities, private funds, banks, venture capital and capital of other firms.

In Italy regional and national institutions are increasingly becoming aware of the importance of supporting innovation and research. Fiscal incentives and programs like "Industria 2015"[1] are among the numerous possibilities of co-financing. Still, Italy is experiencing a significant lack of venture capital activity and the industry is not as developed compared to ones of other European countries. However, venture capital in Italy is starting to grow.

The Italian experience is particularly interesting because of the dominated presence of SMEs in the industrial tissue of the country [14]. A very interesting example of spin-off successful functioning and of the synergy between universities (in particular public resources and founds) industry and finance is the PharmEste Ltd, a spin-off of

---

[1] "Industria 2015" is the name of the synthetic Bill (proposed law) aimed to enhance the competitiveness and industrial policy, approved on 22 September 2006 by the second government lead by Romano Prodi. Industry 2015 provides the strategic lines of the Italian industrial policy, basing them on a conception of industry which integrates not only the manufacturing but also advanced services and new technologies in the medium-long term (2015).

the University of Ferrara. PharmEste, founded as a USOs of the University of Ferrara is a private drug development biopharmaceutical company based on a unique Transient Receptor Potential (TRPs) ion channel technology platform that brings together strong expertise on TRPs area and industrial competences in research & development process applied to small molecule therapeutics [11].

Another Italian reality, famous for its synergy between research and industry is Etna Valley, a large conglomerate of small innovative enterprises (electronics and semiconductors) concentrated in Catania area in Sicily. In 1997, in Catania the new ST Microelectronics factory was opened (the multinational microchip firm created by the merger between SGS Italiana and the components sector of the French enterprise Thomson). Only few years after a solid group of horizontally and vertically integrated firms emerged from just one firm, representing a positive reference point on the Italian and European industrial panorama. Recent developments were caused by the decision of several large companies to establish important production divisions and research centers in the Etna Valley. Vodafone, Nokia, IBM, Nortel and Sicos have all set up business in Catania.

Meanwhile the side industries generated by ST Microelectronics have prompted the development of hundreds of small and very small firms, supplying the microelectronic giant with components and equipment previously imported from abroad. There are also other sectors with a high technological content - but outside the area of electronics, information and communication technology - which find an area for potential development on the slopes of Etna. This particularly applies to Wyeth Lederle, a leading European pharmaceutical firm carrying out important research in the vaccine sector. In just seven years, the Etna Valley has become an essential reference point in Italian economic system: more than 1,200 firms, one thousand of them resulting from initiatives by very young local entrepreneurs; about 200 national firms which have chosen Catania to develop their businesses; and 23 multinationals. This has also resulted from the strong integration which has taken place across firms, local institutions and universities. It has allowed the companies established in the area to identify young people who are adequately trained, as well as providing incentives for new infrastructure and a drastic simplification of the administrative procedures necessary in the establishment of new firms [19]. Even in crisis times this reality showed a stable growth: +14,3% of export in January-September of 2011 [15].

In order to facilitate the transition from bench to market and with the aim of providing brilliant academic scientists with the necessary instruments to best use their innovative ideas and translate them in commercial technologies, 90.7% of the Italian universities are now flanked by a Technology Transfer Office (TTO), each staffed with an average of 4 people (an increase of one employee from 2003). TTOs' main objective is to accelerate the creation of entrepreneurial activities, by offering assistance and valuable instruments to spin-offs venture capital investments in Italy are far less than the US's, but are growing. According to AIFI, the Italian Private Equity and Venture Capital Association, in the first six months of 2010 early stage investments accounted for 51 deals (€41 million), on par to surpass the number of deals registered in 2009 [4].

The spin-offs are majorly diffused in the USA and all the information is gathered by the Association of University Technology Managers. The companies, founded by professors or researchers has no status of spin-off company. By the end of '90s the average number of new companies a year reached 281 firms. From this point of view the example of "Hewlett-Packard" company is rather demonstrative. Almost 90% of all research is being developed in the laboratories of the company itself and only 10% are placed in the university laboratories. The most important here is that HP, for sure, would have been able to fulfill all the tasks independently, but the cooperation with the universities brings other very important advantages. It is the possibility to exchange opinions, exchange new scientific ideas, select best students for work and, the most important, is the positioning of the firm as the company which supports higher education.

Nowadays the similar approach is being carried out in Russia too. It regards the development of Special Economic Zones (SEZ), formalized by the Federal Law about SEZ N° 116 dated 22 of July, 2005. This new form of economic activity for Russia includes, in particular, the so-called SEZ of innovation implementation type which are engaged in promotion, industrial realization and further commercialization of scientific research results. These zones are located in four Russian cities, traditionally strong in scientific field (Tomsk, Dubna, Zelenograd and Saint Petersburg) and the enterprises-residents of these zones have strong relations with the educational bodies present there. The research projects conducted there cover the fields of new materials, ICT, energy-saving technologies, bio- and nanotechnologies and some others. These business agglomerations are characterized by the strong presence of IT enterprises and their share among the total of residents, according to a survey of Ministry of Economic Development of Russian Federation [20] was equal in June 2012 to 46%.

The majority of literature on research parks shows that most university research parks are not effective economic interventions. This is surprising because cluster theory [5] suggests that university research parks ought to have positive effect on economic activity. It is possible that the real implementation of university research park is not following the prescriptions of cluster theory and that addressing this shortcoming may provide more effective economic impact.

4   Clusters Analysis: An Advanced Methodology

In the work [3] a model for evaluating the efficiency of a cluster was proposed. It was determined that there is the number of independent and dependent variables for such type of analysis. We have assumed that the main independent variables are to be:

- university knowledge: R&D expenditures in science and technology;
- university faculty capital: number of faculty members in science and technology fields;
- university human capital: number of degrees awarded in science and technology fields (bachelors, masters, doctors' degrees).

We have also assumed that the main dependent variable was given by the number of technology-based firms in a cluster in each of principal technology fields for the park.

So, three main research hypotheses were included in our investigation:

- H1: there is a correlation between the strength of the university's research capacity in specific technology fields to the technical needs of firms located in the associated university research park. The variable research capacity referred to university's R&D [3].

- H2: there is a correlation between the number of faculty in specific technology fields at the university and the technical needs of firms located in the associated university research park. The variable human capacity refers to the total number of scientists in research and technology fields. Companies obtain knowledge by establishing relations with university scientists.
- H3: there is a correlation between the number of graduating students at the university and the technical needs of firms located in the associated university research park.

The variable of labor pool refers total number of degrees granted at university in science and technology fields. This variable has been used in the studies of [5] authors.

Statistical analysis is the principal instrument for further research. The statistical procedures ought to be done into two steps. In the **first** one the null hypotheses must be formulated for each of the research hypotheses. The following null hypotheses can be formulated:

- NH1: there is no correlation between the strength of the university's research capacity in specific technology fields to the technical needs of firms located in the associated university research park.
- NH2: there is no correlation between the number of faculty in specific technology fields at the university and the technical needs of firms located in the associated university research park.
- NH3: there is no correlation between the number of graduating students at the university and the technical needs of firms located in the associated university research park.

We ought to choose the alpha level for statistical tests. It seems reasonable to choose 0.05: it indicates that null hypotheses are rejected if the sample outcome was among the results that occurred no more than 5 percent. The statistical test is assumed to be the two-tailed test; the region of rejection is located at both left and right tails. The decision to locate the region of rejection in two tails must be based on the hypotheses and the size of the sample. Two tails test are usually more stringent than one tailed test. It indicates that a result which is significant in two tailed test is also significant in a one tailed test (but not vice versa).

At the **second** step descriptive analysis ought to be conducted. The descriptive analysis for variables will include percentages. It is assumed that correlation analysis will be performed using parametric test and Pearson product-moment correlation coefficient. Data ought to be normalized to determine the strength of each university using three variables of research capacity, human capital and specialized labor pool across major technological fields.

Still, all factors considered in the model are factors of internal to the enterprise nature. Our proposal consists in extending its frames by including different external parameters. In particular, we propose to consider the state-of-the-art of the legislative base in this matter and the grade of mutual trust between the economic agents.

The actuality of spin-offs activity analysis in Russia is conditioned by the adoption of Federal Law N° 127 "About Science and the State Scientific and Technical Policy" which permits to institutes and universities to create small innovative enterprises. Still, very often it is not convenient for large companies to invest in spin-off firms, but to open a proper innovative unit with the purpose of new products developing. Recently amendments to this Law have been approved and it permitted to the universities to create enterprises for practical realization of their scientific results without a founder (State) consensus. It also previews the possibility to involve other juridical persons if the share of the university exceeds 25% in the joint-stock company and 33% in limited liabilities. The share of the other persons in the social capital must be paid by money means at least by 50%. This law permits to the authors of a scientific invention created in the State institute or university to carry out the commercial activity in the high-tech sphere.

The innovation risk is the reason by which many large companies don't realize broad-scale investments: they need at least some guaranty of success. So, from the practical point of view the application of research to the industrial process became the niche of small innovative firms. This procedure became possible in Russia after the Federal Law N° 127 "About Science and the State Scientific and Technical Policy" adoption. The main advantages of this Law are the following [6]:

- unemployment reduction;
- the possibility for the universities to develop the own innovative technologies;
- enhancing of the state funds directed to innovation development effectiveness;
- practical realization of ideas in socio-economic sphere.

Different sources [10] mention that the main factor of economic development is represented by the mutual trust between the economic players. From this point of view, Russia is quiet a problematic reality[2] [9]:

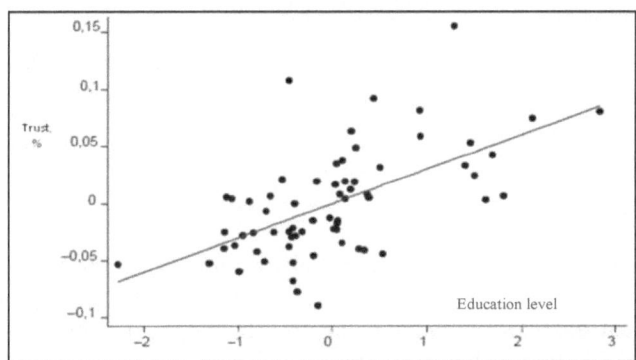

Fig. 1. Correlation between the trust level and education level in Russia

---

[2] This problem was raised recently during the XIII International Academic Conference on Economic and Social Development in the Higher School of Economics in the report of Mikhail Zadornov, President of the "VTB-24" bank. According to his data only 800 thousand persons (of nearly 75 million of economically active population in Russia) allocated part of proper means in Russian stock exchanges. This data is extremely worrying because it indicates not only a low investing activity of Russian population, but first of all its reduced trust level towards the national financial institutes.

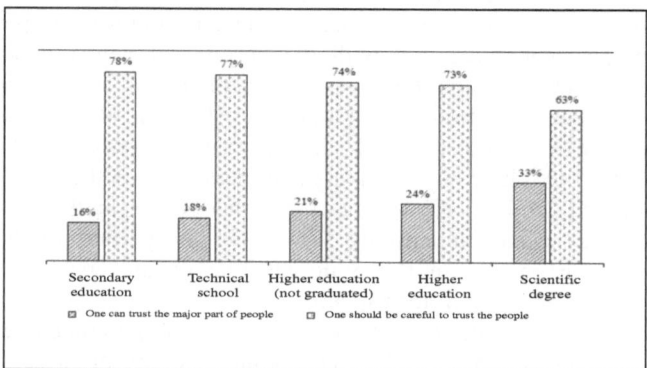

Fig. 2. Trust level by different categories of educated people

So, the model described in [3] can be extended as follows:

- H4: there is a correlation between the grade of mutual trust between the economic agents and the technical needs of firms located in the associated university research park.
- H5: there is a correlation between the grade of legislative base development and the technical needs of firms located in the associated university research park.

The following null hypotheses can be formulated:

- NH4: there is no correlation between the grade of mutual trust between the economic agents and the technical needs of firms located in the associated university research park.
- NH5: there is no correlation between the grade of legislative base development and the technical needs of firms located in the associated university research park.

5   Conclusion

In this work a new methodological proposal for university clusters was formalized. The further development of the research may consist in the data gathering and the further statistical analysis application having the scope to apply it to real known international or Russian technologies parks, clusters or Special Economic Zones in order to determine the correlation of the factors described in it.

References

1. David, P.A., Metcalfe, S.: Universities must contribute to enhancing Europe's innovative performance. Knowledge Economists' Policy Brief (2) (2007)
2. Wright, M., Lockett, A., Clarysse, B., Binks, M.: University Spin-Out Companies and Venture Capital. Research Policy (35) (2006)

3. Litvintseva, M.: Methodology for Cluster Model Analysis for Technical and Workforce Needs of Companies in Universities Research Parks. International Research Journal of Finance and Economics (63) (2011)
4. Italian Trade Commission, Report Research in Italy, 2nd edn., New York (2011)
5. Porter, M.: The Cluster and Competition: New Agenda for Companies, Governments and Institutions. Harvard Business Review Books, MA (1998)
6. Ghuljaevskaja, N., Shumakova, S., Popov, A.: Cooperation of Business and Universities in Development of Innovative Economics. Journal of Saint Petersburg University of Fire Service (3) (2010)
7. Federal Law of Russian Federation № 127 About Science and the State Scientific and Technical Policy (August 23, 1996)
8. European Commission, University Spin–Outs in Europe. Overview and Good Practice, Directorate General for Enterprise, Bruxelles (2002)
9. Natkhov, T.V.: Education and Trust in Russia. Empirical Analysis. Economical Journal of Higher School of Economics (2011) (in Russian)
10. Arrow, K.: Gifts and Exchanges, Philosophy and Public Affairs (1972)
11. Fici, L., Piccarozzi, M.: University Spin-Offs, Venture Capital and Public Funds: a Network For the Creation of Value. In: Business Administration, Finance and New Methods of Management in Organizations, Workshop Proceedings. RIREA (2011)
12. Klimova, N.: Innovative Clusters in Regional Economy. International Research Journal of Finance and Economics (65) (2011)
13. Klimova, N., Litvinseva, M.: Universities Innovation Clusters: Approaches for National Competitiveness Paradigm. European Journal of Social Sciences 19(1) (2011)
14. Kozyrev, O., Malyzhenkov, P.: Industrial Clusters as the Form of the Territorial Organization of Economy in Russia and Italy. European Journal of Economics, Finance and Administrative Sciences (42) (December 2011)
15. National Observatory of Italian Clusters, III Report (2012)
16. Porter, M.E.: The Competitive Advantage of Nations. Free Press, N.Y. (1998)
17. Krugman, P.R.: Geography and Trade. MIT Press, Cambridge (1991)
18. Audretsch, D.B., Feldman, M.P.: R&D Spillovers And the Geography of Innovation and Production. American Economic Review 86(3) (1996)
19. E-source, http://www.italtrade.com/focus/5123.html
20. E-source, http://www.economy.gov.ru/minec/

IS Research Challenges and Needs for Service Networks — A Brazilian-German Perspective

Martin Matzner[1], Armin Stein[1], Carl Stolze[2], Matthias Voigt[1], and Fábio Alexandrini[3]

[1] University of Muenster, European Research Center for Information Systems (ERCIS), Münster, Germany
{martin.matzner,armin.stein,matthias.voigt}@ercis.uni-muenster.de
[2] University of Osnabrueck, Information Management and Information Systems Group, Osnabrück, Germany
carl.stolze@uni-osnabrueck.de
[3] Instituto Federal Catarinense, Rio do Sul, SC, Brazil
fabalexandrini@yahoo.com.br

Abstract. When countries move from manufacture-oriented to service-oriented societies, the service sector becomes ever more important. Through this development, coalitions of industry and service companies play a crucial role to respond to individualized customer demands. Those coalitions are referred to as service networks. A vivid IS community in Europe and the United States emerged, to explore and advance the role of IS in service networks. On their way towards global economic leadership, service networks also play a crucial role for the BRIC countries (Brazil, Russia, India, and China). However, so far research on that topic is at an early development stage in those emerging markets. A Brazilian-German workshop held in 2011 in Florianópolis brought design-oriented researchers from both countries together. In this paper we present the identified research challenges for IS research on service networks, potential contributions to meet these challenges and conclude with a research agenda for the forthcoming years.

Keywords: Service networks, BRIC, IS research, research agenda, design-oriented research.

1 Introduction

A strong service sector is seen as the next step in the development of leading economies, especially to decouple them from the limited availability of natural resources or volatile markets [1]. In the same way the production industry moved from single producers of simple and identical products to complex networks producing highly customizable goods, single service providers have to build up coalitions to shift from uniform services to fit-to-use solutions realized by service networks. These service networks can be composed of multiple independent companies whose goals, processes and IT systems need to be aligned on different levels [2]. The emerging phenomena of service networks is of special interest for

N. Aseeva, E. Babkin, and O. Kozyrev (Eds.): BIR 2012, LNBIP 128, pp. 136–147, 2012.

the Information Systems (IS) and service science disciplines as the various conflicts of flexibility versus efficiency in service development and delivery require specific methods, systems and approaches.

Emerging markets, like the BRIC (Brazil, Russia, India and China), have seen rapid economic growth in recent years. Productivity gains have been fueled by the transition from agricultural to manufacturing labour. The ever growing service sector in all these economies makes productivity improvements harder to archive [3]. However, the service science discipline is not as well established so far in these countries as it is in, e.g., in the European and especially German business and information systems engineering community. Based on this we aimed at closing that knowledge gap by conducting a bi-national workshop in Florianópolis, Brazil, in late 2011. During this workshop, different scientific perspectives from German service science researches were matched with Brazilian service reality. The workshop was guided by the following two research questions:

1. *What are challenges in service networks in Brazil and Germany?*
2. *What are the needs of service networks towards design-oriented Information Systems research?*

The combined answers to these questions allow to draft a research agenda in the field of service networks. Both questions also assure that future research is relevant for practice in the field.

In this paper, we present the process and the outcome of the workshop, pointing towards answers of the research questions motivated above. The paper is structured as follows. To ground our research, we provide an overview about the applied research method in Section 2. We then motivate the areas of interest to be discussed during the workshop in Section 3, leading to a research agenda derived from the input provided by the participants in Section 4. In Section 5, we present the discussion of the agenda and close the paper with our conclusions in Section 6.

2 Research Method

The workshop was subdivided in two divergent and one convergent session. While the first divergent session was dedicated to the development of research challenges, the goal of the second divergent session was to identify research needs. Both sessions were performed in a group of six participants from Germany and Brazil, both with academic (IS) and professional (service sector) background. For the evaluation session, we sought an audience with interdisciplinary research background. Thus, five participants from academia joined the group of the divergent session, again from Germany and Brazil, with research background in engineering sciences and computer science.

The first divergent session for the development of challenges was split in two phases: in the first phase, ideas should be generated individually, whereas the second phase was dedicated to idea generation in groups on the basis of individually identified ideas. This is in line with the finding that the creative performance of groups preceded by individual brainstorms (i.e. nominal groups) is higher than those who develop ideas exclusively in groups [4]. The second divergent session, aiming to identify research needs, was performed as a Group Brainstorming session [5]. On the basis of the priory identified challenges, IS artifacts were identified and grouped. Ideas were contributed by all six group members. Critique should be omitted. As a result of both brainstorming sessions, integrated flip charts for needs and challenges were compiled.

In the convergent session, the best ideas for research needs had to be selected and undergo a creativity assessment. First, the participants of the divergent sessions presented their ideas for challenges and needs to those who had not participated in idea generation. All eleven session participants could then assign up to five credits to each research need (one idea could be assigned more than one credit by one participant). The five ideas that received most credits then were selected for creativity assessment. Each participant had to assess each of the five ideas with respect to novelty, workability, specificity and relevance on a five point Likert skale [6].

3   Design-Oriented Research for Service Networks

Engineering, selling and delivering services is based on rich interactions of providers and customers (co-creation of value). For complex value propositions, companies need to network on nested hierarchical levels—ecosystems, organizations, work group, jobs [7]—in order to tap into complementary resources and core competencies [8]. Complementary resources allow network partners to "collectively generate greater rents than the sum of those obtained from the individual endowments of each partner." [8, p.667]. In consequence, we nowadays observe the emergence of complex networks of institutions that integrate their individual resources and competences in order to provide fit-to custom solutions to their customers. Service networks can be considered as both, an organizational phenomenon comprising of several interacting actors, as well as a means to co-ordinate actors. In this view, the network organization [9] pools the resources and competences that belong to the network [10]. The coordination perspective instead is a responding to problems caused by dependencies [10] between the network actors. It comprises of a set of distinct inter-organizational processes and mechanisms that puts the required co-ordination between actors into action and thus finally facilitates the value creation [2].

In order to achieve tapping into complementary resource endowments among the service network actors and achieving the provision of competitive as well as custom-fit services to the customer service networks have to achieve two goals at the same time—flexibility and efficiency [11]: First, flexibility requires the network organization to allow for dynamic reconfiguration with respect to the customers' demand. Based on the resources and competences required, actors have to be added or removed from the network. The assignment of tasks to specific actors might be changed. Second, the service network still is faced increased competition and thus must be able to deliver custom-fit services in a competitive manner. Accordingly, high performance in dynamic environments such as service networks relies on balancing flexibility and efficiency.

As a sensing device for our analysis of needs towards design-oriented IS, we employed the framework for design research in the service science discipline as proposed by [12] and successfully applied by [13]. The framework is intended to help structuring design-oriented research activities in the area of service management and engineering. The first dimension of the framework classifies design science research result categories according to the four IT artifact types proposed by March and Smith [14]: *Constructs* form the vocabulary of a domain. *Models* are sets of statements expressing relationships between constructs. *Methods* are sequences of steps used to perform a task. *Instantiations* are realizations of constructs, models, or methods in information systems. The second dimension comprises different perspectives on a service [12]. The *potential* perspective considers required resources in order to provide services to clients. The *process* perspective outlines the activities required for service value creation. The *outcome* perspective exhibits the structure and the functional and non-functional properties of a service. The *market* perspective respects the customer as a cocreator of value.

4   Towards a Research Agenda

In this section we will first present the research challenges for service network research in IS from a Brazilian-German perspective. On that basis, we then indicate the needs of organizations towards design-oriented IS research that respond to those challenges.

4.1   Challenges

Information exchange. The efficient exchange of information between the network partners was identified as a major challenge in service network operations. Information exchange facilitates and enables inter-organizational business processes for service provision. IT systems are indispensable in realizing corresponding information flow among the actors. Benefits of this digitization of business relationships, amongst others, are more accurate and faster information flows and potentially increased volume of business [15]. However, those benefits can only be realized when the process of digitization is purposefully planned and executed by the affected network partners. The complexity increases with the number of actors involved. One important step in this process is to select shared standards for data formats—an important strategic step for each participant [16]. Given the context of networks spanning boundaries of political or economic unions (in our case the European Union, EU, and the Common Southern Market, Mercosul), specific local regulations and laws have to be considered. Furthermore, information exchange has to be bi-directional, so that information flows in any direction of the value chain are possible [17].

Coordination mechanisms. While customers often perceive "their solution" to be inseparable, the several service providers and manufactures of the service network are faced with the need to coordinate disparate business processes and resources to create this integrated service experience. Typically, the co-operation in the network starts with a mode of customer-case specific ad-hoc coordination. For a distinct customer project process of initiation, engineering and fulfilment are designed. On a longer perspective and in order to achieve scaling from several customer projects, the inter-organizational processes typically get more formally planned and documented. In these cases, coordination can be achieved through different coordination means—e.g. through conjugate collectives of enterprises [18]. Our experts agreed that the choice of coordination, whether ad-hoc or defined, is a challenge that needs to be addressed with systematic decision support. Furthermore, the process of formalization itself is a particular challenge in service networks.

Resource efficiency. The major global question of resource efficiency was also identified as being an important part for service networks at various levels—from design and strategy over planning to operations and market impact. This assessment is supported by the argument that sustainability initiatives are seen today as an investment rather than being merely cost by a majority of business leaders [19]. This investment is sometimes hard to justify when consumers do not have strong attitudes towards sustainable production or service systems yet. But this number is growing globally. Therefore, service networks as a whole need to get ready to deliver up to the growing sustainability-related expectations.

Reference processes. Reference models can be seen as conceptual models of that are generic and formalize state-of-the-art or best practice in a certain field. Their nature is normative and can, but does not necessarily cover different domains such as industry sectors or functional areas [20]. Due to their universal applicability, researchers and practitioners alike can use them as guidelines for comparing and validating specific existing processes. Reference Models as a blueprint for specific models and procedure exist for a variety of domains and industries [21], however the service sector in general and the area of service engineering in service networks in particular are not sufficiently covered yet by IS research. Facing this problem and developing respectively extending this field might certainly support the development of a stronger service research society.

Service description. In order to effectively discover, understand, and compare services, a unified way to describe services would be required [22]. Here, service description is a means to facilitate the integration between the several providers of a customer solution as well as to integrate the customer as co-creator of value into processes. Further, a purposeful digital representation of a service might allow providers for exploiting new sales channels (e.g., digital service marketplaces), and might even lead to creating and providing entirely new offers that arise from dynamically integrating value offers. Customers can be provided with enhanced functionalists in searching and finding services and composing purposeful solutions. Our experts agreed that the description of services delivered by a service network might be particularly complex. Comprehensive service descriptions would, e.g., have to include information about the actors contributing single service components.

4.2   Needs

Tool for defining information flows. In response to the *challenge of information exchange*, one of the experts highlighted that an information exchange infrastructure will be required to allow network actors to cross their organizational boundaries. Previous research indicated that streamlining business processes across organizations requires an open exchange of information to facilitate common planning and synchronization of activities [23]. However, current research falls short on approaches to systematically identify the information required to be exchanged and especially on methods and tools to purposefully specify those. Having the right information identified, described, and finally exchanged would allow the network partners to cooperate with greater flexibility, at increased speed and at lower cost, the experts agreed. The information flows and coordination need to be supported by appropriate information technology to identify, describe and bring to action the information flows [24]. In the framework of design research, the tool represents an instantiation for the process perspective on services.

Tool for inter-organizational processes. Our experts agreed that flexible and at the same time efficient network structures, as required by the *challenge of coordination mechanisms*, requires an analysis and design of the cross-organizational processes in order to facilitate process planning and coordination based on a mutual exchange of information. In previous research, business processes that cross organizational boundaries have been found to considerably increase the complexity of a network organization [25]. Thus, software tool support would be required in order to help to establish new cross-organizational processes. The introduction of those tools will depend on defined information flows and thus the priory defined research need. Further, such a tools support shall consider that the inter-organizational mechanisms are shared by all network participants [2] and accordingly should allow all the participants to bring their individual interests into the shared design process of their coordinating business processes. As the tool for defining information flows, the tool for inter-organizational processes is an instantiation for service processes.

Method for sustainable services. Our experts established the notion of sustainability to be of major importance for service networks in order to respond to the *challenge of resource efficiency*. Within our workshop, the need for methods to assess, design and delivering sustainable processes across a value-creating network was identified. Although certain parts of these methods have been already developed and prototypically applied (e.g. Boehm et al. 2011), the integration of these approaches still needs to be achieved. Furthermore, it was stated that actors involved in any service network need to be aware of the interdependencies between the partners to succeed in sustainability endeavours [26]. The design of sustainable service networks may well be fostered by reference models. An example of such a model applied in practice is the SCOR (Supply Chain Operations Reference) model [27]. SCOR provides guidance for business process reengineering, benchmarking and structured best practices. Into its version 9.0

first sustainability extensions have been integrated. Nonetheless there is no set of methods tailored specifically at service networks to achieve sustainability goals yet. As to the design research framework, the method addresses the service market perspective.

Reference model for service delivery. In response to the *challenge of reference processes* for service networks, our experts identified the need of adequate reference models. Creating an entirely new reference model would be a time-consuming task. Because of the adaptability of the before-mentioned SCOR model, the participants suggest its extension. According to the SCOR model's structure, each process building block has been assigned exactly one set of metrics and best practices. To make clear that certain of metrics and practices sets are only relevant in the service context, they have to be explicitly added. The literature already suggests approaches for this extension [28, 29]. Extending the core processes indicates that service-specific processes like, e.g. Disposition and Repair [30], have to be added to the existing elements. By doing so, experiences gained in the manufacturing, supply chain, and logistics environment can be utilized to extend a suitable reference model to describe, design, and evaluate service networks. The reference model can be categorized as model for the outcome perspective of services.

Service description language. In order to purposefully describe the property of a service, as indicated necessary in the challenge of service description, the integration of previous work in different areas of related work has to be achieved. In particular a unified approach to a service description language would require adding aspects such as "ownership and provisioning, release stages in a service network, composition and bundling, pricing and legal aspects among others" [22] to a pure technical description of a service as proposed, e.g., in related work on Service Oriented Architectures. This could be achieved by means such as an accompanying description of the pricing scheme, the service level agreement, the terms and conditions when consuming the service and paying for it. A service description language represents an IS model addressing the service outcome perspective.

5   Discussion

In the final convergent phase of our workshop, the five research needs formerly underwent a creativity assessment by eleven experts, stemming from interdisciplinary research background. Each idea had to be assessed with respect to four criteria [6]:

- Novelty: how novel an idea is.
- Workability: how easy an idea can be implemented without violating known constraints.
- Relevance: how effective an idea is to solve the given problem.
- Specificity: how clearly an idea is understandable and worked out in detail.

Table 1. Creativity Assessment Results

Research Need/Assessment Criteria	Novelty	Workability	Relevance	Specificity
Tool for Info. Flow Definition	2.8	3.8	4.3	2.9
Tool for IOS Processes	3.3	4.0	4.2	2.7
Method for Sustainable Services	4.2	3.3	4.1	3.4
Reference Model for Service Delivery	3.3	3.5	3.7	3.3
Service Description Language	3.2	3.5	4.0	3.5

The mean values for all ideas are listed in Table 1.

The interrelationships of the five research needs are presented in research artifact stack for service network research (see Figure 1). Each layer of the stack represents the research needs, where higher level artifacts depend in the next lower level ones (see Figure 1). Similar stacks have been defined in research on electronic standards [31]. We will address the role of each artifact in the following discussion of the evaluation results.

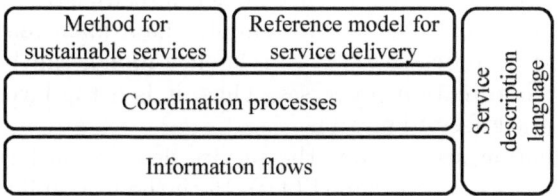

Fig. 1. Research artifact stack for service network

The research need to develop a tool for the definition of information flows received the highest rating in idea relevance (4.3). At the same time, our experts assessed a relatively high value for the workability, i.e. the realizability of the idea (3.8). The comparably low value in novelty (2.8) provides allusion to the fact that several tools have already been developed for conceptual modeling information flows between network partners (Becker et al. 2009). However, the comparably low value of specificity (2.9) may be interpreted in a way that besides a general shared understanding amongst our experts of what such a tool should facilitate to accomplish, the question remains on how the tool should be designed. In our research artifact stack, defined information flows represent the bottom layer, independent on other artifacts identified in the workshop (see Figure 1).

The second research need, the development of a tool for the definition of inter-organizational coordination processes, was assessed quite equally to the first research need. We reason, that this congruence resides from the closeness of both ideas. As stated before, information flows are important facilitators for inter-organizational business processes, thus depending on the information flow layer in our artifact stack [17] (see Figure 1). Only with respect to the novelty, the issue of coordination process support was clearly rated higher than information flow definition (3.3). We reason that currently research has a stronger focus on the data layer of coordination than on the process layer.

The research need for a method to assess, design and deliver for sustainable services was rated as most original idea (4.2). Equally, high ratings were given for the relevance of the idea (4.1). We interpret this assessment against the background of potential resource efficiency gains that can be achieved when multiple actors concurrently and systematically strive for more sustainable services [32]. These gains clearly have a higher magnitude than gains achieved by single actors only. The delivery of sustainable services will depend on appropriate coordination processes within the service network. Consequently, the latter are the basis for the development of the method (see Figure 1). Given relatively high values in workability (3.3) and specificity (3.4), the proposed method should be considered for future German-Brazilian research activities.

The criteria ratings for the idea of a reference model of service delivery reached modest above average values with low variance (3.3-3.7). The relatively highest value was obtained for idea relevance (3.7). A reference model was further deemed to be a rather workable IS artifact (3.6). For novelty and specificity equal values were obtained (3.3). The overall modest value for the idea originality may be due to the fact that reference models already have been proposed for numerous application contexts, e.g. for supply chain management [27, SCOR, see above], or service processes [33]. A reference model can be interpreted as industry specific coordination processes. Thus, it is a top-layer artifact in our research artifact stack (see Figure 1).

The final evaluation artifact was the service description language. Again, a high value for relevance was obtained (4.0). Both the workability and specificity of the idea were rated modestly above average (3.5). As with the idea of a reference model, novelty received the lowest rating of all criteria (3.2). Current work on the Unified Service Description Language (USDL) may give reason for that. With reference to our stack of research artifacts for service science (see Figure 1), a service description language has to facilitate the description of services on all three layers, i.e. information flows, coordination processes and process models.

6   Conclusion

With our paper, we present the results of the German-Brazilian IS workshop on the topic of service networks. We indicated the mode in which the result were developed in the workshop, consisting of divergent (idea generation) and convergent (idea evaluation) sessions. Ideas for challenges in service networks were generated for the fields of network operations and network organization. Moreover the ideas should be generated against the backdrop of balancing flexibility and efficiency in service networks. Ideas for research needs of service networks towards design-oriented IS research was categorized with the framework for design research in the service science discipline. In all, five challenges were identified by our experts: information exchange, coordination mechanisms, resource efficiency, reference processes, and service description. In response to these challenges five research needs have been identified: a tool for defining information flows, a tool for inter-organizational processes, a method for sustainable services, a reference model for service delivery, and a service description language. We presented the evaluation results for the research needs, indicating a high relevance of the results generated. The needs were then subsumed in a research artifact stack for service network research.

Our paper is subject to limitations: firstly, the challenges and needs are by no means meant to be exhaustive. One the one side, given the restriction of length for this paper, only some ideas generated in the workshop could be presented. On the other side, we had restrictions in the number of workshop participants. Future discussions, involving more IS service science researchers from Germany and Brazil, should be conducted to enrich the research agenda. Moreover, the track of this SBSI 2012 symposium on smarter cities could provide further insights relevant for the topic of service networks. Secondly, only in the convergent part of our workshop, participants stemmed from diverse disciplinary background. In future, this should be the case for the idea generating group as well. In that way a constantly evolving, collaborative, multi-disciplinary German-Brazilian research agenda could be developed to foster the transition of both countries to a leading economy and sustain this status.

References

1. Gemmella, N.: Economic development and structural change: The role of the service sector. Journal of Development Studies 19, 37–66 (1982)
2. Zarvić, N., Stolze, C., Boehm, M., Thomas, O.: Dependency-based IT governance practices in inter-organisational collaborations: A graph-driven elaboration. International Journal of Information Management (Article in press, 2012)
3. The Economist: BRIC wall (2011), http://www.economist.com/node/18560195 (last accessed on July 10, 2012)
4. Hill, G.W.: Group versus individual performance: Are N + 1 heads better than one. Psychological Bulletin 91, 517–535 (1982)
5. Osborn, A.F.: Applied imagination: Principles and procedures of creative thinking. Scribeners and Sons, Oxford (1957)
6. Dean, D., Hender, J., Rodgers, T., Santanen, E.: Identifying quality, novel, and creative ideas: Constructs and scales for idea evaluation. Journal of the Association for Information Systems 7, 646–699 (2006)
7. Basole, R., Rouse, W.: Complexity of service value networks: Conceptualization and empirical investigation. IBM Systems Journal 47, 53–70 (2008)
8. Dyer, J.H., Singh, H.: The relational view: Cooperative strategy and sources of interorganizational competitive advantage. Academy of Management Review 23, 660–679 (1998)
9. Ching, C., Holsapple, C.W., Whinston, A.B.: Modeling network organizations: A basis for exploring computer support coordination possibilities. Journal of Organizational Computing 3, 279–300 (1993)
10. Crowston, K.: Organizing business knowledge: The mit process handbook. In: Malone, T.W., Crowston, K., Hermann, G.A. (eds.) Organizing Business Knowledge: The MIT Process Handbook, pp. 85–108. MIT Press, Cambridge (2003)

11. Eisenhardt, K.M., Furr, N.R., Bingham, C.B.: Microfoundations of performance: Balancing efficiency and flexibility in dynamic environments. Organization Science 21, 1263–1273 (2010)

12. Becker, J., Knackstedt, R., Müller, O., Beverungen, D., Matzner, M., Pöppelbuß, J.: A framework for design research in the service science discipline. In: Proceedings of the Fifteenth Americas Conference on Information Systems (AMCIS), San Francisco, CA, pp. 1–9 (2009)

13. Becker, J., Beverungen, D., Matzner, M., Müller, O., Pöppelbuß, J.: Design Science in Service Research: A Framework-Based Review of IT Artifacts in Germany. In: Jain, H., Sinha, A.P., Vitharana, P. (eds.) DESRIST 2011. LNCS, vol. 6629, pp. 366–375. Springer, Heidelberg (2011)

14. March, S.T., Smith, G.F.: Design and natural science research on information technology. Decision Support Systems 15, 251–266 (1995)

15. Salo, J.: Business relationship digitization: What do we need to know before embarking on such activities? Journal of Electronic Commerce in Organizations 4, 75–93 (2006)

16. Becker, J., Matzner, M., Voigt, M.: Selecting interorganizational standards: A management cybernetics perspective. In: Proceedings of the Sixteenth Americas Conference on Information Systems (AMCIS), Lima, Peru, pp. 1–8 (2010)

17. Becker, J., Beverungen, D., Knackstedt, R., Matzner, M., Müller, O.: Information needs in service systems: A framework for integrating service and manufacturing business processes. In: Proceedings of the 44th Hawaii International Conference on System Sciences (HICSS), Kauai, HI, pp. 1–10. IEEE (2011)

18. Astley, W.G., Fombrun, C.J.: Collective strategy: Social ecology of organizational environments. The Academy of Management Review 8, 576–587 (1983)

19. Accenture: Decision maker attitudes and approaches towards sustainability in business in 2011 (2011), http://www.accenture.com/SiteCollectionDocuments/PDF/Accenture-Decision-Maker-Attitudes.pdf (last accessed on July 10, 2012)

20. Janiesch, C., Stein, A.: Adapting standards to facilitate the transition from situational model to reference model. In: Proceedings of the 10th International Workshop on Reference Modelling (RefMod), Brisbane, Australia, pp. 405–416 (2007)

21. Fettke, P., Loos, P.: Classification of reference models: A methodology and its application. Information Systems and e-Business Management 1, 35–53 (2003)

22. Barros, A., Oberle, D. (eds.): Handbook of Service Description: USDL and Its Methods. Springer, New York (2011)

23. Skjoett-Larsen, T., Thernøe, C., Andresen, C.: Supply chain collaboration: Theoretical perspectives and empirical evidence. International Journal of Physical Distribution & Logistics Management 33, 531–549 (2003)

24. Hsu, C., Spohrer, J.C.: Improving service quality and productivity: Exploring the digital connections scaling model. International Journal of Service Technology and Management 11, 272–292 (2009)

25. Sun, S.X., Zhao, J.L., Nunamaker, J.F., Sheng, O.R.L.: Formulating the data-flow perspective for business process management. Information Systems Research 17, 374–391 (2006)

26. Stolze, C., Boehm, M., Zarvić, N., Thomas, O.: Towards Sustainable IT by Teaching Governance Practices for Inter-Organizational Dependencies. In: Nüttgens, M., Gadatsch, A., Kautz, K., Schirmer, I., Blinn, N. (eds.) Governance and Sustainability in IS. IFIP AICT, vol. 366, pp. 70–88. Springer, Heidelberg (2011)

27. Supply Chain Council: SCOR frameworks (2011), http://supply-chain.org/resources/scor (last accessed on July 10, 2012)

28. Baltacioglu, T., Ada, E., Kaplan, M.D., Yurt, O., Kaplan, Y.C.: A new framework for service supply chains. The Service Industries Journal 27, 105–124 (2007)
29. Ellram, L.M., Tate, W.L., Billington, C.: Understanding and managing the services supply chain. Journal of Supply Chain Management 40, 17–32 (2004)
30. de Waart, D., Kemper, S.: 5 steps to service supply chain excellence. Supply Chain Management Review 8, 28–53 (2004)
31. Löwer, U.M.: Interorganisational Standards: Managing Web Service Specifications for Flexible Supply Chains. Physica-Verlag, Heidelberg (2005)
32. Boehm, M., Freundlieb, M., Stolze, C., Thomas, O., Teuteberg, F.: Towards an integrated approach for resource-efficiency in server rooms and data centers. In: Proceedings of the 19th European Conference on Information Systems (ECIS), Helsinki, Finland (2011)
33. CMMI Product Team: CMMI for Services, Version 1.3 CMMI-SVC, V1.3. Technical Report November, Software Engineering Institute, Pittsburgh, PA, Tech Rpt. CMU/SEI-2006-TR-008, 2006 (2010)

Conducting a Privacy Impact Analysis
for the Analysis of Communication Records

Stefan Hofbauer[1], Kristian Beckers[2], and Gerald Quirchmayr[3,4]

[1] University of Vienna, Multimedia Information Systems Research Group, Liebiggasse 4,
1010 Vienna, Austria
stefan.hofbauer@gmx.net
[2] Paluno - The Ruhr Institute for Software Technology – University of Duisburg-Essen,
Oststrasse 99, 47057 Duisburg, Germany
kristian.beckers@paluno.uni-due.de
[3] University of Vienna, Multimedia Information Systems Research Group, Liebiggasse 4,
1010 Vienna, Austria
gerald.quirchmayr@univie.ac.at
[4] University of South Australia, School of Computer and Information Security, GPO Box 2471,
5001 Adelaide, Australia
gerald.quirchmayr@unisa.edu.au

Abstract. Attacks on Voice-over-IP calls happen frequently. The prevention of
these attacks depends on understanding the attack patterns. These can be
derived from communication records. However, these records contain privacy
relevant information of the call participants. These records are also protected by
a number of laws and regulations. One has to consider all these laws and
regulations and the privacy concerns of call participants before an analysis can
be done. We propose a method for changing communication records in such a
way that the forensic analysis for VoIP attacks is possible and the privacy of the
call participants is preserved. We define privacy requirements for
communication records from laws, regulations and concerns of call participants.
We also present patterns of communication records based on real world
examples. Moreover, analysis patterns for VoIP attack states which have
relations to communication records that have to survive the data minimization.

Keywords: Privacy, CDRs, PIA, Communication Records, VoIP, PETs.

1   Introduction

Communication records contain information about telephone calls, e.g., which person
called what person, the duration of the call. This information can be used for different
kinds of security analyses, for instance, to prevent toll fraud attacks (Beckers, K.,
Hofbauer, S., Quirchmayr, G., Sorge, C., 2012). However, communication records
also contain personal information. Hence, the privacy of the callers and callees in
these records has to be preserved. We present a structured approach to elicit privacy
requirements for communication record analysis. In addition, we present privacy
measures that fulfil these measures.

N. Aseeva, E. Babkin, and O. Kozyrev (Eds.): BIR 2012, LNBIP 128, pp. 148–161, 2012.

2   A Privacy Impact Analysis Approach Building on the PIA Guide

According to widely accepted privacy impact analysis guides, the core steps in a privacy oriented analysis of IT projects are the mapping of the information flows and privacy framework, the privacy impact analysis and privacy management. One of the leading examples is the privacy impact analysis (PIA) guide for government agencies (Australian Government, 2010). This assessment tool analyses the flow of personal information and the possible privacy impacts of these flows on individuals of a given project. A PIA has five key stages according to (Australian Government, 2010). We extend it by a sixth step: 1. Project description: Describe the scope of the project including the aims and if there is personal information involved. 2. Mapping the information flows and privacy framework: Describe the personal information flows in the project and document relevant laws and regulations, as well as organisational rules. 3. Privacy impact analysis: Identify and analyse the privacy impact of the project. 4. Privacy management: Choose mechanisms that manage the privacy impact and still achieve the goals of the project. 5. Recommendations: Generate a PIA report that contains recommendations based upon the previous stages. 6. Model scenario: Instantiate a model of the scenario described. We conduct the PIA for the scenario in this paper.

a. Project description:
VoIP calls are conducted between a caller and one or more callees. Both are customers of a telecommunications provider and they use the infrastructure of this provider. These are the stakeholders of this scenario. The data of the calls occurring in this scenario are stored in Call Detail Records (CDR)s. These are stored at a data centre owned by the telecommunication provider. The telecommunication provider analyses the CDR to prevent VoIP attacks. The results of the analysis are used to generate automatic white lists of their clients. We investigate Cisco CDRs, because the vendor is of reasonable practical significance (Gartner Inc., 2010). The data in CDRs can be classified in primary and secondary personal information. Analysis of primary personal information can help identifying a stakeholder directly with reasonable in time and money. Secondary information personal information can derive actions of a stakeholder. For instance, the knowledge of the filled date time might lead to identify the caller's habits or even to identify possible callees.

b. Mapping the information flows and privacy framework:
The information flow in this scenario starts from a callee to the telecommunications provider and results at the callee. The laws in the EU, Germany and the US also demand that telecommunications data is only stored for a specific purpose and deleted after the purpose is no longer valid. The usage of the data beyond this purpose requires an informed consent of the owner of the personal information. We elicit the following privacy requirements for CDRs data from legal norms and laws: Communication records have to be kept confidential

— Communication records can only be stored as long as there is a valid reason, e.g., for billing purposes of the telecommunications provider
— Customers have to provide their informed consent if their communication data is used in an VoIP attack analysis
— Communication records have to be deleted if none of the cases above apply

Our review of the legal aspects and further privacy impact assessment is focused on a business perspective and does not consider any of the special exceptions for law enforcement. Nissenbaum (Nissenbaum, H., 2004) stated the sources of privacy norms are law, history, and culture. According to Art. 6 ePrivacy Directive 2002/46/EC, traffic data must be erased or made anonymous when it is no longer needed. Users of subscribers shall be given the possibility to withdraw their consent for the processing of traffic data at any time. The directive of the European parliament and the council regarding data retention states, that this Directive relates only to data generated or processed as a consequence of a communication or a communication service and does not relate to data that are the content of the information communicated. Data should be retained in such a way as to avoid their being retained more than once. In particular, as regards the retention of data relating to Internet e-mail and Internet telephony, the obligation to retain data may apply only in respect of data from the providers' or the network providers' own services. 'Telephone service' means calls (including voice, voicemail and conference and data calls), supplementary services (including call forwarding and call transfer) and messaging and multi-media services (including short message services, enhanced media services and multi-media services) (Hofbauer et al. 2011). After addressing law, we investigate norms originating from culture briefly. For reasons of space we are not focusing on history. These definitions state that persons shall be able to control which personal information is released, to whom it is released to and in what context. We believe that these needs can be addressed with an informed consent. However, the person shall also be able not to share personal information.

c. Privacy impact analysis:
The privacy impact is the amount of people involved and the severity of a possible leakage of personal information (Cisco Systems Inc., 2010). The amount of people in this case is the amount of people using VoIP services of a telecommunications provider. The personal information contains data from which the person can be identified with reasonable amount of time and money. Thus, this leads to a high privacy impact of this project.

d. Privacy management:
In order to identify suitable privacy enhancement technologies (PET)s, we are presenting a number of misuse cases for privacy in the given scenario. The selection of PETs is based on (Deng et al. 2011, Wuyts et al. 2009, Kalloniatis et al. 2008, Spiekermann et al. 2009). For reasons of space we do not provide a detailed pattern for misuse cases. Moreover, we are not addressing PETs for secondary personal information, because we propose to use pseudonymisation with primary personal information. Hence, secondary personal information is of no use to a privacy attacker, as long as he/she does not have a way to identify the person this information belongs to.

e. Recommendations:
We exclude the fifth step of the guide, since we cannot provide a complete PIA report within the page limits of this paper.

f. Model scenario:
In the following scenario, we describe two possible call flows that we have identified from our industrial experience. It describes that whether SIP or ISDN as telephone technology is used, the CDRs are stored on the Private Branch Exchange (PBX). The Cisco Unified Border Element (CUBE) is placed between the PBX and the Internet and therefore knows about every session. For registering the phones to the PBX, either the Session Initiation Protocol (SIP) or the Cisco proprietary Skinny Client Control Protocol (SCCP) is used. In the SIP scenario, a SIP trunk connects the source to the VoIP provider. Our contribution is based on the use of a Call Detail Records Analysis System (CDRAS) and an Intrusion Detection System (IDS) within the call flow. The H.323 protocol is mainly used to connect the network elements (CDRAS, IDS, voice router) to the PBX in use.

The CDRAS approach relies upon timings of IDS analysis in the internet to generate host lists: white-, grey-, and black-lists for VoIP participants. We derive patterns from different combinations of timings that occur in CDRs, e.g., processing time for a call request, the call duration, and the time to destination. In addition, we relate these timing-patterns to call participants in the CDRs. A timing pattern that can lead to an attack are, e.g., call requests in relatively short time intervals. The timings can also relate to the number of available, busy and idle voice channels. The whitelist in our approach is the summary of all hosts known as valid, whereas the blacklist presents all hosts, which are known to be malicious. A host that is member of the greylist is sent to the quarantine, where an administrator has to check whether the host is allowed or disallowed.

We expect that the detection of malicious users that are sent to quarantine will never be perfect. Hence, we propose a semi-automated approach in which a human operator can correct the mistake of a false positive. This correction can be a recall a short time later. The alarming of a human operator or even the call destination is part of our solution. The difference to fully automated approaches is that in these, false positive are more difficult to reconcile, because the machine makes the final decisions. In case of a host being added to the blacklist, the call will not be passed through and, thus, blocked. Of course, hosts need not always reside on the same list. If a host becomes malicious, he will be moved to the blacklist. The host can as well be changed from the blacklist to the whitelist. With our approach in use, we plan to be aware also of other VoIP attacks. The approach complements existing IDS approaches via detecting timing based attacks and giving a recommendation to existing IDS. The CDRAS approach determines the occurrence of fraudulent usage based upon thresholds. The number of acceptable VoIP sessions from an IP address depends on the available bandwidth, but it should of course also be limited to maintain an acceptable quality of service.

Traditional network traffic detection techniques used by IDS are not sufficient to analyse VoIP specific communication records. A basic installation of IDS like SNORT without VOIP rules does not protect against VoIP attacks, but we are using CDRAS complementary to the IDS SNORT and extend it with the detection of VoIP attacks through extended rules. The difference to SNORT is that our approach uses behaviour based learning, based on Bayesian networks to also protect against novel attacks. We base our work on a hybrid IDS. A hybrid detection system is a signature based IDS combined with an anomaly detection system. Signature-based IDS compare the state of a system against a number of attack signatures, while anomaly based detection systems capture the normal behaviour of a system in a profile and detect when the system diverges significantly from the profile (Pfleeger & Pfleerger, 2007) We and Zhang (Zhang et al., 2008) believe that a hybrid detection system is better compared to a signature based IDS or anomaly detection system alone, in terms of false positive rates and the detection of unknown attacks.

This model can be instantiated and further used for other scenarios and domains. The prerequisite is the use of communication records within the call flow.

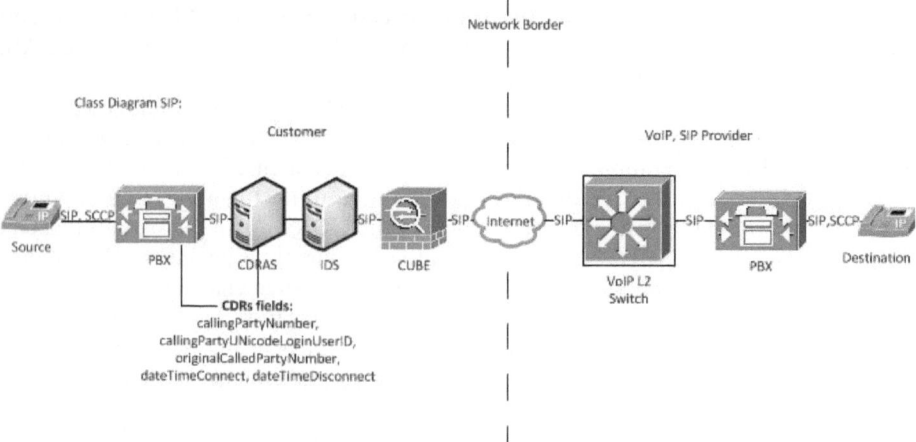

Fig. 1. Class Diagram for a SIP scenario

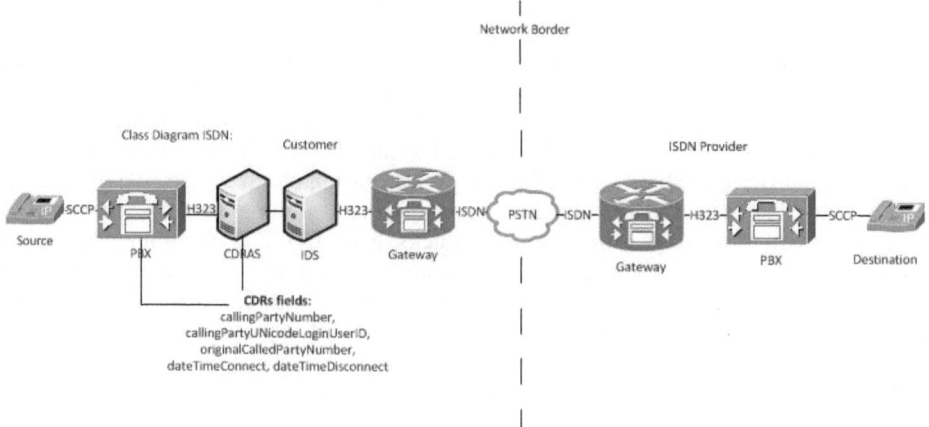

Fig. 2. Class Diagram for an ISDN scenario

In essence, we identify the following privacy requirements for CDRs:

— Confidentiality of the data in CDRs
— Storing CDRs data requires a reason compliant with the law
— Analysing CDRs requires an informed consent of the call participants
— CDRs have to be erased when the previous requirements are not fulfilled

3   Deriving Privacy Requirements for Communication Records

3.1   A Method for Privacy Preserving CDRs Analysis

We present a method for ensuring privacy in a CDRs analysis. Each step of the
method is written in bold and the execution of the step is written in the following.

a. Description of the context and stakeholders

VoIP calls are conducted between caller and one or more callees. Both are
customers of a telecommunications provider and they use the infrastructure of
this provider. The VoIP technology uses VoIP hard phones, physical devices and
soft phones, software running on a personal computer. In some cases, the call
participants might use Public Switched Telephone Network (PSTN) phones and
the call is just transferred to VoIP via a PSTN gateway. The telecommunication
provider has also relations to security analysts that can provide protection from
VoIP attacks. These experts, however, are not employees of the
telecommunication company. The data, of the call occurred, are stored in CDRs.
These are stored at a data center owned by the telecommunication provider. The
telecommunication provider forwards these calls to the security analysts to
analyse possible VoIP attacks. The telecommunication provider uses the results
of the analysis to generate automatic white lists for their clients.

b. Identification of personal information in data

Table 1. CDRs Fields with primary personal information

Field	Relation to Privacy
origIPAddr	Might lead to identfying the caller with reasonable efforts in time and money.
callingPartyNumber	
callingPartyUnicode	
origMediaTransport	
destIpAddr	Might lead to identfying the callee with reasonable efforts in time and money.
originalCalled	
FinallyCalledParty	
destMediaTransport	

Table 2. CDRs Fields with secondary personal information

Field	Relation to Privacy
dateTime Origination	This might lead to identify the callers habits or even to identify possible callees. For instance, most callers would not call their doctors at 8 p.m. on Christmas eve.
dateTime Connect	This might lead to identify the callers habits or even to identify possible callees.
dateTime Disconnect	The duration of the call might allow a guess to what subjects were discussed. For example, agreeing on a meeting point should be quick, while discussing a research matter might take longer.
duration	The duration of the call might allow a guess if the call participants are malicious.

The data in CDRs can be classified in primary and secondary personal information. Analysis of primary personal information can help identifying a stakeholder, while secondary information can derive actions of a stakeholder. Table 1 lists the fields with primary personal information. Table 2 describes CDR fields containing secondary personal information.

c. Elicitation of privacy requirements from legal and cultural aspects

Nissenbaum (Nissenbaum, H., 2004) stated the sources of privacy norms are law, history, and culture. For reasons of space we are focusing on norms from law and culture. Law will be further distinguished into US and German law. We are starting with culture as a source for privacy norms from which we will derive privacy requirements. We use the definition of privacy by Pfleeger and Pfleeger (Pfleeger & Pfleeger, 2007) as a source for a cultural privacy norm.

The definition states that everyone can control the distribution of their personal information. The first part of this method already described the context of the situation and the information in Tab. 1 and Tab. 2 states that the data in the CDRs are personal information. The call participants have to decide if this information can be used by the telecommunications companies or not. In any case should the call participants give their informed consent that this data can be used for a VoIP analysis and protection. In addition, a privacy mechanism has to be used during the analysis (Pfitzmann A., Hansen M., 2011). Pfitzmann further introduces a terminology for privacy via data minimization. The authors define central terms of privacy using items of interest (IOIs), e.g., subjects, messages and actions. Anonymity means a subject is not identifiable within a set of subjects, the anonymity set. Unlinkability of two or more IOIs means that within a system the attacker cannot sufficiently distinguish whatever these IOIs are related or not. Undetectability of an IOI means that the attacker cannot sufficiently distinguish whatever it exist or not. Unobservability of an IOI means undetectability of the IOI against all subjects uninvolved in it and anonymity of the subject(s) involved in the IOI even against the other subject(s) involved in that IOI. A pseudonym is an identifier of a subject other than one of the subject's real names. Using pseudonyms means pseudonimity. Identity Management means managing various partial identities (usually denoted by pseudonyms) of an individual, i.e., administration of identity attributes including the development and choice of the partial identity and pseudonym to be (re-)used in a specific context or role.

We discuss possible mechanisms during the threat analysis part of this method. The laws in the EU, Germany and the US also demand an informed consent for CDRs analysis, e.g., in FIPs, EU Data Protection Directive, BDSG and SCA. Moreover, telephone calls have to be kept confidential according to the Telecommunication laws in the US and Germany. In general, confidentiality is seen as a mechanism to enforce privacy (Danezis, G., Gürses, S., 2011). The SCA in the US, the EUDRD and the German laws TKG and TKÜV demand CDR data retentions. This is in conflict with the cultural privacy requirements, where all persons should be allowed to deny the storage of their personal information. The authors of this paper cannot solve this conflict and the space of it is not sufficient to discuss it in detail. Hence, we consider only the laws for the remainder of this paper. However, this does not reflect the opinion of the authors. We are proposing to use stored CDRs data for security analysis and use the results to protect telecommunication users. When applying satisfying privacy mechanisms and getting the informed consent of the call participants this should be within reason.

d. Conducting a Privacy Threat Analysis

We are using the threat analysis approach by Deng et al. (Deng et al. 2011) in this method. The stakeholder shall reveal only the minimum amount of data that is necessary for performing a specific task. The policy and consent compliance property states the requirement for a privacy policy. Stakeholders, who control personal information of other stakeholders, have to inform these other stakeholders about their privacy policy. They also have to specify consents in compliance with legislation for the stakeholders that shall enter personal information into a system. Stakeholders that enter personal information into the system have to constant to these policies, before their personal information enters the system. The privacy threats for CDRs are listed in Tab. 3. A "+" in Tab. 3 marks a privacy threat to a CDRs field or a stakeholder. However, the free cells of the table do not imply that a CDRs field or stakeholder is not subject to a privacy threat. The threat levels are classifies as following: Serious (S), Normal (N) and Merely (M).

The misuse cases in Tab. 4 are derived from the subjects (Linkability, Identifyability, Non-repudiation, Detectability, Disclosure of information, Content unawareness, Policy and Consent Non-Compliance), while the privacy requirements are proposals from the authors. The privacy requirements state that users shall be informed, if their personal information in CDRs is used for a purpose that differs from the purpose these were collected for. In this case users should be allowed not to participate. The source and the destination are user telephones. Hence, users are located at these locations in our scenario. The destination is assumed to be users inside a company. These can be informed in a meeting before using the telephone system for the first time and their informed consent can be collected or they deny their consent and the system is not used for these destinations.

Collecting an informed consent from the source, however, is difficult. For practical reasons, not every source can be queried. However, there are alternative options: the PBX can repeat an automated recorded message for first time callers, informing the caller of the usage of CDRAS and asks for her/his agreement or disagreement. Alternatively, the callers could be asked by their respective providers, and a PBX could include a list of providers who ask for that consent. If a source does not allow processing of his personal data for purposes of the system, the destination might use a policy to block calls from this source. Similarly, even nowadays, it is possible to block all calls whose caller ID is suppressed. This is not illegal if the destination decides about the policy. In German law, for example, suppression of mailings is a criminal act, but this is not true for suppression of phone calls (Sorge et al., 2010).

Table 3. Privacy Threats to CDRs fields and stakeholders

Privacy Threat Target	L	I	N	D	D	U	N	T
origIPAddr	+	+	+	+	+		+	N
callingPartyNumber	+	+	+	+	+		+	S
origMediaTransport Addr. IP+Port	+	+	+	+	+		+	N
destIpAddr	+	+	+	+	+		+	M
originalCalledPartyNumber	+	+	+	+	+		+	N
finalCalledParty Number	+	+	+	+	+		+	S
destMediaTransport Addr. IP+Port	+	+	+	+	+		+	M
dateTimeOrigination	+	+	+	+	+		+	N
dateTimeConnect	+	+	+	+	+		+	N
dateTimeDisconnect	+	+	+	+	+		+	N
duration	+	+	+	+	+		+	S
stakeholder caller	+	+				+		N
stakeholder callee	+	+				+		M

From the left-hand side to the right-hand side: Linkability(L), Identifyability(I), Non-repudiation(N), Detectability(D), Disclosure of information(D), Content unawareness(U), Policy and Consent Non-Compliance(N), Threat Level (T)

The information in Tab. 1 and Tab. 2 can be classified as privacy stage 1 in the framework of Spiekermann (Spiekermann et al., 2009). The reason is that the information in the CDRs, e.g., origIPAddr can be classified as a pseudonym. In stage 1 the pseudonym is linkable with reasonable and automatable effort.

e. Deriving privacy requirements from the threat analysis and choosing privacy enhancement technologies (PET)s

Several solution strategies exist for fulfilling privacy requirements [9]:

— A solution for low risk threats is to warn users.
— Turning the risk to zero can only be achieved via removing or turning off the feature that causes the privacy threat.
— Using countermeasures for privacy threats in the form of preventive or reactive privacy-enhancement technologies.

Table 4. From misuse cases to privacy requirements and mechanisms

Misuse Case	Privacy Requirements	Privacy Mechanism
1. Identifiability at CDR data store at the telecommunications provider	Pseudonymity so that a call participant cannot be identified from a CDRs Protection of the CDRs data records.	Apply an pseudonymisation technique, such as privacy enhancing identity management systems (Clauß, S. et al. 2005)
2. Identifiability of call participants	Pseudonymise User IDs and call numbers in CDRs (see Tab.1)	Apply an pseudonymisation technique, e.g. privacy enhancing identity management systems (Clauß, S. et al. 2005)
3. Detectability of CDRs data	Prevent an attacker to determine how many data sets exist in the CDRs storage	Allocate the maximum storage for CDRs in the database and fill it with randomly created CDRs, replace the randomly created CDRs with real ones.
4. Information disclosure of the data in storage CDRs	Release of CDRs data store should be controlled according to the call participants privacy preference. Keep CDR records confidential.	Enforce data protection by using access control (American National Standards Institute, 2004) and confidentiality in the form of encryption.
5. Content Unawareness of Users	Users need to be aware that the CDRs data is used for VoIP attack prevention including an informed consent. Users should be allowed not to participate.	Provide feedback to raise call participant's privacy awareness, e.g., via a tool according to Patil et al.(Patil, S. et al. 2009).
6. Policy and consent non-compliance of the VoIP system	Monitor the compliance of the VoIP system with law and guidelines. Call participants are aware of the privacy policy and can recognize and react to a violation. Employees of the tele-communication companies have specified privacy rules and they obey these rules. Security analysts have a specific set of privacy rules and they obey these. They are only allowed to work with pseudo-nymised CDR data.	Hire a legal expert to supervise the creation and operations of the VoIP system. Install logging and monitoring software that documents the lifecycles of all personal information. This lifecycles include the creation, usage, access from persons, and deletion of the personal information. Inform call participants of possible signs of a violation and provide a help desk to who these violations can be reported to. Policy communication can be realized via P3P (Platform for privacy preferences project, 2002) and policy enforcement via XACML (OASIS, 2005). Ensure that employees and security analysts are trained for privacy-enhancing operations of the VoIP system. If any of these persons disclose personal information they are penalized,

The callers and callees shall be warned that their CDRs are analysed for the purpose of preventing VoIP attacks. The feature can be adopted in such a way that users can object to it and is turned off for these users. However, our priority is to apply countermeasures to the privacy threats and enable a privacy preserving analysis feature.

In order to identify suitable privacy enhancement technologies (PET)s, we are presenting a number of misuse cases for privacy in the given scenario. These are derived from the information collected in the method up to this point and the privacy threat tree from Deng (Deng et al. 2011). The selection of privacy enhancement technologies is based on various approaches (Deng et al. 2011, Spiekermann et al. 2009, Wuyts et al. 2009, Kalloniatis et a., 2008).

The privacy of the call participants shall be preserved in the CDR information stored in the database. The authors (Clauß et al., 2005) propose a method for privacy enhancing identity management. In order to achieve privacy for the call participants, it is the unlinkability between persons and their actions. One way of achieving this is to replace the information leading to the identity of a person with a pseudonym. The method of the authors also demands to specify if the data is stored in a database or if the information is also transported over a network. We consider only the stored information in the database. The network transfer of information will be used in the future. We present short misuse cases, derive privacy requirements and resulting privacy mechanisms in Tab. 4. For reasons of space we do not provide a detailed pattern for misuse cases. In comparison, the approach from Spiekermann (Spiekermann et al. 2009) describes that privacy-by-policy implementations have to consider four different areas. We are now describing relations between the Spiekermann et al. approach and Tab. 4. The first area Spiekermann et al. consider is to give users notice and choice. This area is covered by the 6. case. The second area concerns access control. This mechanism is suggested as a result of the 2. case. The third is about the responsibility to inform users about data sharing. This is also part of the mechanisms of case 6. The last area concerns technical mechanisms to audit and enforce privacy. This is covered in the 7. case. Thus, all areas named in the work of Spiekermann et al. are covered in Tab. 4.

We propose to integrate CDRAS in this scenario to fulfil the privacy requirements listed in Tab 4. We assume in this example that all the destinations, the telephone users of the providers or in the company, gave their informed consent to the call filtering. In addition, we also assume that a menace exists to inform the source that CDRAS is used and the source also gave an informed consent. In our system, the CDRs are substituted with pseudonyms. CDRAS will provide a database that is protected with access control that links the pseudonyms to the real values. In addition, the CDRs have a time stamp that states their creation. The database automatically erases the database records that link the pseudonyms to the values of real users after a reasonable time, in this example three days.

f. Reconciliation of legal, cultural and threat driven privacy requirements

The requirements derived from legal and cultural aspects have to be free of conflicts with the requirements derived from privacy threats. We show relations between the legal and cultural requirements and the privacy requirement in Tab. 4. The first legal and cultural requirement is that records have to be kept confidential. Confidentiality is part of the requirements of case 5. We further address the confidentiality requirement for CDRs. This requires the configuration of access control measures in VoIP hard- and soft phones, as well as the PBX, IDS and CDRAS. The configuration has to reflect that only administrators are allowed to investigate CDRs and that the access to the CDRs is recorded in, e.g., log files. These files have to reflect the names of the persons that accessed the CDRs. Hence, non-repudiation of access to CDRs is guaranteed. Otherwise it is not possible to prove that the confidentiality privacy requirement is fulfilled The legal and cultural requirements that CDRs can only be stored for a limited amount of time are in accordance with the requirements from the 7.case. The informed consent legal-cultural requirement is in accordance with the privacy requirements of case 6. The last legal-and-cultural requirement is that CDRs have to be deleted if no legal regulation applies. This is part of the requirements of case 7.

4   Results

The privacy requirements presented in the beginning of this section only apply as long as personal information is stored in the communication records. If the records are anonymised, the personal information is replaced with other content, the storage and analysis would not be affected by the law. However, these would render the records useless for attack prevention, since attacks could no longer be identified and blocked. A compromise between these two is the pseudonymisation of the CDRs. In this case the personal information in these records is replaced with other content. We use an HMAC algorithm as specified in RFC 2104 (IETF, 1997) and based on (Jorns et al, 2007) in order to generate the pseudonym. However, the relations between the original and the replaced content still exist in a database. This database has to be kept confidential via mechanism like access control or encryption. In this scenario a pseudonymisation technique that applies to the CDRs fields containing primary personal information.

5   Related Work

Sorge (Sorge et al. 2010) investigate the legal issues involved with call filtering solutions to prevent Spam over Internet Telephony. The authors describe the legal situation for the US and the German legal system). Deng (Deng et al. 2011) present a comprehensive framework to model privacy threats in software- based systems. They also provide a systematic methodology to model privacy-specific threats. Hofbauer (Hofbauer et al. 2011) present an approach to dealing with Man-in-the-Middle (MitM) attacks in the context of VoIP. Legal aspects are also covered in this paper as well as a suggested approach to risk management. Tartarelli (Tartarelli et al. 2010) describe how information is stored in different types of CDRs and how to check the sanity of telecommunication data stored in these. Fernandez (Fernandez et al., 2010) designed several UML models of some aspects of VoIP infrastructure, including architectures and basic use cases. The authors also present security patterns that describe countermeasures to VoIP attacks.

6   Conclusion

We have established a structured method to conduct a privacy impact analysis for example when analysing communication records for security purposes. The approach provides a structured analysis of privacy requirements from users and laws.

Our approach offers the following main benefits:

A **structured method** to conduct a privacy impact analysis, considering privacy requirements from users and laws, **systematic pattern-based identification** of privacy requirements for communication records, **ease the burden of identifying privacy measures** that fulfill the requirements, **improve the privacy preservation** of call participants during security analysis of communication records, **systematic identification of relevant privacy threats** and determining privacy mechanisms for communication records, improve the outcome of communication systems implementations by adding security from communication record analysis, **re-use the structured techniques** of privacy engineering methods for analyzing and elicitation of privacy requirements to support the lawful operation of communication security systems.

In our future work we will extend the systematic privacy analysis to further security analysis, for instance, the usage of cloud computing services.

References

1. Australian Government – Office of the Privacy Commissioner: Privacy Impact Assessment Guide. Australian Government (2010),
   http://www.privacy.gov.au/materials/types/download/9509/6590
2. Gartner Inc.: Gartner Magic Quadrant for Unified Communications 2010. Gartner Inc. (2010), http://msunified.net/2010/08/09/gartner-magic-quadrant-for-unified-communications-2010/
3. Nissenbaum, H.: Privacy as contextual integrity. Washington Law Review 79(1), 101–139 (2004)
4. Hofbauer, S., Quirchmayr, G., Wills, C.C.: CDRAS: An approach to dealing with Man-in-the-Middle attacks in the context of Voice over IP. In: International Conference on Availability, Reliability and Security, ARES 2011, pp. 353–358 (August 2011)
5. Cisco Systems Inc.: Cisco Call Detail Records Field Descriptions. Cisco Systems Inc. (2010), http://www.cisco.com/en/US/docs/
   voice_ip_comm/cucm/service/8_5_1/cdrdef/cdrfdes.html
6. Deng, M., Wuyts, K., Scandariato, R., Preneel, B., Joosen, W.: A privacy threat analysis framework: supporting the elicitation and fulfillment of privacy requirements. Requir. Eng. 16, 3–32 (2011)
7. Wuyts, K., Scandariato, R., De Decker, B., Joosen, W.: Linking privacy solutions to developer goals. In: International Conference on Availability, Reliability and Security, ARES 2009, pp. 847–852 (2009)
8. Kalloniatis, C., Kavakli, E., Gritzalis, S.: Addressing privacy requirements in systems design: the pris method. Requir. Eng. 13, 241–255 (2008)
9. Spiekermann, S., Cranor, L.F.: Engineering Privacy. IEEE Transactions on Software Engineering 35(1), 67–82 (2009)

10. Pfleeger, C.P., Pfleeger, S.L.: Security in Computing, 4th edn. Prentice Hall PTR (2007)
11. Zhang, J., Zulkernine, M., Haque, A.: Random-forest-based network intrusion detection systems. IEEE Trans. Syst. Man Cybernet. C Appl. Rev., 84–93 (2008)
12. Pfitzmann, A., Hansen, M.: A terminology for talking about privacy by data minimization: Anonymity, unlinkability, unobservability, pseudonymity, and identity management – version v0.34, TU Dresden and ULD Kiel, Tech. Rep. (2011), http://dud.inf.tu-dresden.de/literatur/Anon_Terminology_v0.34.pdf
13. Danezis, G., Gürses, S.: A critical review of 10 years of privacy technology. In: Proceedings of Surveillance Cultures: A Global Surveillance Society?, UK (2011), http://homes.esat.kuleuven.be/~sguerses/papers/DanezisGuersesSurveillancePets2010.pdf
14. Clauß, S., Kesdogan, D., Kölsch, T.: Privacy enhancing identity management. Protection against re-identification and profiling. In: Proceedings of the 2005 Workshop on Digital Identity Management, DIM 2005, pp. 84–93. ACM (2005)
15. American National Standards Institute (ANSI), American national standard for information technology – role based access control, ANSI, ANSI INCITS 359-2004 (2004)
16. Beckers, K., Hofbauer, S., Quirchmayr, G., Sorge, C.: A process for the automatic generation of white-, grey-, and black-lists from Call Detail Records to prevent VoIP attacks while preserving privacy. In: International Conference on Availability, Reliability and Security, ARES 2012 (August 2012)
17. Patil, S., Kobsa, A.: Privacy considerations in awareness systems. Designing with privacy in mind. In: Markopoulos, P., De Ruyter, B., Mackay, W. (eds.) Awareness Systems. Human-Computer Interaction Series, pp. 187–206. Springer, London (2009)
18. Platform for privacy preferences project, W3C (2002), http://www.w3.or/TR/P3P/
19. OASIS, eXtensible Access Control Markup Language TC v2.0 (XACML), OASIS (2005), http://docs.oasis-open.org/xacml/2.0/access-control-xacml-2.0-core-spec-os.pdf
20. IETF, Hmac: Keyed-hashing for message authentication, Internet Engineering Task Force (IETF), IETF RFC 2104 (1997), http://tools.ietf.org/rfc/rfc2104.txt
21. Jorns, Jung, O., Quirchmayr, G.: Transaction pseudonyms in mobile environments. In: EICAR 2007 Best Academic Paper, pp. 49–58 (2007)
22. Sorge, C., Niccolini, S., Seedorf, J.: The legal ramifications of call-filtering solutions. IEEE Security and Privacy 8, 45–50 (2010)
23. Tartarelli, S., d'Heureuse, N., Niccolini, S.: Lessons learned on the usage of call logs for security and management in IP telephony. IEEE Communications Magazine 48(12), 76–82 (2010)
24. Fernandez, E.B., Pelaez, J.C., Larrondo-Petrie, M.M.: Security patterns for voice over IP networks. In: Proceedings of the International Multi-Conference on Computing in the Global Information Technology, pp. 19–29. IEEE Computer Society, Washington, DC (2007)

Gaining Insight in Social Networks
with Biclustering and Triclustering

Dmitry Gnatyshak[1], Dmitry I. Ignatov[1], Alexander Semenov[1],
and Jonas Poelmans[1,2]

[1] National Research University Higher School of Economics, Russia
dignatov@hse.ru
http://www.hse.ru
[2] Katholieke Universiteit Leuven, Belgium

Abstract. We combine bi- and triclustering to analyse data collected
from the Russian online social network Vkontakte. Using biclustering we
extract groups of users with similar interests and find communities of
users which belong to similar groups. With triclustering we reveal users'
interests as tags and use them to describe Vkontakte groups. After this
social tagging process we can recommend to a particular user relevant
groups to join or new friends from interesting groups which have a similar
taste. We present some preliminary results and explain how we are going
to apply these methods on massive data repositories.

Keywords: Formal Concept Analysis, Biclustering and Triclustering,
Online Social Networks, Web 2.0 and Social Computing.

1 Introduction

Online social networks generate massive amounts of data which can become a
valuable source for guiding Internet advertisement efforts. Each registered user
has a network of friends as well as specific profile features. These profile features
describe the user's tastes, preferences, the groups he or she belongs to, etc. Social
network analysis is a popular research field in which methods are developed for
analysing 1-mode networks, like friend-to-friend, 2-mode [1,2,3], 3-mode [4,5,6]
and even multimodal dynamic networks [7,8,9]. We will focus on the subfield of
bicommunity and tricommunity identification.

There is a large amount of network data that can be represented as bipartite or tripartite graphs. Standard techniques like "maximal bicliques search"
return a huge number of patterns (in the worst case exponential w.r.t. the input size). Therefore we need some relaxation of the biclique notion and good
interestingness measures for mining biclique communities.

Applied lattice theory provides us with a notion of formal concept [10] which
is the same thing as a biclique; it is widely known in the social network analysis
community (see, e.g. [11,12,13,14,15,16]).

A concept-based bicluster [17] is a scalable approximation of a formal concept
(biclique). The advantages of concept-based biclustering are:

N. Aseeva, E. Babkin, and O. Kozyrev (Eds.): BIR 2012, LNBIP 128, pp. 162–171, 2012.

1. Less number of patterns to analyze;
2. Less computational time (polynomial vs exponential);
3. Manual tuning of bicluster (community) density threshold;
4. Tolerance to missing (object, attribute) pairs.

For analyzing three-mode network data like folksonomies [18] we also proposed a triclustering technique [6]. In this paper we describe a new pseudo-triclustering technique for tagging groups of users by their common interest. This approach differs from traditional triclustering methods because it relies on the extraction of biclusters from two separate object-attribute tables. Biclusters which are similar with respect to their extents are merged by taking the intersection of the extents. The intent of the first bicluster and the intent of the second bicluster become the intent and modus respectively of the newly obtained tricluster. Our approach was empirically validated on online social network data obtained from Vkontakte (`http://vk.com`).

The remainder of the paper is organized as follows. In section 2 we describe some key notions from Formal Concept Analysis and Biclustering. In section 3 we introduce the model for our new pseudo-triclustering approach. In section 4 we describe a dataset which consists of a sample of users, their groups and interests extracted from the Vkontakte (`http://vk.com`) social networking website. We present the results obtained during experiments on this dataset in Section 5. Section 6 concludes our paper and describes some interesting directions for future research.

2   Basic Definitions

2.1   Formal Concept Analysis

The formal context in FCA [10] is a triple $\mathbb{K} = (G, M, I)$, where G is a *set of objects*, M is a *set of attributes*, and the relation $I \subseteq G \times M$ shows which object possesses which attribute. For any $A \subseteq G$ and $B \subseteq M$ one can define *Galois operators*:

$$A' = \{m \in M \mid gIm \text{ for all } g \in A\}, \tag{1}$$
$$B' = \{g \in G \mid gIm \text{ for all } m \in B\}.$$

The operator $''$ (applying the operator $'$ twice) is a *closure operator*: it is idempotent ($A'''' = A''$), monotonous ($A \subseteq B$ implies $A'' \subseteq B''$) and extensive ($A \subseteq A''$). The set of objects $A \subseteq G$ such that $A'' = A$ is called closed. The same is for closed attribute sets, subsets of a set M. A couple (A, B) such that $A \subset G$, $B \subset M$, $A' = B$ and $B' = A$, is called a *formal concept* of a context $\mathbb{K}$. The sets A and B are closed and called *extent* and *intent* of a formal concept (A, B) correspondingly. For the set of objects A the set of their common attributes A' describes the similarity of objects of the set A, and the closed set A'' is a cluster of similar objects (with the set of common attributes A'). The relation "to be a more general concept" is defined as follows: $(A, B) \geq (C, D)$ iff $A \subseteq C$. The concepts of a formal context $\mathbb{K} = (G, M, I)$ ordered by extensions inclusion form a lattice, which is called *concept lattice*. For its visualization the *line diagrams* (Hasse diagrams) can be used, i.e. cover graph of the relation "to be a more general concept". In the worst case (Boolean lattice) the number of concepts is equal to $2^{\{\min |G|, |M|\}}$, thus, for large contexts, FCA can be used only if the data is sparse. Moreover, one can use different ways of reducing the number of formal concepts (choosing concepts by their stability index or extent size).

2.2 Biclustering

An alternative approach is a relaxation of the definition of formal concept as a maximal rectangle in an object-attribute matrix which elements belong to the incidence relation. One of such relaxations is the notion of an object-attribute bicluster [17]. If $(g, m) \in I$, then (m', g') is called object-attribute bicluster with the density $\rho(m', g') = |I \cap (m' \times g')|/(|m'| \cdot |g'|)$.

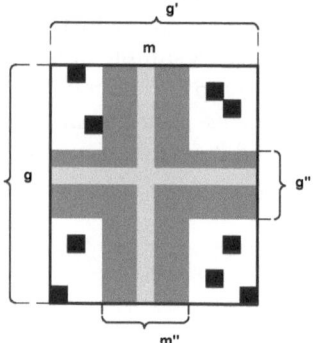

Fig. 1. OA-bicluster

The main features of OA-biclusters are listed below:

1. For any bicluster $(A, B) \subseteq 2^G \times 2^M$ it is true that $0 \leq \rho(A, B) \leq 1$.
2. OA-bicluster (m', g') is a formal concept iff $\rho = 1$.
3. If (m', g') is a bicluster, then $(g'', g') \leq (m', m'')$.

Let $(A, B) \subseteq 2^G \times 2^M$ be a bicluster and ρ_{min} be a non-negative real number such that $0 \leq \rho_{min} \leq 1$, then (A, B) is called *dense*, if it fits the constraint $\rho(A, B) \geq \rho_{min}$. The above mentioned properties show that OA-biclusters differ from formal concepts by the fact that they do not necessarily have unit density. Graphically it means that not all the cells of a bicluster must be filled by a cross (see fig. 1). The rectangle in figure 1 depicts a bicluster extracted from an object-attribute table. The horizontal gray line corresponds to object g and contains only nonempty cells. The vertical gray line corresponds to attribute m and also contains only nonempty cells. By applying the Galois operator, as explained in section 2.1, one time to g we obtain all its attributes g'. By applying the Galois operator twice to g we obtain all objects which have the same attributes as g. This is depicted in fig. 1 as g''. By applying the Galois operator twice to m we obtain all attributes which belong to the same objects as m. This is depicted in fig. 1 as m''. The white spaces indicate empty cells. The black dots indicate non-empty cells. Whereas a traditional formal concept would cover only the green and gray area, the bicluster also covers the white and black cells. This gives to OA-biclusters some desirable fault-tolerance properties.

Algorithm 1. Bicluster computation

Data: $K = (G, M, I)$ is a formal context, ρ_{min} is a threshold density value of bicluster density

Result: $B = \{(A_k, B_k) | (A_k, B_k) - \text{bicluster}\}$

1 **begin**
2     $Obj.Size = |G|$
3     $Attr.Size = |M|$
4     $B \longleftarrow \emptyset$
5   **for** $g \in G$ **do**
6        $Obj[g] = g'$
7   **for** $m \in M$ **do**
8        $Attr[m] = m'$
9   **for** $g \leftarrow 0$ **to** $|G|$ **do**
10   **for** $m \in Obj[g]$ **do**
11   **if** $\rho(Attr[m], Obj[g]) \geq \rho_{min}$ **then**
12             $B.Add((Attr[m], Obj[g]))$

For calculating biclusters fulfilling a minimal density requirement we need to perform several steps (see 1. The first step consists of applying the Galois operator to all objects in G and then to all attributes in M. Then all biclusters are enumerated in a sequential manner and only those fulfilling the minimal density requirement are retained.

3   Model and Algorithm Description

Let $\mathbb{K}_{UI} = (U, I, X \subseteq U \times I)$ be a formal context which describes what interest $i \in I$ a particular user $u \in U$ has. Similarly, let $\mathbb{K}_{UG} = (U, G, Y \subseteq U \times G)$ be a formal context which indicates what group $g \in G$ user $u \in U$ belongs to.

We can find dense biclusters as $(users, interesets)$ pairs in $\mathbb{K}_{UI}$ using the OA-biclustering algorithm which is described in [17]. These biclusters are groups of users who have similar interests. In the same way we can find communities of users, who belong to similar groups on the Vkontakte social network, as dense biclusters $(users, groups)$.

By means of triclustering we can also reveal users' interests as tags which describe similar Vkontakte groups. So, by doing this we can solve the task of social tagging and recommend to a particular user relevant groups to join or interests to indicate on the page or new friends from interesting groups with similar tastes to follow.

To this end we need to mine a (formal) tricontext $\mathbb{K}_{UIG} = (U, I, G, Z \subseteq U \times I \times G)$, where (u, i, g) is in Z iff $(u, i) \in X$ and $(u, g) \in Y$. A particular tricluster has a form $T_k = (i^X \cap g^Y, u^X, u^Y)$ for every $(u, g, i) \in Z$ with $\frac{|i^X \cap g^Y|}{|i^X \cup g^Y|} \geq \Theta$, where Θ is a predefined threshold between 0 and 1. We can calculate the density of T_k directly, but it takes $O(|U||I||G|)$ time in the worst case, so we prefer to define the quality of such tricluster by density of biclusters (g^Y, u^Y) and (i^X, u^X). We propose to calculate this estimator as $\widehat{\rho}(T_k) = \frac{\rho(g^Y, u^Y) + \rho(i^X, u^X)}{2}$; it's obvious that $0 \leq \widehat{\rho} \leq 1$. We have to note that the third component of a (pseudo)tricluster or triadic formal concept usually is called *modus*.

The algorithm scheme is displayed in Fig. 2. Intuitively, we start from two formal contexts from which we extract biclusters fulfilling the minimal density requirement set for each context separately. We then determine the similarity of biclusters' extents and in case of high similarity their intents are used to form a pseudo-tricluster. We select only those pseudo-triclusters whose average density is above a predefined threshold.

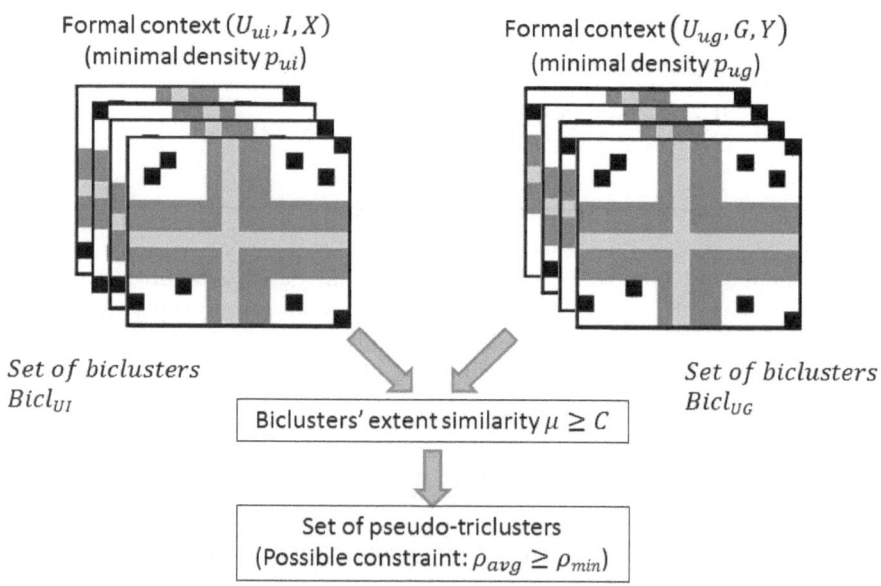

Fig. 2. Pseudo-triclustering algorithm scheme

4   Data

For our experiments we collected a dataset from the Russian social networking site Vkontakte. Each entry consisted of the following fields: id, userid, gender,

Table 1. Basic description of four data sets of large Russian universities

	Bauman	MIPT	RSUH	RSSU
number of users	18542	4786	10266	12281
number of interests	8118	2593	5892	3733
number of groups	153985	46312	95619	102046

family status, birthdate, country, city, institute, interests, groups. This set was divided into 4 subsets based on the values of the institute field, namely students of two major technical universities and two universities focusing on humanities and sociology were considered: The Bauman Moscow State Technical University, Moscow Institute of Physics and Technology (MIPT), the Russian State University for Humanities (RSUH) and the Russian State Social University (RSSU). Then 2 formal contexts, users-interests and users-groups were created for each of these new subsets.

5   Experiments

We performed our experiments under the following setting: Intel Core i7-2600 system with 3.4 GHz and 8 GB RAM. For each of the created datasets the following experiment was conducted: first of all, two sets of biclusters using various minimal density constraints were generated, one for each formal context. Then the sets fulfilling the minimal density constraint of 0.5 were chosen, each pair of their biclusters was enumerated and the pairs with sufficient extents intersection (μ) were added to the corresponding pseudo-tricluster sets. This process was repeated for various values of μ.

Table 2. Bicluster density distribution and elapsed time for different ρ_{min} thresholds (Bauman and MIPT universities).

ρ	Bauman				MIPT			
	UI		UG		UI		UG	
	Time, s	Number	Time, s	Number	Time, s	Number	Time, s	Number
0.0	9.188	8863	1874.458	248077	0.863	2492	109.012	46873
0.1	8.882	8331	1296.056	173786	0.827	2401	91.187	38226
0.2	8.497	6960	966.000	120075	0.780	2015	74.498	28391
0.3	8.006	5513	788.008	85227	0.761	1600	63.888	21152
0.4	7.700	4308	676.733	59179	0.705	1270	56.365	15306
0.5	7.536	3777	654.047	53877	0.668	1091	54.868	13828
0.6	7.324	2718	522.110	18586	0.670	775	44.850	5279
0.7	7.250	2409	511.711	15577	0.743	676	43.854	4399
0.8	7.217	2326	508.368	14855	0.663	654	43.526	4215
0.9	7.246	2314	507.983	14691	0.669	647	43.216	4157
1.0	7.236	2309	511.466	14654	0.669	647	43.434	4148

Table 3. Bicluster density distribution and elapsed time for different ρ_{min} thresholds (RSUH and RSSU universities)

ρ	RSUH				RSSU			
	UI		UG		UI		UG	
	Time, s	number	Time, s	number	Time, s	number	Time, s	number
0.0	3,958	5293	519.772	116882	2.588	4014	693.658	145086
0.1	3.763	4925	419.145	93219	2.450	3785	527.135	110964
0.2	3.656	4003	330.371	68709	2.369	3220	402.159	79802
0.3	3.361	3123	275.394	50650	2.284	2612	332.523	58321
0.4	3.252	2399	232.154	35434	2.184	2037	281.164	40657
0.5	3.189	2087	224.808	32578	2.179	1782	270.605	37244
0.6	3.075	1367	174.657	10877	2.159	1264	211.897	12908
0.7	3.007	1224	171.554	9171	2.084	1109	208.632	10957
0.8	3.032	1188	170.984	8742	2.121	1081	209.084	10503
0.9	2.985	1180	174.781	8649	2.096	1072	206.902	10422
1.0	3.057	1177	173.240	8635	2.086	1068	207.198	10408

Table 4. Number of similar biclusters and elapsed time for different μ thresholds (four universities)

μ	Bauman		MIPT		RSUH		RSSU	
	Time, s	Count	Time, s	Count	Time, s	Count	Time, s	Count
0.0	3353.426	230161	77.562	24852	256.801	35275	183.595	55338
0.1	76.758	10928	35.137	5969	62.736	5679	18.725	5582
0.2	80.647	8539	31.231	4908	58.695	5089	16.466	3641
0.3	77.956	6107	27.859	3770	53.789	3865	17.448	2772
0.4	60.929	31	2.060	12	9.890	14	13.585	12
0.5	66.709	24	2.327	10	9.353	14	12.776	10
0.6	57.803	22	2.147	8	11.352	14	12.268	10
0.7	68.361	18	2.333	8	10.778	12	13.819	4
0.8	70.948	18	2.256	8	9.489	12	13.725	4
0.9	65.527	18	1.942	8	10.769	12	11.705	4
1.0	65.991	18	1.971	8	10.763	12	13.263	4

As it can be seen from the graphs and the tables, the majority of pseudo-triclusters had μ value of 0.3 (or, to be more precise, 0.33). In this series of experiments we didn't reveal manually any interests which are particular for certain universities, but the number of biclusters and pseudo-triclusters was relatively higher for Bauman State University. This is a direct consequence of the higher users' number and the diversity of their groups.

Some examples of obtained biclusters and triclusters with high values of density and similarity are presented below.

Example 1. Biclusters in the form $(Users, Intersts)$.

- $\rho = 83,33\%$, generator pair: $\{3609, home\}$,
  bicluster: $(\{3609, 4566\}, \{family, work, home\})$

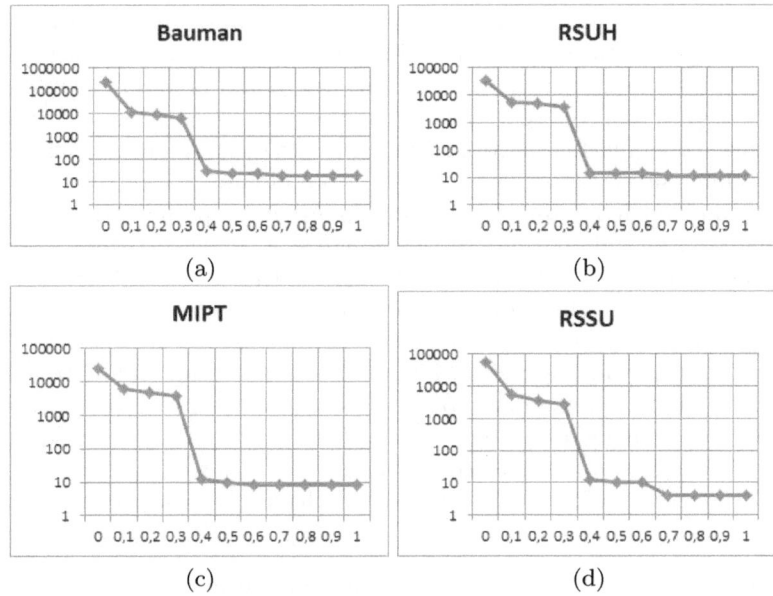

Fig. 3. Density bicluster distribution for the empirical data sets of four Russian universities. (a) Bauman State University (b) Russian State University for Humanities (c) Moscow Physical University (d) Russian State Social University

- $\rho = 83,33\%$, generator pair: $\{30568, orthodox\ church\}$,
  bicluster: $(\{25092, 30568\}, \{music, monastery, orthodox\ church\})$
- $\rho = 100\%$, generator pair: $\{4220, beauty\}$,
  bicluster: $(\{1269, 4220, 5337, 20787\}, \{love, beauty\})$

E.g., the second bicuster can be read as users 25092 and 30568 have almost all "music", "monastery", "orthodox church" as common interests. The pair generator shows which pair $(user, interest)$ was used to build a particular bicluster.

Example 2. Pseudo-triclusters in the form $(Users, Intersts, Groups)$.

Bicluster similarity $\mu = 100\%$, average density $\widehat{\rho} = 54,92\%$.
Users: $\{16313, 24835\}$,
Interests: $\{sleeping, painting, walking, tattoo, hamster, impressions\}$,
Groups: $\{365, 457, 624, \ldots, 17357688, 17365092\}$

This tricluster can be interpreted as a set of two users who have on average 55% of common interests and groups. The two corresponding biclusters have the same extents, i.e. people with almost all interests from the intent of this tricluster and people with almost all groups from the tricluster modus coincide.

6 Conclusions

The approach needs some improvements and fine tuning in order to increase the scalability and quality of the community finding process. We consider several directions for improvements: Strategies for approximate density calculation; Choosing good thresholds for n-clusters density and communities similarity; More sophisticated quality measures like recall and precision in Information Retrieval ([19]); The proposed technique also needs comparison with other approaches like iceberg lattices ([20]), stable concepts ([21]), fault-tolerant concepts ([22]) and different n-clustering techniques from bioinformatics ([23], [24], etc.). We also claim that it is possible to obtain more dense pseudo-triclusters based on conventional formal concepts (even though it is expensive from a computational point of view). To validate the relevance of the exctracted tricommunities expert feedback (e.g., validation by sociologist) is needed.

Finally, we conclude that it is possible to use our pseudo-triclustering method for tagging groups by interests in social networking sites and finding tricommunities. E.g., if we have found a dense pseudo-trciluster (*Users*, *Groups*, *Interests*) we can mark *Groups* by user interests from *Interests*. It also makes sense to use biclusters and triclusters for making recommendations. Missing pairs and triples seem to be good candidates to recommend the target user other potentially interesting users, groups and interests.

Acknowledgments. We would like to thank our colleagues Vincent Duquenne, Sergei Kuznetsov, Sergei Obiedkov, Camille Roth and Leonid Zhukov for their inspirational discussions, which directly or implicitly influenced this study. The study was implemented in the framework of the Basic Research Program at the National Research University Higher School of Economics in 2012 and in the Laboratory of Intelligent Systems and Structural Analysis.

References

1. Latapy, M., Magnien, C., Vecchio, N.D.: Basic notions for the analysis of large two-mode networks. Social Networks 30(1), 31–48 (2008)
2. Liu, X., Murata, T.: Evaluating community structure in bipartite networks. In: Elmagarmid, A.K., Agrawal, D. (eds.) SocialCom/PASSAT, pp. 576–581. IEEE Computer Society (2010)
3. Opsahl, T.: Triadic closure in two-mode networks: Redefining the global and local clustering coefficients. Social Networks 34 (2011) ISSN: 0378-8733, http://www.sciencedirect.com/science/article/pii/S0378873311000360, doi:10.1016/j.socnet.2011.07.001
4. Jäschke, R., Hotho, A., Schmitz, C., Ganter, B., Stumme, G.: TRIAS–An Algorithm for Mining Iceberg Tri-Lattices. In: Proceedings of the Sixth International Conference on Data Mining, ICDM 2006, pp. 907–911. IEEE Computer Society, Washington, DC (2006)
5. Murata, T.: Detecting communities from tripartite networks. In: Rappa, M., Jones, P., Freire, J., Chakrabarti, S. (eds.) WWW, pp. 1159–1160. ACM (2010)
6. Ignatov, D.I., Kuznetsov, S.O., Magizov, R.A., Zhukov, L.E.: From Triconcepts to Triclusters. In: Kuznetsov, S.O., Ślęzak, D., Hepting, D.H., Mirkin, B.G. (eds.) RSFDGrC 2011. LNCS, vol. 6743, pp. 257–264. Springer, Heidelberg (2011)
7. Roth, C.: Generalized preferential attachment: Towards realistic socio-semantic network models. In: ISWC 4th Intl Semantic Web Conference, Workshop on Semantic Network Analysis, Galway, Ireland. CEUR-WS Series, vol. 171, pp. 29–42 (2005) ISSN 1613-0073

8. Roth, C., Cointet, J.P.: Social and semantic coevolution in knowledge networks. Social Networks 32, 16–29 (2010)
9. Yavorsky, R.: Research Challenges of Dynamic Socio-Semantic Networks. In: Ignatov, D., Poelmans, J., Kuznetsov, S. (eds.) CDUD 2011 - Concept Discovery in Unstructured Data. CEUR Workshop proceedings, vol. 757, pp. 119–122 (2011)
10. Ganter, B., Wille, R.: Formal Concept Analysis: Mathematical Foundations, 1st edn. Springer-Verlag New York, Inc., Secaucus (1999)
11. Freeman, L.C., White, D.R.: Using galois lattices to represent network data. Sociological Methodology 23, 127–146 (1993)
12. Freeman, L.C.: Cliques, galois lattices, and the structure of human social groups. Social Networks 18, 173–187 (1996)
13. Duquenne, V.: Lattice analysis and the representation of handicap associations. Social Networks 18(3), 217–230 (1996)
14. White, D.R.: Statistical entailments and the galois lattice. Social Networks 18(3), 201–215 (1996)
15. Mohr, J.W., Duquenne, V.: The Duality of Culture and Practice: Poverty Relief in New York City, 1888-1917. Theory and Society, Special Double Issue on New Directions in Formalization and Historical Analysis 26(2/3), 305–356 (1997)
16. Roth, C., Obiedkov, S., Kourie, D.G.: Towards Concise Representation for Taxonomies of Epistemic Communities. In: Yahia, S.B., Nguifo, E.M., Belohlavek, R. (eds.) CLA 2006. LNCS (LNAI), vol. 4923, pp. 240–255. Springer, Heidelberg (2008)
17. Ignatov, D.I., Kaminskaya, A.Y., Kuznetsov, S., Magizov, R.A.: Method of Biclusterzation Based on Object and Attribute Closures. In: Proc. of 8th International Conference on Intellectualization of Information Processing (IIP 2011), Cyprus, Paphos, October 17-24, pp. 140–143. MAKS Press (2010) (in Russian)
18. Vander Wal, T.: Folksonomy Coinage and Definition (2007), http://vanderwal.net/folksonomy.html (accessed on March 12, 2012)
19. Poelmans, J., Ignatov, D.I., Viaene, S., Dedene, G., Kuznetsov, S.O.: Text Mining Scientific Papers: A Survey on FCA-Based Information Retrieval Research. In: Perner, P. (ed.) ICDM 2012. LNCS (LNAI), vol. 7377, pp. 273–287. Springer, Heidelberg (2012)
20. Stumme, G., Taouil, R., Bastide, Y., Pasquier, N., Lakhal, L.: Computing iceberg concept lattices with titanic. Data & Knowledge Engineering 42(2), 189–222 (2002)
21. Kuznetsov, S.O.: On stability of a formal concept. Ann. Math. Artif. Intell. 49(1-4), 101–115 (2007)
22. Besson, J., Robardet, C., Boulicaut, J.-F.: Mining a New Fault-Tolerant Pattern Type as an Alternative to Formal Concept Discovery. In: Schärfe, H., Hitzler, P., Øhrstrøm, P. (eds.) ICCS 2006. LNCS (LNAI), vol. 4068, pp. 144–157. Springer, Heidelberg (2006)
23. Zhao, L., Zaki, M.J.: Tricluster: an effective algorithm for mining coherent clusters in 3d microarray data. In: Proceedings of the 2005 ACM SIGMOD International Conference on Management of Data, SIGMOD 2005, pp. 694–705. ACM, New York (2005)
24. Mirkin, B.G., Kramarenko, A.V.: Approximate Bicluster and Tricluster Boxes in the Analysis of Binary Data. In: Kuznetsov, S.O., Ślęzak, D., Hepting, D.H., Mirkin, B.G. (eds.) RSFDGrC 2011. LNCS, vol. 6743, pp. 248–256. Springer, Heidelberg (2011)

Developing the Method for Value Assessment of SOA-Based IS Projects

Alexey Likhvarev and Eduard Babkin

Higher School of Economics, Nizhny Novgorod Branch 25/12, B.Pecherskaya str. Nizhny Novgorod, 603155, Russia
likhvarev@gmail.com, eababkin@hse.ru

Abstract. Measuring the value of IT is always a challenge for investors. Market share for service oriented Information Systems (IS) is constantly growing and it creates the demand for methods of measuring the value of SOA-based IS projects. This research is aimed at adopting existing IT Project assessment methods to this growing demand. The work proposes the method that considers the fact that SOA-based IS deployment and evolution could be split in separate flows, one per service. It will allow usage of individual discount rate values per service since project risk values should be different for different services. It should make project value assessment more accurate comparing to existing methods which use the single flow for the entire project. This research also proposes Real Options for calculating the flexibility fraction of the value. The developed method was verified using own simulation model. Both developed method and the simulation model were applied to value assessment of a real-world project.

Keywords: Software Engineering, Investment Appraisal, SOA.

1 Introduction

Service-oriented market share is constantly growing and forecasts predict its growth as well from the current $3.4 billion to $9.1 billion by 2014 (at 17% a year growth) [1]. It means that amount of IT projects involving deployment or evolution of Information Systems (so called IS projects) will be conducted to Service-oriented Architecture (SOA) [2] more and more frequently. It makes adoption of IT project assessment methods to SOA-based projects more valuable. Value measuring methods targeted on IT projects exist but none of them is specifically created for assessments of SOA-based IS projects.

We conduct the research which pursues the goal to develop an effective method for objective value measurement of complex IS projects which intensively use modern features of SOA like Software as Service (SaaS) concept, service outsourcing and others. Demand for such method exists and this method should help investors in decision making while developing an IT projects portfolio. It means the users of this new method are the representatives of the company that wants to develop its IT infrastructure with help of IS project where SOA is involved as an architecture.

N. Aseeva, E. Babkin, and O. Kozyrev (Eds.): BIR 2012, LNBIP 128, pp. 172–186, 2012.

The method being developed will answer the main question involved in decision-making process of such a representative: if the project worth to be kicked-off or not. The main criteria would be a Net Present Value (NPV) provided by the method. The proposed method delivers the NPV discounting cache flows of the project separately per service and taking into consideration the flexibility of the project.

Discounted Cash Flow (DCF) [3] is the major instrument in most of the modern value measurement methods. The most important parameter in this technique is the discount rate which depends on risk. From the point of view of investors risk is variability, be it in the returns in the shares of a company or in the cash flow of a project [4]. Thus the risk factor becomes very significant variable and the importance of it cannot be underestimated. Flexibility is also important and measuring its value should be especially stressed in SOA-based projects since there are alternatives in such projects since services could be developed in-house or obtained using SaaS approach.

This paper proposes new value assessment method for such SOA-based projects, and verifies this method using a simulation model based on System Dynamics approach. The new method takes into consideration specifics of SOA in architecture of IS proposing several modifications to the base assessment method including separate DCF flows for every service and risk assessment-related (project and flexibility components of risk) modifications. The paper is structured as follows. In Section 2 we present conceptual background information for value assessment of IT projects. Section 3 contains description of the proposed assessment method for SOA projects. Then we describe application of the proposed assessment method in the particular case of SOA-based Network Management System in Section 4. The System Dynamics simulation model, verification process and results comparison are discussed in Section 5.

2 Conceptual Background

Investment projects need to be justified and evaluated prior to their start. IT projects are not an exception. There are some common points against IT project valuation [4]:

– resistance from management side
– inadequacy of existing methods, lack of complex approach
– calculation complexity of different risk components and intangible benefits evaluation
– high cost of evaluation process itself because of its complexity

The first point is out of scope of this research. The second and third points are exactly what the method being developed need to deal with. The last point could be covered by valuation process automation with help of decision support systems implementing the valuation method.

IT project valuation methods could depend on one or several IT valuation models from this list [5]:

- NPV models;
- Decision Tree Analysis (DTA) models;
- Financial Options models;
- Real Options models.

The NPV model is based on DCF and it doesn't leave space for managerial flexibility. In real-world applications this type of flexibility usually exists and this is why NPV model is usually used along with some of models especially targeted for flexibility fraction valuation. Combined NPV-DTA model is a popular choice in existing methods of valuation [4,6,7]. One of the main disadvantages of this approach is the need to adjust the discount rate taking into consideration several risk components for every node of the decision tree. It makes this approach to be complicated for practioneers as it was noted by real options method developers [8]. Financial Options models are criticized for inaccurate results and rich set of limitations [9]. Real Options (RO) models are treated as an alternative of DTA approach that solves DTA disadvantages. Some authors point that DTA and RO could provide the same results [10]. This can be achieved if DTA is coupled with utility function estimation and it adds even more complexity to DTA. It makes NPV with Real Options Analysis (ROA) to look like a valid high-level basis for IT project valuation methods. The existing integrated methods are usually proposing NPV-DTA approach [4] while several authors consider using ROA instead of DTA without fitting it into integrated method [10, 11]. This paper proposes using NPV-ROA combination instead of NPV-DTA inside new integrated method that is based on existing integrated method [4] taking into account SOA specifics of projects being evaluated. It is described in details in Section 3.

NPV calculation fraction is affected by SOA architecture as well. Different types of risks are considered in general purpose IT project assessments methods [4]. Company and project risks impact the discount rate while the event risk has impact on Net Present Value (NPV) during flexibility evaluation [4]. SOA brings its own specifics not in IS only but in the assessment techniques as well. In order to take into account specifics of SOA during risk assessment Thomas and vom Brocke [12] propose to extend well-known EPC modeling technique and introduce three-layer diagrams with three separate DCF flows on every Service being considered in the scope of value measurement. Ontology-based approach (OLPIT) was offered on the hand proposing to represent every IT project by the set of atomic and measurable elements defined in the ontology [13]. Separating the main DCF flow of assessment algorithm looks suitable and appropriate for SOA since service orientation leads to high limit of loose coupling and according to SIMM [14] the services are independent entities starting from the low levels of maturity. This is why the EPC-extension-approach [12] with DFC flow separation sounds promising in the scope of value assessment [4]. While separation in several layers does not change discount rate since risks are the same in the scope of one service, but separates outcomes and incomes; the separation of the project in independently assessed services makes believe that discount rate could be different since the risk for every service should be individually calculated.

3   Proposed Assessment Method

In our research the value assessment method of Hares and Royle [4] was selected as a framework. This integrated method is one of the methods based on NPV-DTA and it is logically clear and complete. It uses DCF as an instrument of NPV calculation. This framework method takes into account three types of risk in general: company risk, project risk, event risk. We follow work of Hares and Royle [4] and their approach to relate different types of the risks. The company risk is represented by company *beta* value that could be represented by relative variability of the company shares compared with the variability of the shares of the market as a whole. The project risk is represented by project *beta* factor that is based on the relative variability of the project cash flow to the variability of company shares. Event risk is the one risk that does not have a *beta* factor. And events do not have shares or cash. Their monetary impact on project value is represented by offsetting them via project flexibility. Flexibility valuation is a separate component in the method.

Our research is concentrated on adoption of this framework method to assessment of SOA IS projects. The main idea of modification is to have separate DCF passes for every SOA service involved in the project being assessed instead of one DCF flow for all project contents in the framework method. Since discount rate depends on the company/project risk, those parameters have to be calculated for every service. Event risk in the framework method is accessed via Decision Tree Analysis (DTA) approach. Another crucial point of modification is migration to Real Options Analysis (ROA) in this matter.

3.1   Separating DCF Flows in Respect of Service Orientation

The risk components being used in discount rate definition are (1) the company risk and (2) the project risk. The event risk is used in the separate pass of NVP calculation according to the framework method and it is out of scope at this stage. The company risk is determined using Capital Asset Pricing Model (CAMP) [15] technique. It means that it depends on measure of company's stock's volatility in relation to the market. This parameter is called "company *beta*". The influencing specifics of SOA projects do not change company beta calculation. The common case for such projects is deployment of a service that is indeed owned by another company (provider). Stock's volatilities of two companies still cannot be taken into account because the value assessment is usually taken from one particular side i.e. company and this and only company stock volatility should be taken into consideration.

The project risk is calculated using the Bowater-Scott model [4]. Its value is that it is based on the CAPM [15] but takes into account the variability of money flows in the project. This variability is measured and the *beta* value of the company is adjusted to suit the project. If the cash flow variability is high relative to the company norm the *beta* value goes up for the project (the project is more risky than the company), if it is low it goes down (the project is less risky than the company). Basically the dispersion of variable sources of potential benefits brought by the project is the source of the project *beta* value. Those numbers regarding the variable sources of benefits are supposed to be provided by marketing.

Two main necessary modifications were identified from the literature review:

- Separate DCF flows with individual rates based on individual project risk values should be applied for every service. Summary of NPV values should result in final total NPV for the project.
- The method of project risk calculation mentioned by Hares and Royle [4] itself should be revised and readjusted. The dispersion looks too vague since it takes into account only three points for every outcome component. Instead, the subjective distribution proceeding with Monte Carlo modeling is suggested for use.

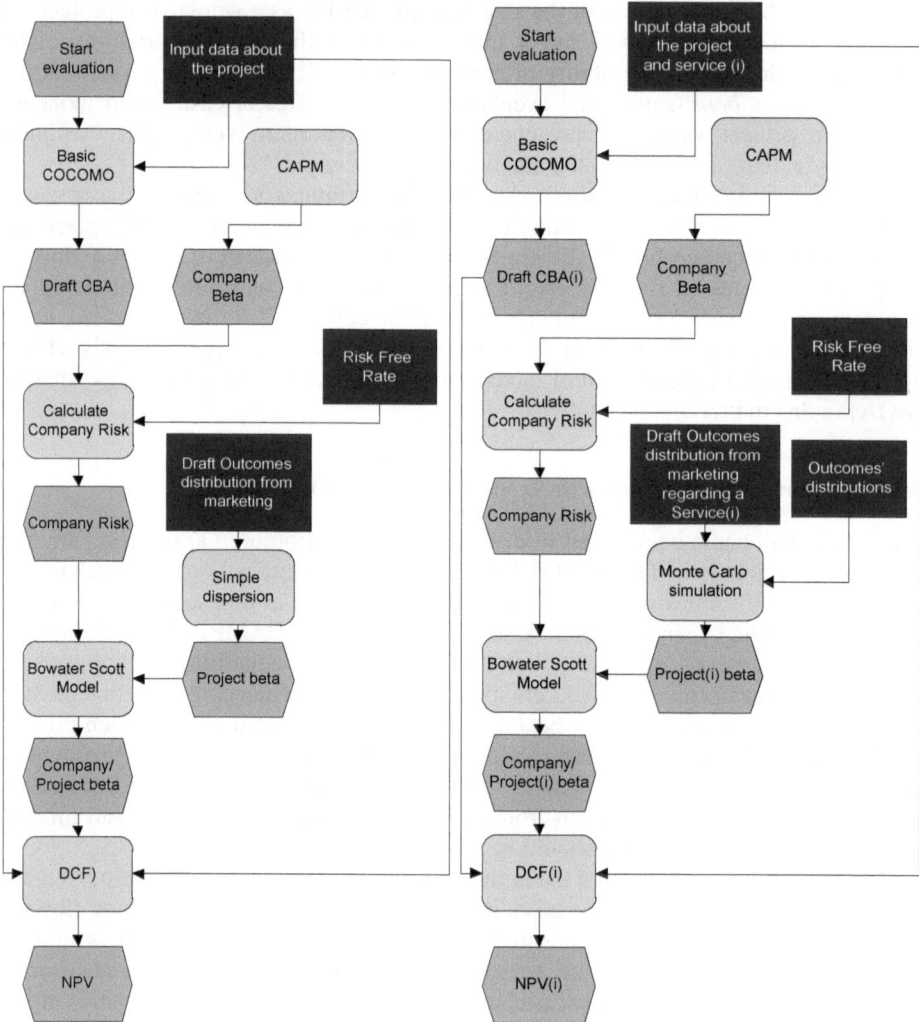

Fig. 1. EPC schemes for assessment methods. The original framework method [4] to the left. The proposed modified method to the right.

The first modification could be illustrated by two schemes (fig. 1). The first one represents the algorithm workflow described in the original framework method. The second schema shows how it is possible to separate DCF flows to form the final NVP.

As we can see the main distinctive feature of our modified method is to have an individual pass of the original framework algorithm [4] for every service (i) resulting in NPV(i). Each service (i) pass will have its own project beta value (i) in scope the project beta calculation. Total NPV could be identified using formula (1).

$$NPV = \sum_i NPV \tag{1}$$

The second modification could be resolved as follows. First of all, the components of outcomes are divided into constant and variable parts. The variable part is estimated in order to determine subjectively low and high mean values. These values can be estimated using input from the market research. This is followed by simple deviation calculation and then it leads to calculation of the project *beta*. Most of researches propose to estimate variability of outcomes more precisely. For example, determination of distributions for outcome components and Monte Carlo simulation has been proposed in [16, 17]. We selected this approach to replace simple deviation technique in the original framework method [4] for calculation of the project *beta*.

3.2   Using ROA to Measure the Flexibility Value

A separate topic of this research is the way to take flexibility into account. Projects which have flexibility can reduce the impacts of event risk and so raise the value of a project. Flexibility enables project managers to take advantage of beneficial change and add value to a project this way [4]. The original framework method has a special phase to determine the NPV brought by the event risk. DTA technique is used for this purpose. Therefore the ROA technique is considered to be the extension and evolution of DTA in particular conditions:

- The key characteristic factors of the company/market should be limited [18].
- The elements of the project should be "tradable". It means, for example, that getting rid of some of the project elements is quite possible (let's say we may eliminate one of the services).

The first requirement looks closely dependent on a particular company or project. Forthcoming application of our proposed method for risk assessment of the project in telecommunication domain seems to fit this requirement since telecom market has transparent and limited set of key characteristics as well as key characteristics of IS in that domain.

The second requirement exactly matches the SOA approach where the system according to SIMM [14] is going to reach its peak in an absolutely reconfigurable eco-system of independent components each of which could be eliminated or postponed in its evolution without significant damage to the system in general.

Such considerations lead to the third modification in the original framework method [4]; namely, it is replacing of DTA with ROA for determination of the event risk specific for the particular project.

4   Applying the Proposed Method

We offer to apply and evaluate our proposed assessment method to a specific project case of Network Management System (NMS) in comparison with the original framework method [4]. We use the case where two new modules are going to be added to the three-tier based legacy NMS for this task. The SOA is considered to be the architectural approach for this, and SaaS could be one of the ways the components could be deployed in the company. The evolution of the existing system using SOA and evaluating in-house development versus SaaS look like the most essential and relevant way nowadays to evolve IT infrastructure for many companies. It stresses the importance of this research.

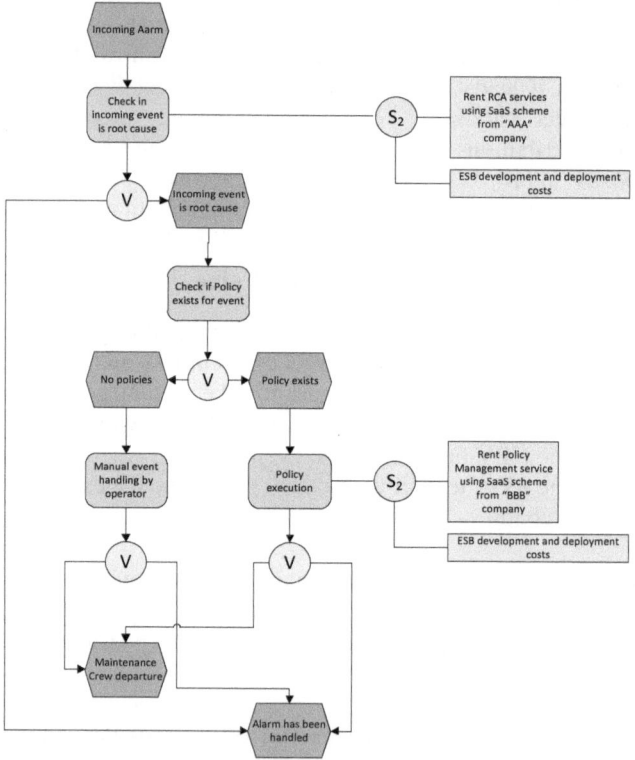

Fig. 2. Extended EPC diagram with RCA and Policy Management services (modules) in the NMS system

The NMS system is installed in a company of large Middle East Telecom provider. The modules (now services) are:

– Policy Management (Policy);
– Root Cause Analysis (RCA).

The Policy service is targeted on automated processing of routine events coming to the system by means of highly configurable rule-based policies. The RCA service is supposed to find the root cause of network breakdowns in the high-rate stream of incoming alerts. Enterprise Service Bus (ESB) [19] is supposed to be used for existing NMS and services coordination. The role and place of these two components in the NMS could be seen on the Extended EPC diagram [12] (fig.2).

Let's go through the algorithms depicted in figure 2. First start with the original framework method (left scheme in figure 2). Then the modified method will be used for assessment of the project described above.

ESB component is the infrastructural component that is the prerequisite for RCA and Policy services. There are two options that could be related to flexibility of the project. Once ESB development and deployment is done, SOA components could be deployed using two approaches:

- in-house development;
- service rental from a SaaS provider.

These alternatives define two branches for calculation of flexibility fraction of NPV. The figure 3 illustrates these alternative options. The p is the probability of particular transition in the tree. It is selected as 0.5 in the original framework method where the DTA is applied in flexibility value assessment stage and it is calculated in new proposed method. Later in this paper we will describe the procedure of its calculation.

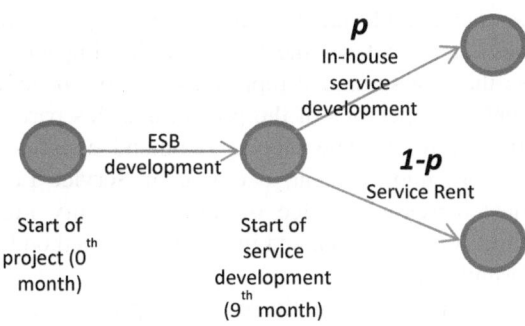

Fig. 3. Alternative project options

The passive NPV needs to be calculated for every branch. Outcomes, incomes and the discount rate are required components for passive NPV.

The main outcomes are ESB development cost plus services development cost in the case of in-house development and service rent in the case of SaaS deployment approach. Development costs are estimated using COCOMO [20]. The following assumptions were taken into account during outcomes identifications:

- There are no software development, maintenance and hardware outcomes for services Policy and RCA because those services are rented from the SaaS services provider.
- Outcomes related to ESB development could be identified using Basic COCOMO method.
- The project period for DCF is 3 years.
- The monthly rent costs for services are fixed: Policy service rent cost is $30 000, RCA service rent cost is $70 000.

Incomes depend mostly on the model of IS components in the production mode. Such model depends on particular project specifics and the domain. Since we consider the real-life project in the Network Management domain, specific production model of new IS components of the NMS was created. This model could be described using the formula (2).

$$I = \upsilon_o \times [(t_o \times w_o \times c_o) + (t_m \times w_m \times c_m)] + \sum_i (I_0 \times w_i \times s_i) \qquad (2)$$

In this formulae: I – the yearly income of IT project, υ_o – the incoming alert rate, t_o – the alert handling time spent by an operator, w_o – the ratio of alerts being handled by a service automatically without operator intervention, c_o – the operator time cost, t_m – the alert handling time spent by a maintenance crew, w_m – the ratio of alerts being handled by a service automatically without maintenance crew intervention, c_m – the maintenance crew time cost, I_0 – the yearly income of IT project before it has been started, i – index of intangible incomes component, w_i – the improvement ratio of i intangible incomes component, s_i – the ratio of service impact on improvement.

As we can see the first summand represents tangible benefits of the project. This summand represents the specifics of the project and this part of the formula (2) was developed specifically for it. The second summand consists of intangible benefits (such as market share improvement, decrease of Service Level Agreement (SLA) violation penalties, increase in price because of quality improvement, etc.). The additivity of such factors was explained in framework method [4] and it is reflected in this part of the formula (2).

The discount rate is based on the company/project *beta*. This dependency is described by formulae (3) [4]:

$$R = R_f + \beta_c \times \beta_{pr} \times (R_m - R_f) \qquad (3)$$

In this formula: R – the discount rate, R_f – the risk free rate, R_f – the industry rate, β_c – the company *beta*, β_{pr} – the project *beta*. This formula is the modification of risk adjusted discounting formula. The beta factor is represented by multiplication of company *beta* and project *beta* factors. It is possible taking into consideration Bowater-Scott approach [4]. The beta parameters need to be calculated. The company *beta* is calculated using CAPM. The project *beta* is calculated using project income volatility. The framework method calculation was based on deviation estimation using three points supplied by marketing department and new method uses the model described by formulae (2). The volatility of I is the project *beta*. The probability distribution and their parameters assumptions were made. The distribution is assumed to be normal for all arguments in formulae (2). The distribution parameters of arguments of the first summand are based in historical data of IS running in the production mode before start of the IT project. The distribution parameters of arguments of the second summand are estimated by a marketing department.

DCF was applied to calculate passive NPV for both options in the original framework method and our newly proposed method. The framework method applies DCF to composite flow of all services involved in the project and uses one discount rate for one option. Our method applies DCF to every service (component) of the project individually with the individually calculated discount rate.

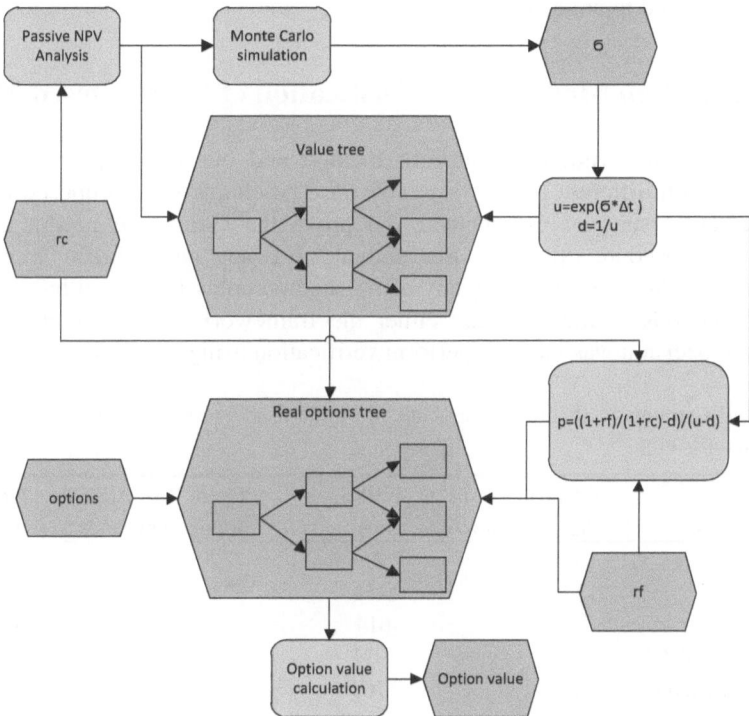

Fig. 4. Measuring the value of the switch option using ROA

Then flexibility fraction of NPV was estimated in the framework method using the DTA technique and the simple tree (fig. 3) with $p = 0.5$. The flexibility fraction of NPV was estimated in our proposed method using the ROA technique. It was assumed that we have a case of switch option [11] where base option is the in-house development and the alternative (switch) option is the case of SaaS. The switch option is an American put option and the binomial lattice technique is suitable for its calculation [11]. Figure 4 depicts the overall ROA procedure [21] and describes how the value of p and the value of this switch option were calculated. Passive NPV analysis, Monte Carlo simulation and determination of volatility σ were already applied during the project beta calculation. The parameters p, u, d are related to the binomial lattice method of real option valuation [11], rf – the risk free rate, rc – the company rate.

In Table 1 we compare the results of NPV valuation produced following the original framework method [4] and our newly proposed method. The new method has DCF flows for every component and this is why there are separate rows for IT project components (Policy, RCA, ESB) along with New Method Total row. The values in this New Method Total row could be compared to values in Framework Method row (and with Simulation model row as well, this would be discussed later in this paper). There columns in Table 1 with NPV without taking into account the value of project flexibility, the value of flexibility and the final NPV column that is the most important value to obtain and to compare.

5   Simulation Modeling for Verification of the Proposed Method

Application of the original Framework method and our newly proposed method provided us with different results (see table 1). The claims were proposed regarding more accurate results of our method. To prove the claims we need a thorough verification procedure. Because the authors did not have direct access to a comprehensive data set describing any of finished complex IT project based on SOA that could be post-evaluated using either the framework method or the proposed method, the decision was made to perform verification using simulation modeling.

Table 1. NPV summary. Results were obtained by the framework Method, New Method and Simulation modeling.

	Company/Project discount rate,%	NPV, thousands $	Event Risk Added Value, thousands $	NPVa, thousands $
Policy	18.24	127	232	359
RCA	17.80	2458	435	2894
ESB	-	-614	-	-614
New Method Total	-	1971	667	2638
Framework Method	18	1703	876	2578
Simulation Modeling	-	1868	820	2688

The simulation model was developed. It takes into consideration an external environment (i.e. the market process such as market share redistribution) along with an internal environment (i.e. running IS in the production mode and the software development process). System Dynamics [22] was chosen as a simulation modeling approach. This selection is caused by the following: System Dynamics is good enough when the level of details in the model is not high (this is acceptable since the simulation model being developed should not replace the assessment method but rather verify the method); there is a lot of already developed models in System

Dynamics notation for the areas involved in our model domain. iThink [23] software developed by iSee Systems was used as an instrument for modeling process since this is one of the most powerful and feature-enabled products for modeling following System Dynamics notation.

To verify the new assessment method the simulation model was applied to the same real-life IT project (the case of NMS extension via adding two new SOA services).

The main structure of the model is shown on figure 5.

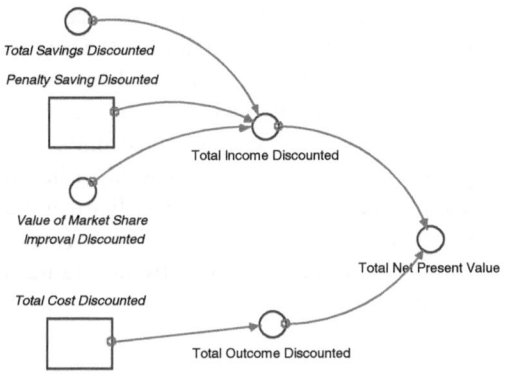

Fig. 5. General structure of the simulation model

Part of the simulation model that represents the IS running in the production mode (Total Savings Discounted on fig.5) allows to determine cost reduction of network operation. This part of the model was fully developed by the authors of this paper because it is tightly coupled with specifics of the particular real-world project and takes into account specifics of the domain. The main components of this sub-model are operator time reduction and maintenance crew incidents reduction. The ongoing results of it are: the customer loyalty shift (it would be needed in the market share movement sub-model) and SLA penalty reduction (Penalty Savings Discounted on fig.5).

Part of the model that considers the market behavior allows determining the income generated by market share increase (Value of Marker Share Improvement Discounted on fig.5). This part of the model is based on existing System Dynamics model called "Bass Diffusion with Type 1 and Type 2 Rivalry" [24]. The sub-model combines two copies of this existing model. Those copies have different customer switching matrices. The first copy represents the situation in the market before the start of IT project. The second copy shows how situation has changed after the IT project was deployed. This change happened because deployment improved of quality of service and it increased the customer loyalty (fig.5).

Modeling of costs related to software development process (Total Cost Discounted on fig.5) is handled by the part of the main model that is implemented using an existing System Dynamics model for inspection-based software development process [25,26].

Parameters of the model related to software development process were set as they were in the existing model except the lines-of-code value that was set according to the project. Parameters of the model related to IS running in production (such as the incoming alert rate, the operator time cost, the maintenance crew cost and others) were set according to statistical data of a particular company involved in the project. Parameters of the market share shift model were set mostly based on the existing diffusion model [24] since the number of main players in the telecom market (three) in it matches what it is in the real project.

To determine the flexibility value the assumption was made that there is a company (the SaaS provider) that develops the same services and this company would have started selling them for rent with probability 0.5 by the moment the ESB component is deployed in NMS. The simulation model was run for this case the same way as it was run for in-house services development but the difference was in the outcome-related part (ESB-related costs were counted only, but the service rent was added) and in income parts (IS production phase started earlier and market share shift started earlier because the production phase started earlier using the SaaS approach).

In our case the main result of simulation modeling is calculating the final NPV. The comparison of it with NPV values produced by the framework method and new method could be seen in table 1.

6   Conclusion

The new value assessment method was developed by authors. This method is targeted for IT projects where the IT infrastructure is developed using SOA as an architectural approach. The method takes into consideration the SOA specifics. This new method along with the original framework method [4] was applied to the real-life IT project. The NPV values were achieved. They were different. To justify the value of new method against the existing one the verification had to be performed. The simulation model was developed by the authors in order to perform verification. This simulation model was developed following System Dynamics approach and it was applied to the same IT project to fulfill the verification goal.

The NPV value produced by the simulation model is closer to the NPV value provided by our proposed method in comparison with the value of the framework method. It shows that verification has passed successfully. The robustness of new assessment method as well as developed imitation model needs to be verified and this is what is going to be done in nearest future. The modeling experiment was performed for the real-world IT project what was used for assessment method application. This way the verification of this method was performed only and not the imitation model itself. Verifying the robustness would allow determining if the developed method and imitation model are suitable enough for wide range of IT project where SOA architecture is involved.

Our new method requires more data than the framework method because modified method needs to prepare separate incomes and outcomes for every service (and ESB as a non-service component) while the original framework method only demands for cumulative incomes and outcomes. Moreover our method needs to perform income sensitivity analysis for every service and it also adds complexity (the framework method does this analysis once). An assumption could be made that having more data involved in analysis could lead to more precise results. This statement requires verification and verification of results is important direction of the research. Important phase in verification has been accomplished via developing imitation model and proving the results of new method with help of this model.

The increased complexity of the new method could be eliminated by development of decision support system (DSS) that is supposed to automate all steps of the algorithm involved in the modified method. This DSS is in a prototype phase now.

Such DSS system could be a useful for companies demanding IT infrastructure development using SOA as an architecture approach and SaaS as the deployment method. Market trends show that evolution of existing IS is done exactly this way. Gartner Group is forecasting the enterprise application software market to surpass $12.1 billion in 2011. (That is up 20.7% compared to 2010) [27]. It means that the assessment method being developed in this research has demand for it and the NMS example could be a good reference case study for many companies. The last but not the least result of the research is developed prototype of DSS that automates the new assessment method. Moving this DSS to the phase when it could be used by investor representatives is another area of effort.

References

1. Services Oriented Architecture (SOA) Infrastructure Market Shares, Market Strategy, and Market Forecasts, 2008-2014. Wintergreen Research, INC. TOC-6, Lexington, Massachusetts (2008), ftp://ftp.software.ibm.com/software/soa/pdf/ Service_Oriented_Architecture_SOA_Infrastructure_all.pdf
2. MacKenzie, C., Laskey, K., McCabe, F., Brown, P., Metz, R.: OASIS Reference Model for Service Oriented Architecture 1.0. Advancing open standarts for the information society (2006), http://docs.oasis-open.org/soa-rm/v1.0/soa-rm.pdf
3. Kruschwitz, L., Loeffler, A.: Discounted Cash Flow. A Theory of the Valuation of Firms. John Wiley & Sons (2005)
4. Hares, J., Royle, D.: Measuring the Value of Information technology. John Wiley and Sons, England (1994)
5. Pendharkar, P.C.: Valuing interdependent multi-stage IT investments: A real options approach. European Journal of Operational Research 201, 847–859 (2010)
6. Dixit, A.K., Pindyck, R.S.: Investment Under Uncertainty. Princeton Univercity Press (1994)
7. Santos, D.: Justifying Investments in New Information Technologies. Journal of Management Information Systems 7(4), 71–89 (1991)
8. Hodder, J.E., Mello, A.S., Sick, G.: Valuing real options: Can risk-adjusted discounting be made to work? Journal of Applied Corporate Finance 14(2), 90–101 (2011)
9. Copeland, T., Antikarov, V.: Real Options: A Practitioner's Guide. Thomson-Texere, New York (2003)
10. Smith, J.E., Nau, R.F.: Valuing risky projects: Option pricing theory and decision analysis. Management Science 41(5), 795–816 (1995)

11. Trigeorgis, L.: Real Options: Managerial Flexibility and Strategy in Resource Allocation (1996)
12. Thomas, O., Brocke, J.: A value-driven approach to the design of service-oriented information systems-making use of conceptual models. Information Systems and E-Business Management (2009)
13. vom Brocke, J., Braccini, A.M., Sonnenberg, C., Ender, E.: A Process Oriented Assessment of the IT Infrastructure Value: A Proposal of an Ontology Based Approach. In: Abramowicz, W. (ed.) Business Information Systems. LNBIP, vol. 21, pp. 13–24. Springer, Heidelberg (2009)
14. Arsanjani, A., Holley, K.: Increase Flexibility with the Service Integration Maturity Model (SIMM). IBM Developer Works (2005),
    http://www.ibm.com/developerworks/webservices/library/
    ws-soa-simm/
15. Ross, S.A.: The Capital Asset Pricing Model (CAPM), Short-sale Restrictions and Related Issues. Journal of Finance 32 (1977)
16. Borison, A.: Real Options Analysis: Where are the Emperor Clothes? In: Real Options Conference, Washington, DC (July 02, 2003)
17. A Guide to the Project Management Body of Knowledge. PMI (Project Management Institute) (2004)
18. Mauboussin, M.J.: Get Real: Using Real Options in Security Analysis. Credit Suisse First Boston (1999)
19. Richards, M.: The Role of the Enterprise Service Bus. Info Queue (2006),
    http://www.infoq.com/presentations/Enterprise-Service-Bus
20. Boehm, B.: COCOMO II. Center for Systems and Software Engineering. University of South California,
    http://sunset.usc.edu/csse/research/COCOMOII/
    cocomo_main.html
21. Roth, T.: Application of Real Options Analyses for Service Oriented Computing Projects, University of Zurich, Faculty of Economics (September 2007)
22. Sterman, J.: Business Dynamics. Irwin McGraw-Hill (2000)
23. Richmond, B.: An Introduction to Systems Thinking with iThink. iSee Systems (2004)
24. Morecroft, J.: Strategic Modelling and Business Dynamics. John Wiley and Sons (2007)
25. Abdel-Hamid, T., Madnick, S.: Software project dynamics: an integrated approach. Prentice Hall (1991)
26. Madachy, R.: Software process dynamics. John Wiley and Sons (2007)
27. Lawinski, J.: Worldwide SaaS Revenue to Grow 21 Percent in 2011: Gartner. Channel Insider (July 7, 2011), http://www.channelinsider.com/c/a/Cloud-Computing/Worldwide-SaaS-Revenue-to-Grow-21-Percent-in-2011-Gartner-486968/

Face Recognition in Real-Time Applications: A Comparison of Directed Enumeration Method and K-d Trees

Andrey V. Savchenko

National Research University Higher School of Economics,
Nizhniy Novgorod, Russian Federation
avsavchenko@hse.ru

Abstract. The problem of face recognition with large database in real-time applications is discovered. The enhancement of HoG (Histogram of Gradients) algorithm with features mutual alignment is proposed to achieve better accuracy. The novel modification of directed enumeration method (DEM) using the ideas of the Best Bin First (BBF) search algorithm is introduced as an alternative to the nearest neighbor rule to prevent the brute force. We present the results of an experimental study in a problem of face recognition with FERET and Essex datasets. We compare the performance of our DEM modification with conventional BBF k-d trees in their well-known efficient implementation from OpenCV library. It is shown that the proposed method is characterized by increased computing efficiency (2-12 times in comparison with BBF) even in the most difficult cases where many neighbors are located at very similar distances. It is demonstrated that BBF cannot be used with our recognition algorithm as the latter is based on non-symmetric measure of similarity. However, we experimentally prove that our recognition algorithm improves recognition accuracy in comparison with classical HoG implementation. Finally, we show that this algorithm could be implemented efficiently if it is combined with the DEM.

Keywords: Real-time object recognition, HoG (histogram of gradients), directed enumeration method, k-d tree, Best Bin First.

1   Introduction

Nowadays, the video surveillance systems are widely used in information security field [1]. However, sometimes their quality is not satisfactory. For instance, these systems are only best for movement detection and afterwards inquiries. Commercial systems do not have early-warning functionality without human intervention.

With the grow of modern information technologies, intelligent image and video content analysis has become a key component in video surveillance system. It is also significant in security video and image forensic [2]. Really, person cannot concentrate on video after approximately 3 hours. Because of the evident disadvantages of manual analysis, human capability cannot meet the requirement to understand and analyze such a huge quantity of video data collected in reality. Hence, the popularity of automatic systems has recently grown. These systems are usually based on the algorithms of image recognition and computer vision.

N. Aseeva, E. Babkin, and O. Kozyrev (Eds.): BIR 2012, LNBIP 128, pp. 187–199, 2012.

One of the most practically important surveillance systems include facial recognition engine. Automatic face recognition [3] is a challenging task because factors such as pose, illumination, facial expression make it difficult to achieve high accuracy. One of the most important practical cases of face recognition is video-based recognition [4]. Although current systems of face recognition in video have reached a certain level of maturity [4], their development is limited by the conditions brought about by many real applications [3]. For instance, it is still difficult to implement the requirement to recognize faces with large database [5], [6] (hundreds of persons) in real-time (25-30 frames per second).

An interesting application here includes a biometric authentication for e-learning web applications [7]. Really, the lack of efficient authentication algorithms at login time and throughout the session restricts the reliability of distance course learning. Unfortunately, if the amount of students for all courses is high, it is quite difficult to implement an existing recognition algorithms in real-time.

To achieve better performance, approximate algorithms [8], [9] (in the sense that they return the closest neighbor with high probability) were offered. K-d tree [10] (and its modifications such as Best Bin First (BBF) [5]), spill tree, triangle tree [11] are widely used in object recognition. Unfortunately, all such algorithms require the nearest neighbor be quite closer to query image than the second-nearest neighbor. Thus they cannot be used to solve the most difficult cases in which many neighbors are at very similar distances [5]. However this problem is quite acute in several object recognition tasks such as face recognition. Really, this task is substantially different from conventional object recognition [11], [12] - the shapes of the objects are usually different in an object recognition task, while in face recognition one always identifies objects with the same basic shape.

To overcome this problem we proposed the directed enumeration method (DEM) [6]. It was shown that this method improves recognition performance if Kullback-Leibler [13] and chi-square discriminations [14] are used to compare color and gradient histograms. Meanwhile, the method's capabilities have not been fully exploited. In particular, almost no studies have addressed the advantages of our method over k-d trees in object recognition using conventional measures of similarity. The present paper seeks to fill this gap. Inspired by the ideas of BBF [5], we present here the novel modification of DEM. We show that our method increases recognition speed with L_1 metric and gradient orientations feature set.

The rest of the paper is organized as follows: Section 2 presents our face recognition using a modification of well-known HoG (Histogramof Gradients) algorithm [15]. In Section 3, we recall BBF k-d tree and present its limitations. In Section 4, we introduce our DEM modification. In Section 5, we present the experimental results of face recognition with FERET [16] and Essex [17] datasets and compare the DEM with k-d tree implementation from OpenCV [18]. Finally, concluding comments are given in Section 6.

2   Automatic Face Recognition

Let a set of $R>1$ greyscale images $X_r = \left\| x_{uv}^{(r)} \right\|$ ($u = \overline{1, U_r}, v = \overline{1, V_r}$) be specified.

Here R is a database size, $x_{uv}^{(r)}$ is the intensity of an image point with coordinates

(u,v); $r \in \{1,...,R\}$ is the image number, U_r and V_r are the rth model image height and width, respectively. Each image X_r corresponds to a class $c(r) \in \{1,...,C\}$, $C \leq R$ is an amount of classes. It is required to assign a query image $X = \|x_{uv}\|$ ($u = \overline{1,U}, v = \overline{1,V}$) to one of the C classes where U and V are the query image width and height, respectively. The problem can be factorized into two essential parts [12]: (1) feature extraction; (2) similarity measure and classifier design.

There are various feature sets which are widely used in computer vision - color intensities, HSV representation of color, texture representation, shape, etc. In this paper we will focus on gradient orientation defined by Roberts [11], [19] - illumination invariant texture feature showed good results in object recognition [19]

$$\theta_{u,v}^{(r)} = tg^{-1} \frac{x_{u+1,v+1}^{(r)} - x_{u,v}^{(r)}}{x_{u+1,v}^{(r)} - x_{u,v+1}^{(r)}} \tag{1}$$

The second part of object recognition is classifier design. The conventional procedure for constructing decision rules is based on the nearest-neighbor criterion - image X is assigned to the class $c(\nu)$ where

$$\nu = \arg \min_{r \in \{1,...,R\}} \rho(X, X_r) \tag{2}$$

Here $\rho(X, X_r)$ is a similarity measure of images X and X_r. The classifiers are developed in accordance with some deterministic or histogram approach. In deterministic approach feature values are compared directly (e.g. Euclidean metric). However, this approach does not always provide satisfactory results. The first reason is well-known [12], [20] variability of visual patterns. The second reason is the presence of noise in the query image, such as unknown intensity of light sources or random distortions of some pixels. These difficulties are overcome by a histogram approach [15], [20]. According to it local histograms of selected features are compared.

The local features are calculated by dividing images into a regular grid to provide illumination and outlier robust appearance-based correspondence with some leeway for small spatial deviations due to misalignment after object detection. In this paper, each image is divided into $K \times K$ equal cells (K rows and K columns).

The gradient orientation (1) definition range $[-\pi; \pi]$ is divided into N regular segments (thus each segment has width $\frac{2\pi}{N}$). Then the HoG (histogram of gradient orientation) $\left[h_1^{(r)}(k_1,k_2),...,h_N^{(r)}(k_1,k_2) \right]$ of each cell with coordinates (k_1,k_2), $k_1,k_2 \in \{1,...,K\}$ is evaluated. We propose to use relative gradient magnitude as a weight

$$h_i^{(r)}(k_1,k_2)=\frac{K^2}{U_r\cdot V_r}\sum_{u=1+(U_r\cdot(k_1-1))/K}^{(U_r\cdot k_1)/K}\sum_{v=1+(V_r\cdot(k_2-1))/K}^{(V_r\cdot k_2)/K}\frac{m_{uv}^{(r)}+\Delta m}{m^{(r)}+\Delta m}\times$$
$$\times\left(H\left(\theta_{uv}^{(r)}-\frac{2(i-1)-N}{N}\pi\right)-H\left(\theta_{uv}^{(r)}-\frac{2i-N}{N}\pi\right)\right)$$
(3)

Here

$$H(x)=\begin{cases}0, & x<0\\1, & x\geq0\end{cases}$$

is a Heaviside function,

$$m_{u,v}^{(r)}=\frac{\left|x_{u+1,v+1}^{(r)}-x_{u,v}^{(r)}\right|+\left|x_{u+1,v}^{(r)}-x_{u,v+1}^{(r)}\right|}{2}$$
(4)

- gradient magnitude evaluation, $\Delta m=const<\dfrac{1}{2}$ is a summand to include in the histogram points with zero magnitude ($m_{u,v}^{(r)}=0$) – we found that good recognition results could be obtained with $\Delta m=0.1$, and

$$m^{(r)}=\max_{u=1,U;v=1,V}m_{u,v}^{(r)}$$
(5)

After that nearest-neighbor rule (1) is used to compare corresponding histograms. For instance, L_1 metric is widely used

$$\rho_\Delta(X,X_r)=\sum_{k_1=1}^K\sum_{k_2=1}^K\sum_{i=1}^N\left|h_i^{(r)}(k_1,k_2)-h_i(k_1,k_2)\right|$$
(6)

If the cell size is low ($K>>1$), the criterion (6) could show poor recognition accuracy. It is possible to perform mutual alignment of HoG features and compare histograms in Δ-neighborhood of cell (k_1,k_2)

$$\rho_{\Delta,\Delta}(X,X_r)=$$
$$=\sum_{k_1=1}^K\sum_{k_2=1}^K\min_{\substack{|\Delta_1|\leq\Delta,\\|\Delta_2|\leq\Delta,\\|\Delta_1^{(r)}|\leq\Delta,\\|\Delta_1^{(r)}|\leq\Delta}}\sum_{i=1}^N\left|h_i^{(r)}\left(k_1+\Delta_1^{(r)},k_2+\Delta_2^{(r)}\right)-h_i\left(k_1+\Delta_1,k_2+\Delta_2\right)\right|$$
(7)

It is equivalent to (6) if $\Delta=0$. However, this expression is $(2\Delta+1)^2$-times slower than the original distance (6). Moreover, as we show in the experimental study (see Section 5), the accuracy of (7) does not exceed the accuracy of (6). Hence we decided use partial alignment of all model images to a query image X

$$\rho_\Delta(X, X_r) = \sum_{k_1=1}^{K} \sum_{k_2=1}^{K} \min_{\substack{|\Delta_1|\leq\Delta \\ |\Delta_2|\leq\Delta}} \sum_{i=1}^{N} \left| h_i^{(r)}(k_1+\Delta_1, k_2+\Delta_2) - h_i(k_1, k_2) \right| \tag{8}$$

Thus, expressions (1), (9)-(11), (8) define the proposed object recognition algorithm. It differs from the known HoG algorithm by partial aligning the features in Δ-neighborhood (8) and by weighting (3) of the gradient orientation histogram relative gradient magnitude (5) with $\Delta m > 0$ parameter.

3   Best Bin First Algorithm

We consider the most important and difficult case $R >> 1$, where the database contains hundreds or thousands of images. For the specified conditions, practical implementation of the decision rule (1) encounters the obvious problem of its computational complexity and even feasibility.

Conventional approach to speed up object recognition is based on an approximate algorithm which returns the nearest neighbor for a large fraction of queries and a very close neighbor otherwise. These algorithms widely use the k-d tree data structure, which is built as follows [5], [10]. Beginning with a complete set of points, the data space is split on the dimension i in which the data exhibits the greatest variance. A cut is made at the median value m of the data in that dimension, so that an equal number of points fall to one side or the other. An internal node is created to store i and m, and the process iterates with both halves of the data. This creates a balanced binary tree.

The well-known limitation of conventional k-d trees is their ineffectiveness in very-high-dimensional spaces. To overcome this problem, Best Bin First (BBF) method was designed [5]. It exploits the following ideas: 1. Backtracking according to a priority queue based on closeness; and 2. Search a fixed number of nearest candidates and stop. BBF showed such good performance in object recognition that has been implemented in OpenCV (*cvCreateKDTree* method) [18].

Unfortunately, the k-d tree (and BBF) cannot be build for measures of similarity which does not satisfy all metric properties [8]. For example, it cannot be implemented with the measure (8) if $\Delta > 0$. Really, $\rho_\Delta(X, X_r)$ is not a symmetric because

$$\min_{|\Delta_1|\leq\Delta, |\Delta_2|\leq\Delta} \sum_{i=1}^{N} \left| h_i^{(r)}(k_1, k_2) - h_i(k_1+\Delta_1, k_2+\Delta_2) \right| \neq$$

$$\neq \min_{|\Delta_1|\leq\Delta, |\Delta_2|\leq\Delta} \sum_{i=1}^{N} \left| h_i^{(r)}(k_1+\Delta_1, k_2+\Delta_2) - h_i(k_1, k_2) \right|$$

For such cases directed enumeration method was developed [4].

4   Directed Enumeration Method Modification

First, we transform criterion (2) to an approximate nearest neighbor [9] form suitable for practical implementation [6]:

$$\rho(X, X_\nu) < \rho_0 = const \tag{9}$$

Here ρ_0 is the threshold for the admissible distance on the set of similarly-named images from one class. The value of this threshold could be found experimentally by fixing the false-accept rate (FAR) $\beta = const$ from the following equation

$$\sum_{i=1}^{R} H\left(\rho_0 - \min_{i \neq j} \rho_{ij}\right) = \lceil \beta \cdot R \rceil \tag{10}$$

where $H(x) = \begin{cases} 0, x < 0 \\ 1, x \geq 0 \end{cases}$ is a Heaviside step function, $\lceil \cdot \rceil$ is a ceil round function and

$\rho_{ij} = \rho(X_i, X_j)$ are the elements of $(R \times R)$ distance matrix $P = \left\| \rho_{ij} \right\|$. The evaluation of this matrix needs to be made only once for each database $\{X_r\}$.

At first, the empty queue Q is initialized and the resulted image X_μ is set to undefined. We always refer to the closest to X already checked model image as X_μ.

Then we repeat the following procedure while the termination condition (3) is not met and the count of checked database images is less than R. If Q is empty we put one random database image X_{rand} that has not been checked previously. This action ensures that the algorithm is finite. Then the first element X_i is extracted from the queue Q. If X_μ is undefined or $\rho(X, X_i) < \rho(X, X_\mu)$ then we assign i to μ.

Based on the matrix P the set of $M = const < R$ images $X_i^{(M)} = \left\{ X_{i_1}, ... X_{i_M} \right\}$ is determined from the expression :

$$\left(\forall X_j \notin X_i^{(M)} \right)\left(\forall X_k \in X_i^{(M)} \right) \qquad \Delta\rho\left(x_j\right) \geq \Delta\rho\left(x_k\right) \tag{11}$$

Here $\Delta\rho(X_j) = \left| \rho\left(X_j, X\right) - \rho_{ji} \right|$ is the deviation of the discrimination $\rho_{ji} = \rho\left(X_j, X_i\right)$ relative to the discrimination between the pair of images X and X_j P should be stored as a matrix of pairs $\left\| \left(j_{i,k}, \rho_{j_{i,k}} \right) \right\|, i = \overline{1, R}, k = \overline{1, R}$ where $\{j_{i,k}\}$ is a permutation of numbers $\{1,..., R\}$, $\rho_{j_{i,k}} = \rho(X_i, X_{j_{i,k}})$ and

$\rho_{j_{i,1}} \leq ... \leq \rho_{j_{i,R}}$. In such a case the binary search could be used to obtain $X_i^{(M)}$.

Then, all computations of the first step are repeated cyclically until, in some step, an element X_μ meets the termination condition (3). A decision is made in favor of the closest pattern X_μ or, at worst in the absence of a solution from (3), the conclusion is drawn that the query image X cannot be assigned to any class from the database and that it is necessary to switch to the decision feedback mode (i.e. ignore the frame in video recognition or use the reject option [21]). Anyway, X_μ still refers to the X closest database image.

Thus, expressions (3)–(5) define DEM in the image recognition problem. Its key difference from the existing algorithms is the usage of P distances matrix to choose the next database image to check (5).

In this article we propose the enhancement of the DEM using two key ideas of BBF [5]. First, the queue Q becomes heap-based priority queue. We arrange images $\{X_i\}$ in the queue Q in a decreasing order of their distances $\rho(X, X_i)$ to a query image X - "Best Model First" strategy (i.e. the same BBF priority queue based on closeness). So the first element in the queue is the closest checked model image to a probe X (in terms of used similarity measure).

Second, we terminate the search with X_μ as a returned value if either condition (9) was met or after examining $E_{\max}$ model images. For fairly small values of $E_{\max}$, the method discovers the exact decision a large percentage of the time, and a very close neighbor in the remaining cases. The next section provides experimental evidence to support this claim.

We summarized the described procedure in the following algorithm (Table 1).

Table 1. The Directed Enumeration Method Modification

Data: query image X, database $\{X_r\}$, matrix of database images distances P

Result: image X^* from the database which is either the nearest neighbor to query X or meets condition (9)

1. Define image X_μ as undefined

2. While X_μ is undefined OR $\rho(X / X_\mu) \geq \rho_0$ AND (count of checked database images is less than $E_{\max}$) do

    2.1. If queue Q is empty

        2.1.1. Insert random database image X_{rand} into the queue Q

    2.2. Pull the highest priority item from the queue Q into X_i

    2.3. Fill the set $X_i^{(M)}$ based on matrix P and formula (11)

    2.4. For each image X_j in the set $X_i^{(M)}$

        2.4.1. If X_j has not checked previously (distance $\rho(X / X_j)$ has not been calculated), then

            2.4.1.1. Insert X_j into queue Q.

            2.4.1.2. If X_μ is undefined OR $\rho(X / X_j) < \rho(X / X_\mu)$, then

                2.4.1.2.1. Define image X_μ as X_j

Put X_μ into result X^*

---

5   Experimental Results

In the experiment FERET and Essex datasets are used. The images were preliminarily processed with OpenCV library [18] to detect faces. After that the median filter with window size (3x3) was used to remove some noise in detected faces. The face images were divided into 400 fragments ($K=20$). The conventional [20] value $N=8$ of bins in gradient orientation histogram is used. These parameters provide the best recognition accuracy for both FERET and Essex datasets.

From FERET dataset 1432 face-to-face images of 994 persons populate the database (i.e. a training set), other 1288 photos of the same persons formed a test set. From Essex dataset the $R=900$ images were selected as the training set $\{X_r\}$ from the 6400 photographs of $C=395$ different people. Other 1500 photos of the same people were used as a test set to evaluate recognition accuracy.

Table 2. Comparison of face recognition results for criterion (2) with measures of similarity (6)-(8), $\Delta = 1$.

Dataset	Quality measure	(6)	(7)	(8)
FERET	Accuracy	9.08%	8.46%	**4.89%**
	Average time	**5.55 ms**	404714.3 ms	59.05 ms
Essex	Accuracy	0.17%	1.473%	**0.08%**
	Average time	**20. 6 ms**	1461894.8 ms	224.9 ms

The accuracy and average time (in ms) of face recognition using nearest neighbor rule (2) and similarity measures (6)-(8) with $\Delta = 1$ are shown in Table 2.

Based on this table, we could draw the following conclusions. First, the proposed similarity measure (8) achieves the best recognition accuracy. However, its average recognition time is 10-times more than the average time of conventional distance (6). Second, it is impossible to implement the distance (7) in real-time applications. Moreover, there's no need in such mutual alignment of HoG features as achieved accuracy is even worth than the accuracy of (6) for Essex dataset. And third, the recognition time t of brute force (2) may be unsatisfactory in real time face recognition if face detection takes much time or frame contains several faces.

In the next experiment we compare the performance of OpenCV implementation of BBF (for measure (6)), proposed DEM and exhastive search (both for measures (6) and (8) with $\Delta = 1$). We evaluate the error rate (in %) and the average time t (in μs) to recognize one test image using modern laptop (4 core i7, 6 Gb RAM) and Visual C++ 2010 compiler with optimization by speed.

In the preliminary experiments [6], [22] we found that the choice of parameter M is much more important. M should not be very closed to 1, otherwise the directed enumeration procedure (6), (7) could miss the nearest neighbor in a couple of iterations. Also M should be much less then the database size R, otherwise the proposed method will be equivalent to the random search. After several experiments [6] the best (in terms of speed) value of parameter M was chosen $M=64$.

At first, we discover FERET dataset. We fix the FAR $\beta=3\%$ as the brute force accuracy is essentially higher (see Table 2).

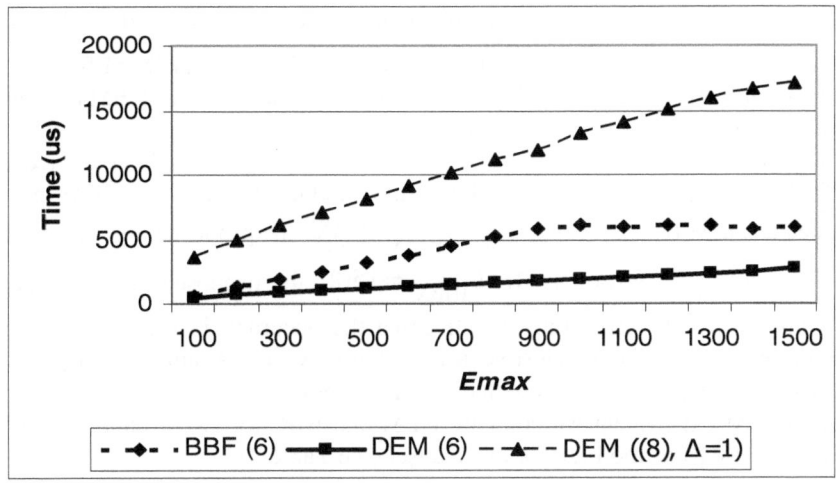

Fig. 1. Dependence of Average Recognition Time t (in μs) on E_{max} , FERET dataset

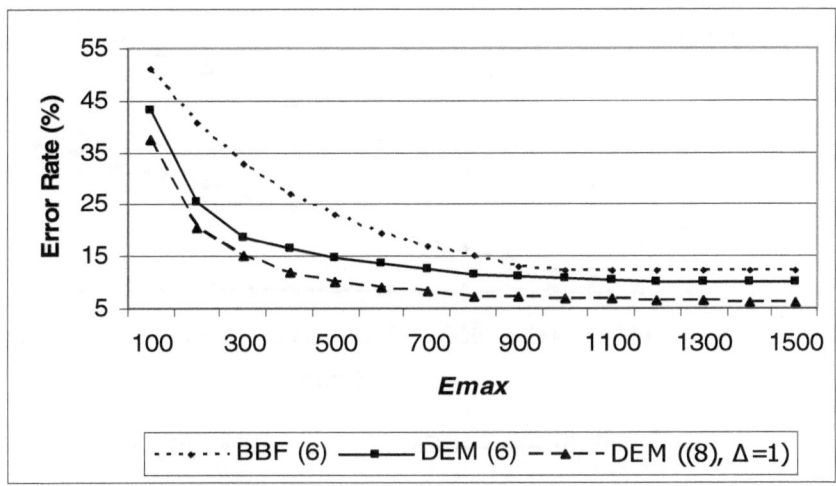

Fig. 2. Dependence of Error Rate (in %) on E_{max} , FERET dataset

In the first case the distance (6) was used. It is a symmetric measure thus BBF and proposed DEM (9)-(11) could be applied. The experiment results (time t and error rate) are shown in Fig. 1,2 (marked as BBF(6) and DEM(6)). The recognition with k-d tree takes even more time than the exhaustive search. It is not surprising as BBF requires the nearest neighbor be quite closer to input image than the second-nearest neighbor. Hence it cannot be used to exactly solve this difficult recognition task. On the other hand, DEM needs $t=1.8$ ms to provide error rate equal to 10.5%

if $E_{max} = 1000$. The decrease of recognition accuracy is caused by the usage of approximate search with termination condition (3). The original DEM [6], [22] takes $t=3.5$ ms with error rate 10.1%. Hence we could conclude that our DEM enhancement caused the increase of recognition performance.

In the second case the criterion (2), (8) was used with $\Delta = 1$. As we stated earlier, the BBF cannot be used there. We show time t and error rate of the DEM in Fig. 1,2 (marked as DEM ((8) $\Delta = 1$)). When $E_{max} = 800$ the proposed algorithm demands $t=11$ ms with 7.2% error rate. If $E_{max} = 1500$ the proposed algorithm demands $t=17$ ms with 6.2% error rate. In all cases the accuracy is much better than the recognition rate of the exhaustive search with $\Delta = 0$. Again, the original DEM performance is worse: $t=21$ ms with error rate 6.25%.

In the next experiment we compare DEM and BBF for Essex dataset. We fix the FAR $\beta=1\%$ as 3% is too high for this dataset (see Table 2).

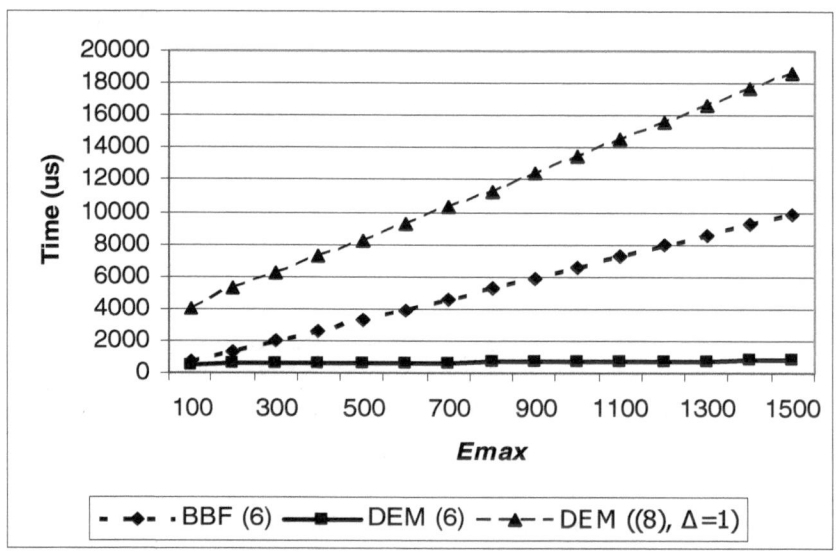

Fig. 3. Dependence of Average Recognition Time t (in μs) on E_{max}, Essex dataset

In the first case the measure (6) was used with the BBF and proposed DEM. The experiment results (time t and error rate) are shown in Fig. 3,4. Here the recognition with k-d tree takes less time than the exhaustive search (Table 1). At the same time, DEM needs $t=0.6$ ms to provide error rate equal to 0.99% if $E_{max} = 600$. The accuracy of DEM is a bit worth than the accuracy of the BBF because the FAR was fixed to 1%, i.e. we suppose 1% error rate is enough for our application. The original DEM takes $t=2.1$ ms with error rate 0.4%. Hence we could conclude that our DEM enhancement caused the increase of recognition performance.

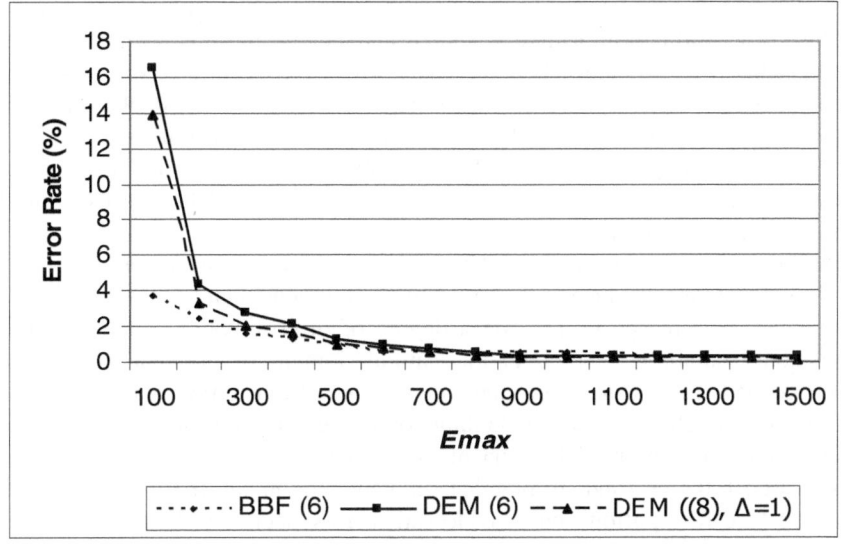

Fig. 4. Dependence of Error Rate (in %) on $E_{\max}$, Essex dataset

In the second case the criterion (2), (8) was used with $\Delta = 1$. We show time t and error rate of the DEM in Fig. 3,4. When $E_{\max} = 700$ the proposed algorithm demands $t=10$ ms with 0.5% error rate. In all cases the accuracy is much better than the recognition rate of the exhaustive search (see Table 2). Again, the original DEM performance is worse: $t=35$ ms with error rate 0.08%.

6   Conclusion

In this paper we proposed a modification of HoG (6) image recognition algorithm by aligning the model features to a query image features. We also suggested to reuse the key ideas of BBF search in DEM to improve recognition performance with large database. Such modification provides additional flexibility by the choose of $E_{\max}$ and the order of priority queue Q.

The most significant concern of applied approach is scalability. For instance, in the experiments 1400 images from the FERET database are used and the recognition with the DEM required 11 ms in the modern laptop. It is obvious that the recognition time increases dramatically with much larger databases. As a matter of fact, the DEM has practically no limitations to be used with bigger database except the additional memory required to store the part of distance matrix P [22]. Unfortunately, modern image feature sets used nowadays seem to be not satisfactory for complex image recognition tasks. Even the recognition quality of gradient-orientation histograms comparison is not so good for the FERET dataset. Moreover, if the one image per person is stored in the database, the recognition rate is really bad (75-80%).

An increase of the number of classes in the face database usually leads to a significant decrease of classification accuracy. As we understand, there is no need to speed up the algorithm if its efficiency is poor. That's why we concentrated on more important practical tasks with hundreds of classes and thousand images in the database. We define the database to be large if the nearest neighbor algorithm with an exhaustive search cannot be implemented in real-time applications, such as face recognition from video where 20-30 frames should be processed in a second. Thus, FERET and Essex datasets are practically important examples.

To this end, we presented an efficient, approximate nearest neighbor algorithm which makes real-time face recognition in high-dimensional spaces practical. High-dimensional feature spaces provide a degree of discrimination that is essential for large model databases, which is the natural domain of application for indexing techniques [5], [20]. Our experiments demonstrated that DEM search is capable of finding close neighbors over a wide range of dimensions and for large faces database, by examining only a small fraction of the model images. We also showed that the widely used k-d tree (and its practical implementation in BBF) cannot be used to speed up face recognition and provide satisfactory accuracy. Moreover, other tree-based indexing techniques cannot be implemented with measures of similarity like (8) because it does not met all metric properties [8]. However, our experiment showed the increase of accuracy of criterion (2) if we put $\Delta = 1$ in (8). And our method does not have special requirements on used measure of similarity or image database.

Finally we could conclude that the proposed enhancement of HoG algorithm and modification of directed enumeration method appears to be more efficient than the approximate nearest neighbor methods currently used for real-time face recognition. Our approach could be used in any modern video surveillance system, which demands image recognition engine.

It is important to emphasize that the proposed DEM modification is not restricted by the face recognition task It could be applied in any practically important problems of business informatics [1]. [2] which refers to a classification task with thousands of classes.

References

1. Yi, M.: Abnormal Event Detection Method for ATM Video and Its Application. In: Lin, S., Huang, X. (eds.) CESM 2011, Part II. CCIS, vol. 176, pp. 186–192. Springer, Heidelberg (2011)
2. Nusimow, A.: Intelligent Video for Homeland Security Applications. In: Proceedings of the 7th Technologies for Homeland Security, pp. 139–144 (2007)
3. Zhao, W., Chellappa, R. (eds.): Face Processing: Advanced Modeling and Methods. Elsevier/Academic Press (2005)
4. Shan, C.: Face Recognition and Retrieval in Video. In: Schonfeld, D., Shan, C., Tao, D., Wang, L. (eds.) Video Search and Mining. SCI, vol. 287, pp. 235–260. Springer, Heidelberg (2010)

5. Beis, J., Lowe, D.G.: Shape indexing using approximate nearest-neighbour search in high dimensional spaces. In: Conference on Computer Vision and Pattern Recognition, Puerto Rico, pp. 1000–1006 (1997)
6. Savchenko, A.V.: Directed enumeration method in image recognition. Pattern Recognition 45(8), 2952–2961 (2012)
7. Penteado, B.E., Marana, A.N.: A Video-Based Biometric Authentication for e-Learning Web Applications. In: Filipe, J., Cordeiro, J. (eds.) ICEIS 2009. LNBIP, vol. 24, pp. 770–779. Springer, Heidelberg (2009)
8. Arya, S., Mount, D.M., Netanyahu, N.S., Silverman, R., Wu, A.Y.: An optimal algorithm for approximate nearest neighbor searching. Journal of the ACM 45, 891–923 (1998)
9. Liu, T., Moore, A.W., Gray, A.G., Yang, K.: An Investigation of Practical Approximate Nearest Neighbor Algorithms. In: NIPS (2004)
10. Bentley, J.L.: Multidimensional binary search trees used for associative searching. Communications of the ACM 18(9), 509–517 (1975)
11. Shapiro, L., Stockman, G.: Computer vision, 752 p. Prentice Hall, Upper Saddle River (2001)
12. Theodoridis, S., Koutroumbas, C.: Pattern Recognition, 4th edn. Elsevier, Amsterdam (2009)
13. Kullback, S.: Information Theory and Statistics. Dover Pub., New York (1978)
14. Srisuk, S., Kurutach, W.: Face Recognition using a New Texture Representation of Face Images. In: Proceedings of Electrical Engineering Conference, pp. 1097–1102 (2003)
15. Dalal, N., Triggs, B.: Histograms of Oriented Gradients for Human Detection. In: International Conference on Computer Vision & Pattern Recognition, pp. 886–893 (2005)
16. FERET dataset, http://face.nist.gov/colorferet/request.html
17. Essex dataset, http://cswww.essex.ac.uk/mv/allfaces/index.html
18. OpenCV library, http://opencv.willowgarage.com/wiki/
19. Roberts, L.: Machine Perception of 3-D Solids, Optical and Electro-optical Information Processing. MIT Press (1965)
20. Lowe, D.: Distinctive image features from scale-invariant keypoints. International Journal of Computer Vision 60(2), 91–110 (2004)
21. Chow, C.K.: On optimum error and reject trade-off. IEEE Transactions on Information Theory 16, 41–46 (1970)
22. Savchenko, A.V.: Image Recognition with a Large Database Using Method of Directed Enumeration Alternatives Modification. In: Kuznetsov, S.O., Ślęzak, D., Hepting, D.H., Mirkin, B.G. (eds.) RSFDGrC 2011. LNCS, vol. 6743, pp. 338–341. Springer, Heidelberg (2011)

Author Index